CREATIVITY AND THE MIND

Discovering the Genius Within

CREATIVITY AND THE MIND

Discovering the Genius Within

THOMAS B. WARD
RONALD A. FINKE
and
STEVEN M. SMITH

PLENUM PRESS • NEW YORK AND LONDON

Library of Congress Cataloging-in-Publication Data

On file

ISBN 0-306-45086-0

© 1995 Thomas B. Ward, Ronald A. Finke, and Steven M. Smith
Plenum Press is a Division of Plenum Publishing Corporation
233 Spring Street, New York, N.Y. 10013-1578

10 9 8 7 6 5 4 3 2 1

Printed in the United States of America

For
Nancy, Deana, and Connor
Pam, Noah, and Dara

ACKNOWLEDGMENTS

Many people contributed ideas and advice during the course of this project, and we thank them one and all. Indeed so many people helped in so many ways that we will undoubtedly forget to mention someone. Nevertheless we gratefully acknowledge the help of the Creative Cognition Research Group, including Steve Balfour, Jeff Brown, Jay Schumacher, Cindy Sifonis, Debbie Tindell, Jyotsna Vaid, and Missi Wilkenfeld; our mechanical engineering colleagues, Harvey Brock, Chris Burger, and Sridhar Condoor; our ever-patient and helpful editors, Melicca McCormick and Linda Greenspan Regan; the countless researchers who have inspired us; and individuals who have helped with ideas for one section or another, including Ken Gray, Kary Mullis, Pam Plate, Nancy Rhodes, Robert Rhodes, Pam Swartz, Paul Ward, and John White. Most particularly we thank the ones closest to us who inspired, endured, and tolerated us while we plodded on through various drafts: Nancy Rhodes, Dara Smith, Noah Smith, Pam Swartz, Connor Ward, and Deana Ward.

CONTENTS

PROBING THE CREATIVE MIND

In the shimmering heat along the Olduvai lakeside in ancient Africa, an anonymous ancestor picks up a sharp rock. He runs his fingers across its jagged edge and wonders if it will scrape meat from the bones that lie at his feet. Nearly two million years later, Deana Ward, age four, handles a very different rock—one that humans have brought back from the lunar surface. One that has been smoothed by the touches of countless children's hands. Deana ponders her rock too, perhaps not so differently from that earliest human. She wonders when and how she might visit the moon.

Stone tools and moon rocks are greatly separated in time and distance, but between them stretches the continuous thread of human creativity. The progress that moved us from the Olduvai lakeside to the moon and beyond is testament to a simple fact: the human mind is designed to create. Underlying all we achieve, as individuals and as a species, is an elegant

1

machine—a mind with an enormous capacity to make use of our experiences and to produce new ideas.

This book is about that machine. What are its basic elements? By what principles does it operate? How does it take the raw materials of experience and transform them into creative thoughts?

How does the mind leap ahead to stagger us with brilliant achievements in science, the arts, and technology? How does it satisfy us so thoroughly with handy solutions to our problems? How does it sometimes become mired in past mistakes, and leave us trudging along through the same old ruts? Most importantly, how can we fine-tune it so that we can leap more and trudge less?

We will see that answers to these important questions are beginning to emerge from careful scientific studies of the mind, conducted in the field of cognitive psychology. Before looking for those answers, however, let's take a brief excursion through the importance of creativity in our lives, our creative heritage, and some different ways of thinking about creativity.

OUR CREATIVE NEED

Creativity plays a vital role in a host of human activities. It can enrich our lives when it reveals itself in soothing or exhilarating music, breathtaking or shocking paintings, joyous or sobering movies, and thought-provoking or titillating novels. It can bring us new tools that eliminate the drudgery of mundane chores, and new toys or gadgets to amuse and entertain us. It can provoke advances in science and medicine, and it can provide great personal satisfaction. Understanding and fostering creativity, then, can certainly enhance our lives, and it can even help save lives.

Aside from its obvious role in spurring musical, artistic, and inventive achievement, creativity is essential to solving a wide range of problems. As a society, we face an enormous number of complex problems that demand creative solutions. We must find cures for deadly diseases, such as cancer and AIDS, and solutions to pressing global concerns such as hunger, poverty, and violence.

As individuals, we also face challenges, ranging from the trivial to the monumental, from breaking into a soda can whose pop-top device is defective, to searching for meaning in our lives. These challenges are not on as grand a scale as societal problems, but they too can benefit from creative thinking.

Creative thinking is also crucial as we adapt to our changing world. We must cope effectively with continual changes in our work situations and in our personal lives if we are to continue participating actively in society. By one estimate, for instance, the typical worker in the United States will change jobs eight times. The days of sticking with the same job in the same stable company for all of one's working life are over. Change is the norm. What this means is that most workers will be unable simply to learn a single set of habits or skills that they will perform throughout their careers. They will have to cultivate innovative ways of responding to interminable changes in their lives.

Continual changes in the world around us also force us to confront novel situations, even if we keep the same jobs. Spurred by numbingly rapid advances in computer technology, the ways in which we communicate with one another, purchase products, and find information are all undergoing persistent, radical change. We must constantly contrive adaptive strategies to contend with these changes.

On a broader scale, corporations also must adapt to changing market conditions if they are to remain competitive. U.S. corporations in particular have lost ground to international competitors over the last 20 years, and are sorely in need of innovative solutions.[1] Consequently, knowing how to enhance innovative thinking is crucial to their continued economic growth and competitiveness in the global marketplace.

Finally, in the largest sense, whole societies also must realign and redefine themselves now that the central structuring force of the last four decades, the Cold War, is behind us. How imaginatively we resolve these issues will determine our likelihood of living together peacefully.

We do not pretend to hold the answers to all of the challenges that confront individuals, corporations, and societies. We do believe, however, that humans will continue to solve such problems, because *it is in our nature to be inventive*. We possess the requisite mental tools to be creative, even though we may not always wield them as effectively as we could.

We may be able to hone our mental skills to cope more inventively with challenging problems, or to behave more creatively in any number of arenas, such as music and art. Identifying the fundamental principles of creative thinking will help us accomplish these lofty goals. Because creative thinking underlies successful problem solving in general, unveiling its secrets may prove beneficial to solving any one of the individual problems. Further, by laying bare these principles, we will be in a position to prepare people more constructively for the future.

OUR CREATIVE NATURE

Shortly after that first human ancestor picked up a sharp rock and pondered its usefulness, *Homo habilis* began to fashion their own primitive stone tools by chipping away at ordinary rocks to sharpen them. By crafting their own tools, these early humans freed themselves from depending on the good fortune to find a suitable rock, and began to make their own luck. This seemingly simple act of creation was a first step on the path toward ever more advanced creative inventions, insights, and discoveries, and it set us apart from the rest of the animal kingdom. More than any other trait, it is our creativity, expressed through invention, language, art, music, science, and technology, that makes us uniquely human.

Homo habilis used stone knives to cut meat from the bones of other animals. Through successive generations, their descendants crafted ever more sophisticated stone tools for acquiring and preparing food. Comparatively recently, beginning in about 4500 B.C., we learned to form copper, then bronze, then iron and steel into a wide variety of tools. More recently, of course, we have invented the Swiss Army Knife, electric knives, and food processors.

This sequence of progressive change is repeated in many spheres of human activity. For instance, early humans surely looked up in wonder at the heavens. Their early curiosity was supplanted by the first systematic observations in ancient China, Egypt, and Mesopotamia, and these observations, in turn, gave way to more detailed celestial charts (570 B.C.), and to innovative instruments such as the astrolabe (130 B.C.) and the telescope (1608 A.D.).[2] Along the way, we accepted the view of the Earth as a sphere rather than a flat surface, and as one of many celestial bodies in motion rather than as the stationary center of the universe.

Now, of course, we scan the skies with giant optical telescopes and radio astronomy, we have set foot on the moon, and we have launched probes to the planets in our solar system and beyond. We now regularly peer down at ourselves from satellites, rather than merely gazing outward into space.

Consider just the last two centuries and the multitude of talented people who shaped our world through their well-known accomplishments in science, the arts, and technology. To note just a few, Darwin put forth his revolutionary theory of evolution, Kekule envisioned the elegantly simple nature of the benzene ring, Einstein formulated his mind-bending theory of relativity, and Crick and Watson identified the graceful, double-helical structure of DNA. Monet and the French Impressionists found a vivid new way to depict the world, Stravinsky composed his alternately raucous and serene *The Rite of Spring*, and Jules Verne anticipated exhilarating breakthroughs in space exploration, such as the Apollo moon landings, through brilliantly conceived fiction. In addition, determined innovators such as Thomas Edison, the Wright brothers, and Seymour Cray brought us a host of world-changing inventions, such as the light bulb, the airplane, and, more recently, the modern supercomputer. All of these familiar yet earth-shaking accomplishments are clear examples of creativity, but they seem to be quite different from one another. Can we explain them all in the same way? Do the minds of the celebrated people who accomplished these amazing feats work differently than ours? We think the answers to these two questions are "yes" and "no," respectively, and we will try to show why.

Our contemporary world is also teeming with the products of creativity. Inventiveness is all around us today. Consider, for example, that the U.S. Patent Office alone issues about 70,000 patents each year. In fact, George Basalla, a historian at the University of Delaware, used patent statistics to make the case that there is as much diversity in the set of things made by humans as in the set of living things on Earth.[3]

Furthermore, patent statistics capture only a small portion of the devices people actually invent and fabricate. And they miss entirely all of the songs, books, paintings, and scientific theories people create.

But, creativity pertains as much to the ordinary as it does to the extraordinary. While dramatic discoveries are being made and revolutionary inventions are being fashioned, ordinary people encounter problems in their daily lives that also call for creative solutions. For instance, Lola Lopes faced a problem when she needed to remove and repair her car's fuel pump. The peculiar arrangement of her engine parts had the fuel line running downhill into the pump. Consequently, if she extracted the pump, gravity would blithely do its allotted task and drain Lola's gasoline all over her driveway. How was she to plug up the fuel line?

As we will find, Lola devised a highly creative solution. The path she trekked to reach her solution tells us a great deal about how to overcome blocks to everyday creativity.

Lola's case is not an isolated one. Millions of people have, in fact, found imaginative ways to cope with problems in their daily lives, such as spreading butter or cutting cheese without a knife, opening a reluctant twist cap without a bottle opener, finding a subtle way to persuade another person, concocting an original recipe to make spaghetti more interesting, or working out a technique for keeping children entertained on a long car trip.

When we fasten curtains closed with a safety pin, substitute a paper clip for a key chain, or wrap Velcro straps from worn-out handball gloves around pant legs to keep them from being ensnared by a bicycle chain, we are being inventive. When we dream up different words to lampoon a familiar song, spin personalized fairy tales for our children, or paint or write stories for our own pleasure, we are being creative.

These observations reinforce the point that humans are essentially a creative species. This simple statement carries with it a striking implication that forms the central thesis of this book: creativity arises from ordinary mental processes that are part of the daily cognitive repertoire of normal human beings. An earlier observer put it more bluntly: "It would appear that genius is not at all a divine and rare gift. . .but is the destiny of everyone who has not been born a complete idiot."[4]

This blunt statement is too extreme, but it underscores a key point. The fundamental processes we need to be creative exist within all of us.

Being creative is such a natural part of being human that we can view creativity much the way we view language; no human cultures, no matter how isolated, have ever been found that do not use language. The same may be said of creativity. Of course, some cultures may boast more extensive technological, scientific, literary, or artistic accomplishments, but this depends on the relative value societies place on innovation, not differences in the basic mental processes of which people are capable.[3]

Since creativity is an intrinsic capability of ours, why are we often stumped by difficult problems that cry out for more creative solutions? We have claimed that humans are, by nature, creative thinkers who constantly rise to such challenges. Why do we sometimes have such trouble doing so? Answering these questions provides telling insights into the nature of creativity.

First, even though many people handle their relatively simple everyday problems creatively, many real-world problems are so complex that the path to a creative solution is more obscure. Finding a way to spread butter without a knife is, after all, simpler than discovering a way to produce large quantities of DNA from a small sample. Understanding the principles by which the creative mind operates, however, can help thinkers to ferret out even these more well-hidden paths.

Second, many people fail to take advantage of their creative potential, even in attacking simpler everyday problems. They are perfectly capable of using the basic mental processes that underlie creativity, but do not always see how to do so. They possess what might be called *latent creative potential*. By identifying what others do when they achieve creative solutions, it is possible to help people live up to their creative potential.

Finally, as we will see shortly, even obviously creative solutions to problems are not always as innovative as they could be. Strikingly creative advances often incorporate what in retrospect are fairly obvious limitations. By understanding the processes that lead to new ideas, we can help to make creative ideas even better.

THE CREATIVE COGNITION APPROACH

Our approach to creativity provides answers to some of the most basic questions about creativity: What brings it about? What inhibits it? How can it be enhanced? We call the approach *creative cognition* because we adapt the scientific theories and procedures from modern cognitive psychology to better understand and heighten creativity.

Creativity has for centuries remained a nearly impenetrable mystery, and it may seem surprising that it would yield its secrets to a scientific method of inquiry. However, cognitive psychology itself is a science that has already successfully probed many of the enigmatic workings of the human mind, and we have simply extended its methods into the realm of creativity. Cognitive psychology focuses on how people interpret the world around them; how they accumulate knowledge, organize their experiences, and recall memories; how they put their knowledge to work to make important decisions and solve problems from the simplest to the most complex; how they consider and plan for the future; and how they carry out actions from as basic as walking to as complex as piloting a supersonic aircraft.

By formulating theories and rigorously testing their predictions in carefully controlled laboratory experiments, cognitive psychologists have unlocked many of the mysteries of human knowledge and thought. Our central assumption is that the same scientific approach can help us to unveil the secrets of human creativity, because creativity is based on the same kinds of cognitive processes that we all use in ordinary, everyday thought: retrieving memories, forming mental images, and using concepts—the very processes that cognitive psychologists have learned so much about. We simply execute those processes differently when we act creatively.

Creativity is one of our most impressive abilities, and it often evokes strong emotions. When you do something creative you feel good. When you ponder great scientific and artistic accomplishments you have a sense of excitement and wonder.

But creativity is not entirely mysterious. Using the methods of creative cognition, we can better understand how the intricate workings of the human mind bring it about. And, like a spectacular sunrise or the birth of a child, the creative process is no less inspiring for being understandable.

THE FOUR P'S OF CREATIVITY: PRODUCTS, PEOPLE, PRESSURES, AND PROCESSES

Because creativity can thrill us with its great accomplishments, and because it is essential for solving practical problems, it has been studied in many ways. In this section, we show how our creative cognition approach complements those other ways of thinking about creativity.

PRODUCTS

A traditional way to approach creativity is to try to specify what counts as a creative product. What properties must an idea, a work of art, a piece of music, a problem solution, an invention or discovery have in order to be considered creative? Almost everyone would agree on two criteria: *appropriateness* and *novelty*. The idea must yield a workable solution to some relevant problem,[5] and it must be original, at least in the mind of the creator.

The first criterion is obvious enough. After all, if we ask you "how much is two plus two?" and you say "spaghetti," your answer is remarkably original, but not very helpful. We would not deem it to be creative. Only if a novel idea begets a useful invention, a valid discovery, a cure for a disease, an emotional response through art or music, or some other accomplishment would it count as creative.

The criterion of novelty, however, deserves further comment. Nobody would dispute the statement that there must be something new about an idea for it to be creative. The problem with focusing on novelty, however, is that it can mislead us into thinking that creative ideas are *only* novel. In reality, however, the ways in which creative ideas resemble old ideas are just as important as the ways in which they differ.

To see this point, consider the truism that the rate of scientific and technological change continues to accelerate. It took over one and a half million years to progress from stone to metal knives, but less than seven thousand years to advance from the first metal knives to the first electric ones. This implies that new ideas are constantly being built on the foundations of older ones.

What we call innovative ideas are never completely novel. They are always a marriage of old and new. To fathom creativity, then, we have to examine not just how new ideas break with the past, but how they carry it forward. Doing so demands that we probe the nature of human knowledge and how it is used. This is where creative cognition comes in.

Throughout this book, we will focus on this central theme. What can cognitive science reveal about the nature of creative ideas? How are they original, how are they familiar, and what determines the balance between these properties?

PEOPLE

A second traditional approach to creativity emphasizes differences between people. In this approach, some people are judged inherently more creative than others, and there is little one can do to improve one's creative standing. An extreme version of this individual differences approach, called the "genius view," holds that some people come into the world endowed with an enormous creative capacity. Their minds are assumed to work differently from those of ordinary humans. They experience flashes of insight in which scientific discoveries, whole works of poetry, complete symphonies, and so on, come to them unpredictably. They may or may not be able to identify the source of their own ideas. And all that's left for the rest of us is to observe and be moved by their accomplishments.

Many have attacked the "genius view," especially its assumption that creative ideas spring forth from obscure and unpredictable sources. Robert Weisberg, for example, a noted creativity expert at Temple University, has traced the origins of a wide range of highly creative accomplishments, including Edison's wizardly inventions, Picasso's evocative paintings, and Watson and Crick's illuminating discovery of the structure of DNA.[6] Weisberg has demonstrated that they all emanated from a deliberate application of previously acquired knowledge, not some mysterious, unobservable processes.

Research focused on the lives of acknowledged geniuses does help us to keep in mind the heights to which people can rise. Indeed, some excellent recent treatments along these lines allow us to celebrate the accomplishments of some of the world's most noted innovators[7,8] Certainly we should honor and revere their deeds, and we can all be inspired by them. We can also try to learn how to improve our own thinking. If we examine what extraordinarily creative people do, perhaps we can learn to emulate them.

It is also vital and empowering, however, to focus on the genius. . . . or at least the potential genius, in all of us. Thus, we are concerned more with what people have in common than with how they differ. We can celebrate the extremes of creative achievement—the stunning brilliance of Mozart's symphonies or Einstein's theory of relativity—without denying the potential that we all share. We also can examine why some people behave more creatively than others, and why some achieve results that dazzle and uplift us. Most importantly, we can assess how each of us might move toward our highest creative potential.

As we will find, individual differences in creativity are based on the amount of knowledge people accrue, and the ways in which they judiciously apply and reject that knowledge. The differences are not based on "divine inspiration," or some set of inexplicable mental abilities available only to the Einsteins of the world. Why do we say this? Because of the simple fact that we are all human, and as such, we are much more alike in our cognitive abilities than we are different. The mind of every reader of this book is much more similar to Einstein's than to that of the most creative member of the most creative nonhuman species. We all possess a human brain, descended in some way from that first tool maker, and capable of carrying out roughly the same basic mental processes of storing, retrieving, considering, and combining information.

Our approach is at once hopeful and challenging: hopeful because it encourages those who say, "I'm just not very creative," to reconsider their potential, and challenging because it forces those who see themselves as creative to recognize that their creativity derives from cognitive skills that they deliberately exercise, not from the sheer luck of having been born creative.

PRESSURES

Clearly, external pressures can motivate us either to cultivate or to quash creative ideas, to share them with other people or to keep them to ourselves. Several noted thinkers have provided in-depth treatments of these pressures,[9] and we acknowledge their significance in fostering or inhibiting creativity. It does a person no good to know how to be creative if he or she is constantly in a situation that discourages creativity. Nevertheless, our primary focus is on the creative workings of the human mind itself, rather than on those external pressures.

PROCESSES

Our approach to mapping the territory of creativity concentrates on the immense bodies of knowledge we all carry around in our heads, and the basic operations the mind performs on that knowledge. Although many factors influence creativity, knowledge and the processes that manipulate it are the fundamental materials from which we form creative ideas. Knowledge is the bricks and mortar, the wood and nails. Processes are the tools—the hammers, saws, and trowels. Creative thoughts are the houses we build and dwell in.

GENERATING IDEAS AND EXPLORING THEIR CREATIVE POTENTIAL

Many creative activities can be broken down into two phases. First, a person generates an idea, and second, the person explores the creative possibilities of that idea. Some of these ideas may be generated deliberately, and others may arrive unbidden. When explored, some of the ideas will be found to be silly or unworkable, but others will yield important advances.

In a way, creativity resembles evolution. Many variations of ideas, like the variations of traits in a species, originate from combinations and mutations of what has come before. When tested or explored against the demands of the environment, some variations fail miserably and are not passed on. Some new ideas fail to move us or solve our problems, just as some traits reduce a creature's chance of survival. Other variations convey some distinct advantage. They advance us. They survive. Importantly, however, *creative cognition* provides a way to increase the creative potential of newly spawned ideas, much as genetic engineering attempts to improve on evolution by deliberately designing species that are more adaptive.

The history of invention and discovery is brimming with examples of this generate-and-explore process. Many people have reported receiving flashes of insight, and then seizing on those insights to exploit their full potential. For example, while dozing by the fire one evening in 1865, the famed chemist Friedrich August Kekulé beheld an image of a snake swallowing its own tail. When he explored the significance of that unconsciously generated form he came to the creative discovery that the benzene molecule is shaped like a ring. Until that time, organic chemists had assumed that all carbon-based molecules must be made from carbon units linked in a series or chain. This notion limited the molecular arrangements they considered, and led to a nagging mystery about the actual nature of benzene, which could not fit any known chain. Kekulé's dramatic vision allowed scientists to overcome this inhibiting idea, and it provided a foundation for modern organic chemistry.

Of course, there is no guarantee that newly hatched ideas will prove fruitful. Many people have had apparent insights that turned out to be wrong on further consideration. We tend to forget these failures, and history seldom records them. But they do show us that scrutinizing ideas to test their usefulness is as critical to creativity as initiating the ideas in the first place.

Creative ideas do not always spring themselves on an unsuspecting thinker in the dramatic and seemingly unconscious way that Kekule's snake did. Nor do we have to wait around for an insight to pop into our mind. Instead, we can gain control of the creative process by deliberately inducing ideas that have creative potential. When Lord Rutherford considered the possibility that the structure of the hydrogen atom resembles the structure of a planetary system, his idea did not leap upon him unbidden in a dream. Like Kekulé's insight, however, Rutherford's was a powerful idea that provoked much research.

The model of creativity we call *Geneplore* captures the two phases of generation and exploration.[10] By separating creativity into these two phases it is easier to isolate some of the mental processes that are involved and determine how to wield them most effectively. For example, by exploiting simple mental activities such as recalling information, combining concepts, and crafting analogies, one can bring to life ideas that may lead to unexpected and penetrating insights. One can then probe these ideas by using other simple processes such as interpretation, inference, and searching for limitations.

The Geneplore theory tells us that, to be creative, we should generate ideas with creative potential and then explore them. But how are we to do this? Coming up with creative ideas may seem a mysterious process open to only a few special individuals, but, in fact, all of us are capable of developing truly interesting and novel ideas. We simply have to exploit, in a different way, some of the basic cognitive processes that we use all the time. What follows is an account of how our thinking can sometimes produce good, creative ideas, and sometimes fixate us on old ideas. Knowing how to use basic mental processes to do the former and avoid the latter is what being creative is about.

THE IMPACT OF OLD IDEAS ON NEW ONES

Mr. Speer was a conductor for the Paterson Railroad. On a warm September evening in 1835 he was sitting on a railroad car as it approached the Paterson depot. When an axle broke, he was thrown off the car and crushed to death under its weight.

Why was Mr. Speer seated atop a moving train car rather than safely inside it? Was he just being reckless, taking a risk to enjoy the warm summer air? No. According to the newspaper account he was "a very industrious and sober man," not prone to recklessness:

> Accident.–As the locomotive on the Paterson Railroad, with a train, composed of transportation and passenger cars, was approaching the depot at Paterson, on Monday evening, an axle of the leading transportation car gave way, which overturned that and the next car, and threw the third off the track. The locomotive and passenger cars remained upon the track uninjured, though the passengers felt a shock by the concussion. Mr. Speer, the conductor of transportation, a very industrious and sober man, was seated *on* the car at the break, and unfortunately was crushed to death under the load. [emphasis added]—*American Railroad Journal*, 1835

Mr. Speer sat on the car because a basic flaw in the design of early railroad cars required him and his fellow conductors to ride outside. That design flaw is a good place to start because it sets the backdrop for depicting both the positive and negative influence of old ideas.

As detailed in John White's classic, *The American Railroad Passenger Car*, early train cars were almost direct replicas of stagecoaches, complete with running boards and brakes that were operated by a conductor seated atop the vehicle in the front.[11] An example of one of these cars is shown in Figure 1.1. Like stagecoaches, they did not have central aisles between the seats. The design forced conductors and baggage handlers to climb all around the outside of the cars to do their jobs. And they rode on the outside all the time, even though this was clearly unsafe. Consequently, many of them fell off and were killed. This is what happened to Mr. Speer.

Only later did car designs incorporate central aisles through which railroad employees could walk more safely. Even though they were safer, these new designs met with some resistance. In fact, some people worried that the central aisle would become one long spittoon.[12]

Railroads are such a familiar part of our world today that it is easy to miss an important aspect of this example. In the 1830s

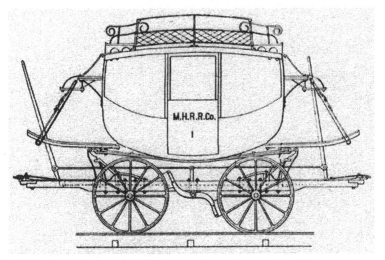

FIGURE 1.1. Example of early railroad car resembling a stage-coach (adapted from White, 1978).

the railroad was a striking technological advancement that was poised to revolutionize the way people traveled. So, adhering to old ideas from stagecoaches happened in spite of the fact that rail travel was an enormously creative idea. The point is a very general one: even plainly imaginative ideas tend to be heavily influenced by the old ideas that have preceded them.

There are many other examples of how imagination is influenced by what we already know. For instance, early forms of automated mining equipment duplicated the action of a person swinging a pick, and only later gave way to the more efficient continuous belt design. More recently, the fact that many modern computer terminals display exactly 80 columns of text is a direct outgrowth from the era when we literally fed data into computers by way of 80-column punch cards. A quick survey of science fiction will also convince you that most space aliens preserve many of the features of animals on Earth. Even serious speculative science shows how existing knowledge can guide or constrain the shape of new ideas. For instance, Frank Drake, the noted astronomer involved in the Search for Extraterrestrial Intelligence (SETI), believes that intelligent creatures from other planets will look basically like humans. Although such creatures could take virtually any form, even our scientific imaginations tend to consider only certain possibilities. Indeed the entire SETI project is based on the idea that intelligent beings somewhere else in the universe will be pretty much like us, including the way they communicate. This might be seen as just an interesting quirk were it not for the fact that we have spent millions of dollars on such projects.

Why do new ideas often look so much like old ideas? The answer is simple. When you develop an idea, you tend to recall something you are familiar with and pattern the new idea after that. The result is that many features of old ideas crop up in new ideas even when those features are unnecessary and potentially dangerous. We call this phenomenon *structured imagination*, and it colors the thinking of designers, scientists, business people, and artists alike. Indeed it influences each of us. It can lead to deadly consequences as we've seen in the case of engineering design, to failed businesses when corporations adhere to old procedures rather than searching for innovative ways to stay competitive, and to inhibited creativity in people as they face everyday situations and strive to fulfill their goals.

Sometimes we need to overcome old ways of thinking to achieve better solutions. Let's now return to Lola Lopes and her fuel line for an everyday example of moving beyond standard interpretations of objects in the world. Have you thought of a solution yet? Her path to a solution is an informative one, and you may have followed a similar line of reasoning. She first considered objects designed to perform a standard *function*: plugging holes. She wanted to find something to put *into* the end of the fuel line. Nothing she thought of would fit. Then she contemplated standard means of sealing things such as aluminum foil and plastic wrap, but none of these seemed workable. Finally she hit on the solution. She jammed the end of the fuel line into a potato. It wedged in nicely, formed a tight seal, and allowed her to get on with her repairs.

Lola had to get away from thinking about objects that normally plug into openings to envision what else could possibly do the job. She had to consider plugging the fuel line into something rather than vice versa. And, she certainly had to escape from the most typical uses of potatoes to realize that one could serve as a seal for a fuel line.

At the same time, however, we do not want to reject the past completely. Basing new ideas on old information can also convey distinct advantages. The details of stagecoach designs provided an expedient way of getting rail travel off and running. The properties of Earth animals furnish science fiction authors with a way of depicting space aliens so that audiences can readily comprehend them. The dramatic advances in simple tools and space exploration that we alluded to earlier occurred because people used old ideas as a springboard for new ones. Even Lola had to consult her knowledge about the properties of potatoes to know that one might solve her problem.

Creative ideas, then, typically emerge from a skillful blending of old and new information. Being creative demands that we judiciously employ and reject earlier knowledge. How can we identify the features of old ideas that we should retain and those that we should discard? Can we recognize when it might be good to deliberately use old ideas and when it would be better to try to avoid them entirely? To answer these provocative questions, we must plumb the very nature of human knowledge.

METACOGNITION: TAKING CONTROL

If creativity can result from applying ordinary mental operations in special ways, then being creative demands that we take charge of our own ideas. To do so, we have to practice the art of monitoring our own thinking, called *metacognition*.

Paying attention to what's going on in our own minds is not really all that difficult. Indeed this form of standing outside ourselves and looking in comes quite naturally in some circumstances. Most of us have had the maddening experience of knowing just the word we're looking for but being unable to pluck it out of the mists of our mind. It taunts and tantalizes us, but it will not come out in the open. And we are certain that if we hear the word, we will recognize it instantly. Being able to examine our knowledge this way is a form of metacognition, just as its embarrassing cousin: seeing a familiar face and being temporarily unable to recall the person's name.

We know that people who monitor their understanding of what they read tend to be better readers. When they bump up against confusing material, they go back and retrace their steps to find out where and how they got lost. Poorer readers plunge ahead recklessly, failing to notice that they haven't a clue about what they're reading. Likewise, monitoring your own thought processes and deliberately altering them when they are not creative can help you to function more creatively.

You can take charge of a host of cognitive processes. You will see that you can deliberately pose your problems in the most abstract and general way to avoid getting hung up on the specific details of old solutions. Are you trying, for instance, to make a more durable vinyl record album, or are you really trying to find a way to store high-quality sounds over a long period of time?

You can also deliberately combine two different concepts and playfully explore alternate interpretations of their union. Sometimes, gloriously unpredictable novel ideas spring forth from combining even mundane words, such as tree and car. What after all is a tree car?

You can deliberately suspend your knowledge and mentally doodle with visual forms in interesting ways, and then later interpret their significance. In doing so you might discover a new invention or a new way of thinking about some problem.

You can deliberately try to forget the things that are blocking your path to a creative idea, by simply getting up and going somewhere else either physically or in your imagination. You can also try to apply analogies and test mental models. There are many other deliberate actions that you can take, but they all have something in common: they involve basic cognitive processes that one can learn to use more creatively.

STALKING THE CREATIVE MIND

The creative mind is an elusive quarry. How are we ever going to pin it down? How can we grasp it in our hands long enough to take its measure, to weigh, sort, catalogue, and classify it? Throughout this book we use a two-part approach.

We turn on the twin beams of laboratory findings and real-world examples to shed light on creativity. In the next three chapters we describe laboratory-based studies of creativity that help to elucidate some of its most basic principles. In the remainder of the book we survey how those principles operate in real-world settings, such as invention and product development, business, science fiction writing, science, and art.

The laboratory studies we describe have the advantage that they precisely manipulate and control all the details of a problem situation and measure the effect on creative performance. For instance, if we ask some people to work continuously on a problem and others to take short breaks at specified intervals, we can then compare their rates of success to determine which procedure is most beneficial.

However, these laboratory-based approaches have serious drawbacks. The most obvious one is that to achieve a modicum of control over the situation, it is often necessary to utilize somewhat artificial tasks. There is always the risk that we might eliminate the very essence of what we're after in our urge to control and measure it. The question naturally arises as to whether the results from laboratory studies have any applicability to the real world. Do we bag our quarry, only to find that we have captured an impostor?

Only in real-world settings can we determine if there are truly important ways to apply theoretical principles we derive in laboratory studies. One of the ways is to assess what creative people do, or say they do in mastering their real-world problems. In this way we can garner information about the various avenues people can travel to reach solutions to the most important problems.

However, examining creativity in these real-world settings has its own shortcomings. The first is that creative people may not be able to see into the workings of their own minds. Observing our own mental processes may not always provide reliable information.

A more serious shortcoming of the real-world approach is the "compared-to-what" problem. Even if creative people can correctly pinpoint the origins of their ideas, we have no way of knowing whether they might have crafted even more creative ideas employing some other procedure. Likewise, if a company successfully markets a product, or becomes more profitable by reorganizing its basic structure, we have no way of knowing how much better a product or more successful a reorganization might have occurred with some other approach.

Consider an analogy to the "compared-to-what" problem. One of the authors sometimes teaches developmental psychology and covers the topic of parental discipline. Invariably, at least one student will defend physical punishment by saying something like, "My father hit me a lot when I was growing up, and I turned out OK." The obvious question is, "OK compared to what?" How much more curious, inventive, motivated, or accomplished might the student have turned out if his father had not beaten him? We do not know, because we have no way to compare the student with who he might have been. Likewise, we have no way to know how much more creative a specific individual or company might have been if they had approached a problem differently.

Only by setting up direct comparisons can we determine the best approaches. This is where laboratory research comes in. By giving two groups of individuals the same problem and instructing them to adopt different approaches, we can be sure which approach is better for that particular type of problem.

The true nature of the creative mind should reveal itself in the two converging approaches. Neither laboratory studies nor real-world observations of creative behavior alone can capture all that is important about creativity. But, together they complement one another, and each helps to overcome the shortcomings of the other. If a laboratory study hints that some technique is useful, workers on the frontiers of innovation can try it to see if it stands the test of real-world application. If highly creative individuals report using a certain strategy, we can try to duplicate it in the laboratory to see if it is truly better than other approaches.

By analogy, one searcher might flush our quarry into the open so that the other can photograph it in all its exquisite and colorful detail. Come with us as we employ these two powerful allies in our quest to observe the creative mind.

NOTES

1. National Research Council, *Improving Engineering Design: Designing for Competitive Advantage* (Washington, DC: National Academy Press, 1991); M. E. Porter, *The Competitive Advantage of Nations* (New York: Free Press, 1990).
2. Kevin Desmond, *A Timetable of Inventions and Discoveries* (New York: M. Evans & Company, 1986).
3. George Basalla, *The Evolution of Technology* (London: Cambridge University Press, 1988), p. 2.
4. P. K. Engelmeier as quoted in G. S. Altshuller, *Creativity as an Exact Science: The Theory of the Solution of Inventive Problems*, trans. Anthony Williams (New York: Gordon & Breach Science Publishers, 1984), p. 5.
5. We use the word *problem* here very generally. It refers to any gap between what one desires and what currently exists. A composer who wants to write a symphony to make people feel the sense of

sorrow that results at the end of an ill-fated love affair has a problem in the exact same sense that a medical researcher who seeks a cure for cancer has a problem. Both need creative solutions to reach their goals.

6. Robert W. Weisberg, "Case Studies of Creative Thinking: Reproduction versus Restructuring in the Real World," in *The Creative Cognition Approach*, eds. Steven M. Smith, Thomas B. Ward, & Ronald A. Finke (Cambridge, MA: MIT Press, 1995), pp. 303–326.

7. Dean K. Simonton, *Greatness: Who Makes History and Why* (New York: Guilford, 1994).

8. Howard Gardner, *Creating Minds: An Anatomy of Creativity Seen Through the Lives of Freud, Einstein, Picasso, Stravinsky, Eliot, Graham, and Gandhi* (New York: Basic Books, 1993).

9. Teresa Amabile, *The Social Psychology of Creativity* (Berlin: Springer-Verlag, 1983); Todd I. Lubart & Robert J. Sternberg, "An Investment Approach to Creativity" in *The Creative Cognition Approach*, eds. Steven M. Smith, Thomas B. Ward, & Ronald A. Finke (Cambridge, MA: MIT Press, 1995), pp. 303–326.

10. Ronald A. Finke, Thomas B. Ward, & Steven M. Smith, *Creative Cognition: Theory, Research, and Applications* (Cambridge, MA: MIT Press, 1992).

11. John H. White, *The American Railroad Passenger Car* (Baltimore: Johns Hopkins University Press, 1978).

12. John H. B. Latrobe, *The Baltimore and Ohio Railroad: A Personal Recollection* (Baltimore: The Sun Book and Job Printing Establishment, 1868).

CONCEPTS AND CREATIVITY

New ideas, whether wondrously creative or merely unusual, are almost always constructed from the building blocks of prior knowledge. Truly creative ideas arise when we wisely preserve and extend what is worthwhile from existing knowledge, and reject only the ideas that constrain our thinking. The old knowledge roots our new ideas in what has worked in the past, and the new variations supply the novelty that is the hallmark of creativity. In creative endeavors, recognizing what to retain and what to reject can make the difference between success and failure.

Here we will explore the nature of old knowledge and how it can affect new ideas. Gaining an understanding of human knowledge in all its intricate complexity and stunning variety can help us to wield it more effectively as we approach our creative efforts.

YOUR VAST STOREHOUSE OF KNOWLEDGE

Reflect for a moment on how much you know about the world. You will see quickly that you hold the deed to a vast storehouse of knowledge, filled with an enormous number and variety of facts, ideas, thoughts, and beliefs.

Consider even just the small portion of that knowledge that you can bring to mind in the next few seconds. You know that you are reading a book. You may be seated on a chair or sofa, in an office or a living room. You may have a cat curled up next to you, or a dog at your feet. If you choose to, you can reflect on different styles of music, foods you like, the ideas of truth and justice, or our place in the solar system, galaxy, or universe.

We could go on forever, but suffice it to say that you know many things. Cognitive scientists would say that you have many concepts. You boast concepts about books, living rooms, cats, rap music, Italian restaurants, justice, the Earth, the universe, and so many other things that we could fill many books just with the list of those things, let alone explanations of what they are.

Concepts are essential for making sense of the world, and without them we would have no chance of being creative. Even the simple act of reading a story would be impossible without concepts. When you read the sentence, "Zelda loves pepperoni pizza," you can understand it only because you know what pepperoni pizza is; you hold a concept of "pepperoni pizza." You also possess a concept of love that is complex enough to tell you that Zelda's love of pizza is different from Romeo's love of Juliet, or a mother's love for her child. So when you comprehend what you read, hear, or see, when you reason, and when you create, you are drawing on your fund of concepts. But, what are concepts like, and how do they affect your ability to be creative?

SIMPLE CONCEPTS

Let's begin with some very simple concepts about tangible things, such as snakes and snails, and yes, even puppy dog tails. What are these concepts like?

When you visit a friend who has just gotten a pet boa constrictor you immediately recognize it as a snake without the slightest hint of having to work to identify the creature. If a waiter inadvertently brought you stuffed mushroom caps instead of the escargot appetizer you ordered you would notice right away. And if a four-legged, furry creature of medium size bounded up to you wagging its tail and barking, you would conclude at once that it was a dog.

Your concepts about snakes, snails, dogs, and any of the myriad of objects in the world you are familiar with give you the power to know one when you see one. Concepts, then, are like little packages of knowledge. When we open them up and look inside we see that they must contain, among other things, information about the properties that make an object what it is.

There are legitimate philosophical debates about whether any such properties are truly essential to the meaning of a concept—if that proverbial leopard really could change its spots, would it still be a leopard? But you know that when you stroll through a new park you readily classify those tall, leafy brown things that have trunks and branches as trees, even though you have never seen those particular trees before. Those properties are central to your concept of tree.

Rather than trusting their own intuitions about such things, however, researchers try to uncover the central properties of concepts by asking people to list characteristic attributes.[1,2] For example, if you were to jot down the properties that most guitars have in common, your list would probably consist of things like strings, tuning keys, a neck, a hole, frets, and so on. Most people cite these attributes, and so we think of them as central to the concept of guitar.

How do these central properties impact on creativity? To a large extent, they tend to limit our imagination, and impose a structure on the new ideas that we develop. This phenomenon, called *structured imagination*, operates in real-world settings as well as in controlled laboratory situations.[3] Before reading about the research findings, however, try the following task for yourself: Imagine a planet somewhere else in the universe that is very different from Earth. Now imagine an animal that might live on that planet. What does your creature look like and how does it behave? How would you draw this alien being?

If you are like most college students tested in this type of experiment, you gave your creature eyes, located in a distinct head, and either two or four legs (see Figure 2.1). You most likely also made it symmetric. In other words, you endowed it with the central properties of Earth animals.

Even though there is no reason why creatures living on another planet would have to look this way, people seem to have trouble thinking of other possibilities. What they know about Earth animals colors their imagination about extraterrestrials.

This structuring comes about because when we must develop new ideas, we recall old ideas and use them as a starting point. Since central properties are such integral parts of our concepts, they work like implicit assumptions. They are part of our unconscious baggage. We do not even consciously question whether they are essential to the old concept, much less the new idea we are trying to formulate. We just import them directly into the territory of the new concept without declaring them at customs, or even stopping to have our old baggage inspected.

It is not surprising, then, to find the central properties of old concepts cropping up in otherwise novel creations. The very same properties that serve us so well in deciding whether an object is a dog, a cockroach, a computer, or something else, encroach on our ability to innovate.

FIGURE 2.1. Drawings of imaginary creatures produced by college students (adapted from Ward, 1994).

A cynical reader might observe that the college students we test are not going to come up with imaginative extraterrestrials; they're a pretty dull lot. A debatable point, no doubt. What is striking, though, is that this structuring phenomenon pervades so many creative activities, even among highly imaginative individuals. For instance, *Barlowe's Guide to Extraterrestrials* contains a marvelous collection of extremely imaginative creatures from science fiction.[4] If you study those examples, however, you will notice that they exhibit symmetry, legs, and eyes. In fact, three fourths of the creatures in *Barlowe's Guide* are equipped with these properties.[4] The same is true for creatures in the wonderfully creative "Star Wars" and "Star Trek" series.

Science fiction writers occasionally bring to life creatures that challenge our most basic assumptions about animals, such as Fred Hoyle's "Black Cloud," a huge intelligent cloud of hydrogen, or Piers Anthony's "Polarian," a being with a teardrop shape and no standard appendages or senses. However, these are clearly the exceptions, and are all the more remarkable for their rarity. Our imagination is ordinarily much more structured than we might think.

Earlier we saw how this same tendency of old properties to infiltrate new concepts gave rise to train cars with the unsafe features of running boards and external seating for conductors.[5] Those features had been central properties of stagecoaches. When designers fashioned the first train cars, they patterned them directly on stagecoaches, with which they were intimately familiar. Consequently, railway cars mimicked that prior mode of transportation, despite posing some dangers for the people who operated the trains, not the least of which was falling off.

Generally, the central properties of old concepts can insinuate themselves into new ideas and limit innovation whether in science fiction, invention, product development, business organizations, art, or science. In all of these pursuits, old knowledge influences even the most highly imaginative ideas.

Deploying old knowledge in the service of new ideas certainly does have benefits. It can bring forth expedient solutions, set the stage for further developments, and prevent us from becoming hopelessly mired in frivolous pursuits. When Kekulé had his insight about the benzene ring, he didn't first have to invent the concept that carbon atoms would join together. Rather, he had to specify the particular way in which they united with one another. Soft drink makers of today concoct an astonishing range of delicious and refreshing carbonated beverages. But they don't have to first dream up the notion of infusing liquids with carbon dioxide. Joseph Priestley did that for them in 1767.

However, as in the case of train travel, which represented a distinct break with past modes of transportation, or in the more modern case of corporations needing to adapt to changing market conditions, there are times when we want to shun the influence of certain central properties. There are times when it might be better to forget about what has come before and start over.

Through the tools of cognitive psychology, we can unveil the central properties of existing concepts. Then, armed with that information, we can predict what new concepts will look like. We can pinpoint the exact bits of old knowledge that are most likely to hang us up or hold us back in our quest to be more innovative. As we have seen, previous studies revealed that people consider eyes[6] and legs[2] to be central properties of animals, and so we could readily predict that most of our college students, as well as most science fiction writers, would insert those properties into their imaginary creatures.

Knowing about central properties also can help us predict what people will change when they generate new ideas. The central properties serve as the basic themes on which we can play new variations, or the skeletons that underlie and give form to the flesh of new ideas. Oftentimes people modify and build on central properties. Thus, the students imagined creatures that had the central property of eyes, but experimented with their shape, number, size, and locations. Some drew many eyes at the ends of long tentacles, others a single eye placed squarely in the center of the creature.

Most importantly, we can also open our minds and become aware of these central properties that we hold so tightly yet tacitly. By dragging the central properties of a concept out into the open, we can assess their worth, take their measure, and decide whether to accept, reject, or transform them as we craft new ideas. We can stop them at a customs checkpoint on the border of the new concept, and confiscate them if they appear to be contraband. This can help us to contrive more innovative concepts, whether in business, art, science, or day-to-day living.

Central properties also provide us a means by which to gauge the originality of a new idea. We can tally how many key features of the old concept are preserved and how many are excluded. We can also draw a distinction between modifying an attribute and rejecting it entirely. Rejecting a central property would, in most cases, count as a more dramatic change.[7] If you endowed your alien with an organ that senses variations in gravity, but gave it no traditional sense organs, we would judge it to be more original than if you simply placed normal eyes and ears in unusual locations. If a soft drink maker infused water with some other gas, say helium or oxygen, we might judge the new concoction more original than if they simply added new flavors to the same old carbonated water.

ATTRIBUTES THAT CO-OCCUR

Suppose that you just happen to catch a two-wheeled vehicle out of the corner of your eye. When you turn to look more closely you are surprised to see that it has a steering wheel, just as you would be if a four-wheeled vehicle sported a set of handlebars. Bicycles and motorcycles are "supposed to" have handlebars, and cars, trucks, and vans are supposed to have steering wheels. We just naturally expect some features to go together.

In fact, if you consider the central properties of many of your own concepts, you will notice that some attributes seem inextricably linked with others. A lifetime of experiences has taught you well that where you find certain features you are bound to find others. Where there's smoke there's fire, so to speak. Our observations of nature, for instance, tell us that wings belong more with feathers than with fur, and gills more with scales than with either feathers or fur.

How might this aspect of our concepts influence creativity? If people carry over one central property to a new idea, they might also throw in other properties that just happen to be correlated with it, whether or not it makes sense to do so.

Recent experimental research provides direct evidence for exactly this possibility.[3] When college students were told that the imaginary creature was feathered, they designed animals having wings and beaks, and when they were told it had scales, they incorporated gills. When told it was furry, they avoided wings, beaks, and gills entirely (see Figure 2.2 for some examples). Extraterrestrials need not contain these correlated properties, but our knowledge of their co-occurrence in Earth animals is so powerful that people inject them into new ideas anyway.

Since cognitive psychology can unveil the subtle correlations between known properties, it can put us on the lookout for their impact on our creative efforts. By shining the light of conscious awareness on those connections we also can learn to avoid them in our new ideas if we deem it desirable. In designing a new two-wheeler, for instance, we might be able to consider whether to steer it with a wheel, a joystick, a knob, or some other device rather than being held tightly in the grip of handlebars.

TYPICALITY

Which is the more typical breed of dog, a collie or a basenji? What are more typical pizza ingredients, pepperoni and mush-

FIGURE 2.2. Imaginary creatures produced by college students given no special instructions (a), or told the creature was feathered (b), furry (c), or scaled (d) (from Ward, 1994).

rooms or eggplant and pineapple? We answer these questions easily, and most often agree with other people about the best answers.

Some things just seem to be better representatives of a concept than others.[8,9] Generally, the more central properties a thing has, the more representative it is of its category or concept. How might this impact on our efforts to be creative?

Research shows that we call up typical instances of a concept faster than less typical ones.[9] To see this for yourself, quickly name the first five birds you can think of. Your list is likely to be populated with very typical birds, such as robins, bluejays, and sparrows, and less likely to contain unusual birds, such as pelicans, ostriches, and penguins.

Because more typical instances of a concept spring to mind first, we naturally tend to seize on them as starting points in developing new ideas.[3,5] And because the most typical members of a concept are the ones that have all of its central properties, this can reduce innovation even further. For instance, robins fly, lay eggs, and build their nests in trees, but penguins do not. If you base a novel alien on the more typical robin, it will resemble a stereotyped bird more than if you base it on a penguin.

Thus, by opening and expanding our minds to explore the outer limits and dazzling variety of our concepts we can go beyond the typical and concoct novel ideas that are wonderfully unusual. But this might take a bit of effort and patience. We might have to inhibit a strong desire to jump on the first idea that comes to mind, and we might have to forcibly dredge up less typical examples of a concept. The reward of more innovative ideas is worth the price of the additional effort.

Science fiction writers wield this technique to great effect. Most of them recognize that there exist more wild varieties of life on Earth than most people could dream up for other planets. And they gather a rich harvest of ideas from the seeds of these most extraordinary instances. By embracing the knowledge we already have rather than rejecting it, we can develop new and innovative ideas. And by drawing on less typical concepts we have more to work with to enhance the originality of new ideas.

FLEXIBILITY

So far we have focused mostly on how our stock concepts can limit creativity. But let's see how exploiting concepts more effectively can boost our creativity.

First, think about the concepts you actually bring to mind. Are they rigid structures that you simply retrieve when you need them? Or do you actively construct them from bits and pieces of information in your vast storehouse of knowledge?

By the first view, your concepts are like books in a library. When you need one, you simply pick it up from the right shelf. By the second view, you construct a different "book" each time you need it from a library of separate pages. The first system would be more efficient, but the second would be more flexible, and would foster more creativity.

For many years, cognitive psychologists accepted the "fixed structure" view without question. But recently the "active construction" view has become more popular. To see why, read the two following passages.

> As Mary reached the third floor landing she could hear the familiar clicking of nails on the linoleum floor of her tiny apartment. She could picture Muffy scurrying to reach the door to greet her. As she unlocked the door, she let out a sigh and thought, "It's nice to be home with my dog."

> As John set his shotgun in the gun rack and stepped out of his truck he could hear the familiar scratching of nails on the hardwood floor of his cabin. He could picture Gus bounding toward the door to greet him. As he unlocked the door, he let out a sigh and thought, "It's nice to be home with my dog."

Did you picture the same dog for each of these passages? Probably not. You would probably be surprised if Muffy turned out to be a Saint Bernard and Gus turned out to be a toy poodle.

Why? Because the events in each passage led you to construct very different images of dogs. In other words, what you retrieve from your memory as a "typical" dog is not fixed, it is flexible.

The way you think about any concept may be slightly different every time you think about it. This is partly related to the fact that the exact concept you bring to mind depends on your immediate situation, and no two situations, no matter how similar, are ever identical. Even if you eat the same type of hamburger, at the same fast-food restaurant, with the same friends every night, you will not have the exact same experience every night or hold the same conversation, word for word. The events leading up to the meal will change from day to day, and they will influence your experience of the meal and the nature of the ideas you conjure up. Perhaps your favorite team just moved within a game of first place, or your preferred candidate just moved down in the polls, or your sink was clogged that morning, or you were slapped with a parking ticket or summoned to jury duty.

These recent experiences impact on exactly what we bring to mind. If you've just seen the popular movie "Beethoven," about a lovable Saint Bernard, the image you get from the sentence, "John petted the dog," will be different than if you have just seen "101 Dalmatians." Similarly, your immediate thoughts about pollsters, pundits, and politicians will waver with the standing of your candidate, and your concepts of police officers and the justice system will reflect the reasons you are headed to court.

Research verifies that the exact concepts we construct change from one time to the next. In one experiment, Francis Bellezza of Ohio University had people provide definitions for a set of words, and then return a week later to define the same words a second time.[10] He found that people's definitions changed greatly from one week to the next. In other words they constructed their concepts differently on the two occasions.

You may have a few typical versions of most concepts that you call on for certain standard situations, but it is unreasonable to think that you have an infinite supply of fixed, prestored structures ready to go in anticipation of every possible situation in which you will need to dredge up every concept you know. It is more reasonable to believe that you have the ability to construct exactly the concept you need when you need it.

This is good news for creativity. Since it is very natural for us to construct familiar concepts, we can seize on the same basic process to construct novel ones. What we need to do is take control of the process and deliberately use it to develop more innovative concepts.

So now let us design a novel alien, using the concept of "dog" as a starting point, but not a whole standard, prestored example of a dog, rather a construction of a dog from its central properties. Think about the properties that most dogs have in common and combine them in some pleasing way to get a completely novel animal. Perhaps when we consider that dogs have four legs, for example, we can deliberately ask whether our novel creature might have some other number of legs, such as three or five. Similarly, we might systematically vary other central attributes of known dogs. Do they really need to be a certain size, or have two ears, and one tail?

What we see is that by working with the central properties of our concepts we can make our implicit assumptions become explicit. We can bring them to light and then either retain, reject, or modify them.

This same approach can be used to develop creative ideas for inventions, as in the procedure called morphological forced connections.[11] In that procedure, for example, one might take an existing invention, mentally chop it into its basic attributes, and then consider all the possible variations on those attributes. By playing with the different variations, one might come up with an interesting idea for a new invention. For instance, we might develop a new eating implement by taking the familiar fork and varying the length and shape of its handle, the material from which it is made, the number, size, and separation of its tines, and so on. We might assemble a tasty new sandwich by experimenting with different combinations of all the types of breads, meats, cheeses, vegetables, and condiments we can think of. Only our taste buds would tell us if pastrami and provolone on six-grain bread with onions and French dressing would produce a delightful new taste sensation.

GETTING DOWN TO BASICS

One other aspect of our concepts that limits innovation is that we seem to think of our concepts in very concrete ways. Consider the picture in Figure 2.3. What is it? Most likely you said it was a cat. You could have called it a Siamese, a mammal, an animal, a living thing, a tangible thing, a furry thing, a thing, or any of an infinite number of other possibilities. Yet your first reaction was to think of it as a cat.

FIGURE 2.3. Siamese cat.

Eleanor Rosch, a prominent cognitive psychologist at the University of California at Berkeley, pointed out that most people classify objects in the same way, as cats, dogs, birds, fish, and so on.[8] She called this the "basic level" of categorization. This very powerful tendency impels us to think of most things on a very concrete level. We seem to be drawn to the wealth of directly observable features such as legs, wings, and fins that help us to distinguish between objects at this level of abstraction. It is simply easier for us to do so.

The consequence for creativity is that, when we try to develop new ideas, we also tend to rely on the basic level, and to get stuck on concrete observable properties. The majority of people who generate imaginary creatures in laboratory experiments claim that they base their creatures on specific Earth animals, such as dogs and elephants.[3] The people who drafted these "basic level" animals into service were the ones whose aliens were the most similar to Earth creatures.

ABSTRACTION

One essential aspect of our concepts that we can capitalize on is their potential flexibility. Even though we tend to think on a basic level, we are not bound to that level. For instance, you can readily think of the cat in Figure 2.3 as an animal, a furry thing, a member of the class of things that weigh between 5 and 15 pounds, and so on. A friend, who shall go nameless, thinks of his dog as a furry thing, and slides her around on his wooden floors to pick up dust bunnies.

One way to exploit the flexibility of concepts is to recast them in more abstract terms. When we want to design a new alien creature, we do not have to base our ideas on specific Earth animals, such as dogs and elephants. Instead, we can reach beyond the limits of concrete images and can cobble together a more general concept of animals and their fundamental properties.

What are animals like in their most abstract sense? They must extract information from the environment, obtain an energy source to carry on biological processes, protect themselves from hazards, and survive long enough to reproduce. What happens if we construct a novel creature using this abstract representation of the concept of "animal"?

Suppose that, instead of basing an imagined animal on your pet dog, you considered only the more abstract idea that living things need some way to take in information about the world around them. Posing the problem this way might evoke all sorts of innovative ideas, including organs to sense magnetic fields, wind speed, gravity, heat, humidity, and so forth. The more abstract approach leaves more room for the imagination, and is likely to inspire us to call up ingenious variations on the senses.

Our studies confirm that abstraction leads to more innovation.[3] The college students who developed more innovative creatures stated that they had considered abstract ideas such as what the planet was like and what the animal would need to survive there. Examples of more unusual creatures are shown in Figure 2.4.

The students who thought more abstractly went beyond the familiar physical characteristics of Earth animals to consider the bigger picture. By establishing the rough outlines of the planet first they were then able to fill in exotic details to tailor their aliens to its conditions. By pondering the essence of what it means to be an animal, they escaped the bonds that might have tied them to any one specific animal.

Thus, old information can help us to develop new ideas, particularly if we pull it up in an abstract form. Forming abstract thoughts is not that difficult because of the way we naturally organize information in our memories. It is relatively easy to think of your pet dog in more abstract ways, as a mammal, an animal, or a living thing. You have already wired the connections between those levels of abstraction through a lifetime of experience with living things. For the same reason it is also easy to think of eyes and ears more abstractly—as devices for getting information from the environment.

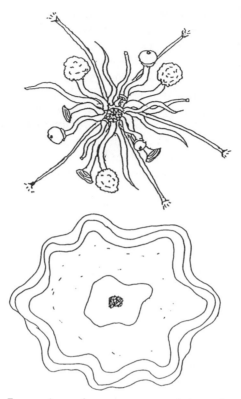

FIGURE 2.4. Examples of more unusual imaginary creatures produced by college students.

It seems that bringing to mind *specific* old ideas, such as dogs and stagecoaches, locks us into the details of those objects, making it difficult to think of highly original new ideas. Concentrating instead on general, abstract information in one's mind leaves room for more pointed and original innovation.

Abstraction also aids in the task of making our assumptions explicit. To get to the abstract levels, we have to consider our most fundamental assumptions. In the process we learn more about our own concepts, our most deep-seated beliefs about what's important in the world. We also set the stage for extending and expanding on our concepts.

Abstraction also helps crystallize what we are trying to accomplish. Consider the store owner, for example, who viewed himself as selling records and tapes, a very specific, narrow idea. The recent trend toward putting music and video on CDs could have threatened to put him out of business. On the other hand, if he viewed himself as a provider of home entertainment, a more abstract characterization, a switch in the medium would not have been threatening, and might even have opened up new opportunities.

Abstraction is vital to creativity. It allows people to dodge the inhibiting properties of more specific concepts. We will see that abstraction is a very general principle that elicits greater innovation in problem solving, product development, and science fiction writing.

AD HOC OR GOAL-DERIVED CATEGORIES

Another aspect of concepts that can expand our creative potential is that we readily form new ones as we need them for new situations. Lawrence Barsalou, a noted cognitive psychologist at the University of Chicago, refers to these concepts we construct on the spot as ad hoc or goal-derived categories.[9] To get a sense of one such concept, consider the following items: children, important documents, pets, money, and clothes. At first they do not seem to form much of a concept, but when you hear that they are things to take from your home in the event of a fire, the concept emerges clearly out of the mist. You also can summon up other items, such as photographs and jewelry.

Notice also that this new, "ad hoc concept" includes items that we usually place in different groups. Children and pets, for instance, might be members of the group "living things," whereas money and documents might exemplify the group "nonliving" or "paper artifacts." In conjuring up ad hoc concepts, we have to be flexible in reorganizing our existing concepts.

Barsalou's research reveals that people easily contrive and comprehend ad hoc concepts. This shows that a basic process of creative thought is readily available to all of us.

This ability to reorganize our concepts may spark creative solutions, particularly in many day-to-day situations that call for creative flexibility. Let's return, for instance, to Lola and her fuel line. She had to forge an ad hoc category of "things to plug a car's fuel line." Her choice of a potato required a clever reorganization of our concepts. We constantly face similar tasks, as when we have to think of things to stand on to change a light bulb, objects to hold papers in place on windy days, and activities to entertain children on long car trips.

ESSENTIAL PROPERTIES

One aspect of concepts that restricts our potential for novelty is that many may possess essential properties. A concept may have certain features that are of such supreme importance that changing those properties alters the concept completely.

Consider a task that Frank Keil, a noted cognitive developmentalist at Cornell University, gave to his subjects.[12] Suppose some scientists got a raccoon, painted it black, dyed a white stripe down the middle of its back, and sewed in a scent gland that would release a foul odor. Would this creature still be a raccoon, or would it now be a skunk? If you were like most adults in Keil's study, you'd say that it was still a raccoon. Why? Because you believe that there is some essence of raccoon that remains. If the scientists could have changed that essence, perhaps by manipulating the genetic structure of the raccoon, they might have changed it to something else.

Similarly, if we don't endow our imaginary aliens with certain properties, other people might not think of them as animals at all. Thus, there are constraints on just how unusual ideas can be and still remain workable.

Let's take a slightly different example that shows how quickly people change their minds if we change the essence of an object. Suppose these same scientists took a coffeepot, sawed off the handle and spout, sealed the top, cut an opening in the side, and filled it with bird food. Would the object be a coffeepot or a bird feeder? Again, like most adults, you probably would say it was now a bird feeder. Why? Because the changes altered the basic function of the object, and function is the essence of an artifact. Any change in the function will change the concept of an artifact.

Together these results tell us that there are some limits on flexibility. We can bend and twist our concepts in many ways, but if we cross the line and change their essences we risk breaking them. Even highly creative people are unlikely to think about changing the essence of a concept in developing a new idea, and if they do alter it, we may not even recognize their creation for what it is supposed to be.

CONCEPTUAL COMBINATION

As we have seen, one way to generate more creative ideas is to use very abstract knowledge. Another way is to amalgamate two separate concepts into a single new idea. In fact, we merge ideas constantly as we try to make sense of the world around us. Prior to the development of microcomputers, for instance, you probably had never heard of a "computer table," but you had no difficulty making the leap to combine your concepts of "computer" and "table" to understand what computer tables were. Nor did you stumble when you first encountered other expressions, such as "religious right," "cautious optimism," "shuttle pilot," or "head banger."

Even young children expand their vocabularies by coupling together separate words to express a new thought. Deana Ward was only two years old when she reported that she had a "soggy nose." She certainly knew what soggy diapers were, but nobody had ever told her that, when you had a cold, noses got soggy too. She came up with this delightful novel expression on her own. Connor Ward entered the fray at about the same age with "alligator car" to refer to a favorite green toy car of his. It is not at all unusual for children of these ages to push the limits of their language this way.

We call this melding of two ideas *conceptual combination*. What makes this seemingly simple ability so exciting is that it can lead us to generate novel and surprisingly creative possibilities.

As an analogy to the power of conceptual combination, think for a moment about hydrogen and oxygen. Put them together in the right combination and you have something entirely different from either of the gases alone, namely water. From knowing about either gas alone, you could not have predicted that ice would float, a hot shower would feel so relaxing, or a cool drink would be so refreshing. Simple concepts are like these simple gases. Alone, they have known and obvious properties. Put them together, and seemingly magical transformations can occur. But, it is not magic; it is simply a creative aspect of ordinary cognition.

Research verifies the seemingly obvious point that from a combination can emerge new properties that were not evident in either of the original concepts. For example, Gregory Murphy of the University of Illinois had people rate how true certain properties were of individual concepts and their combinations.[13] One set of concepts consisted of the individual words *empty* and *store* and their combination, *empty store*. Consider the property "losing money." Like subjects in Murphy's study, you probably recognize that losing money is typical of empty stores, but not of stores in general or of things that are empty. Something changes when we draw the concepts together.

One of our favorite examples of conceptual combination is a "computer dog." Ponder for a moment what that might be. You may have thought about one or more of the following: a virus protection program that barks when it detects an intruder, a simulated or virtual dog, a hacker or computer nerd, a robotic dog, or a hot dog prepared in a computer-controlled device. The point is that many new possibilities emerge that might never have occurred to you had you thought only of dogs and computers *separately*. Perhaps you've thought of a completely different, and more interesting possibility.

A particularly stimulating interpretation is that a computer dog is a peripheral device, similar to a mouse, for interacting with a computer. This last idea highlights the fact that conceptual combination can be a source of ideas for new inventions. It also underscores the importance of the exploration phase of the Geneplore theory we introduced in the first chapter. Like most new concepts, our "computer dog" is just a vague idea until we bring it to life through further exploration.

We asked students to envision what a computer dog would be like if it were a variant on a mouse. They produced several innovative ideas, one of which is shown in Figure 2.5. This idea evolved because one student suggested that the device should

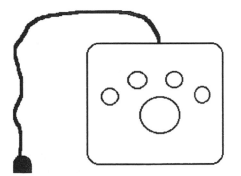

FIGURE 2.5. Sketch of computer input device developed by college students who explored the combination "computer dog."

resemble a dog's footprint. A second followed with the idea that the individual pads would be buttons with different functions, and a third proposed that the central pad could be a rolling trackball. The idea naturally leads to more playful explorations. What are the functions of the different buttons? What can you do with four buttons that you cannot do with the usual two buttons of a mouse? What is the trackball for? How do the functions of the buttons and ball interact? The point is that a potentially useful and clever invention could originate from these simple efforts.

Conceptual combination is not limited to putting together simple object concepts, such as "computer" and "dog." Consider, for example, the hilarity, the wisdom, and the inspiration that blossom forth when people pool their talents. What would Laurel have been without Hardy, Abbott without Costello, or Moe without Larry and Curly? Would Sherlock Holmes have been the same without Watson? Would Crick have found the structure of DNA with a different Watson? And wouldn't the world be a poorer place if not for the pairings of Rogers and Hammerstein and Gilbert and Sullivan? The humor, suspense, discovery, and beauty that emerge from these sorts of alliances speak volumes about the power of combinations.

Conceptual combination can be applied to help develop new products, literature, art, and scientific concepts. Combos snacks that roll cheddar cheese into an outer shell of pretzel are one such food product, and the works of pop artists, such as Andy Warhol, that combine art with commonplace objects from popular culture give us a hint of the possibilities in the art world.

Those who give advice about how to be creative have often mentioned the importance of combinations,[11] but we are only now beginning to find out why they work. We also are finding out why some types of combinations lead to more creative possibilities than others. We no longer have to rely on a "brute force" procedure of randomly testing a huge number of combinations.

One factor that matters is how close or compatible the two concepts are. Generally, the further apart the concepts are, the more they allow for original ideas to emerge.[14] In other words, combining two similar animals, say a "squirrel possum," is less provocative than combining a tool and an animal, say a "hatchet gorilla."

More original ideas may also spring forth when we combine opposites.[15] This style of combination is called Janusian thinking in reference to Janus, the Roman deity who was depicted as having two faces on opposites sides of his head. Intriguingly, Janus was the god of doors and gates, which points to a tantalizing symbolic link to creativity. By invoking this mode of thinking we may open doors to a world of new possibilities.

Shakespeare evoked powerful and poignant emotions with his enduring literary notion that "parting is such sweet sorrow." Many a would-be comic has earned at least a mild chuckle by noting that "military intelligence" is an oxymoron, combining two seemingly contradictory concepts. And Newt Gingrich recently blasted the Americorps program as being "coerced volunteerism." The program is designed to help young people attend college when they have given of themselves to help our country. But however you feel about its merits, you can see that Newt's nugget combines conflicting concepts into a catchy phrase that is bound to swing some votes. It is clear that there is something inherently enticing about combinations of opposites whether they lead to actual inventions, vivid literary images, or just snappy expressions.

METAPHOR

Metaphors are a kind of conceptual combination that can be used to express ideas creatively, and that can lead to creative change in the mind of the person who hears them. Stating that football is the demolition derby of athletics cleverly expresses the energy and violence inherent in football. Saying that golf is the antique car show of athletics captures the relative tranquility of that sport. In either case, the concepts of athletics and automobiles are combined, leading us to view each one a little differently.

Research documents that new properties and concepts can emerge from metaphors.[16,17] The properties that pop into your mind for golf and antique car shows separately will differ from those that strike you when you combine them into a metaphor. Similarly, when you comprehend a metaphor, such as "my job is a jail," you may construct a completely new, ad hoc category, such as the set of items that are unpleasant and confining. You can then probe that concept more deeply and develop new examples, such as a large mortgage or an unsatisfying relationship.

Metaphors can help to overcome some of the constraints of our staid concepts. By allowing us to view objects in a new way, with new properties, and as members of new concepts, we can free ourselves of the bonds of the past and move off in entirely new directions.

SCHEMAS

Our knowledge is also arranged into complex structures called schemas. Schemas play a crucial role in the organization of our memories by telling us how our simpler concepts relate to one another. You probably have a "living room" schema comprised of many simpler concepts, such as a sofa, chairs, a coffee table, lamps, and possibly a television, VCR, and stereo equipment. Your schema provides a map of how those items are organized. They are not just piled together in the middle of the room. The coffee table may rest in front of the sofa which faces the television, and so forth.

You probably also have a schema that depicts a typical visit to a restaurant: a hostess greets you, guides you to a table, and hands you a menu. Following that you may peruse the menu, order a dish, receive and eat your food, obtain a check, pay, and leave.

Schemas allow us to behave efficiently. We know what to expect and how to behave when we walk into a living room or eat at a restaurant. We have difficulties only when something violates our expectations, and those problems disclose the power of our schemas. To take just one example, if you were to wander into a restaurant in Germany and wait by the door for a hostess to seat you, you would wait a long time. It is customary in Germany for patrons simply to seat themselves at an empty table. Further, in many restaurants, if no tables are empty, the norm is to approach a table that is already occupied and ask if an empty chair at that table is "free." If the reply is "yes," the custom is to sit down in that chair at the table. Try doing this in a restaurant in the United States.

The problem with schemas is the same as that regarding simpler concepts. When our goal is to produce something new, our schemas can constrain us as much as they can help us. Roger Schank, a well-known expert on schemas at Northwestern University, described the pitfalls of schema-based thinking.[18] Because they can be applied nearly automatically, they allow us to behave very efficiently. But, for the very same reason, schemas allow us to stick mindlessly with old ways of interpreting situations and solving problems.

As with simpler concepts, a way to overcome the influence of schemas is to recognize their central properties. By making explicit the underlying assumptions that are built into a schema, we put ourselves in a position to challenge and change it.

ANALOGIES

One of the great resources for artistic, technological, and scientific advancement is *analogy*, taking concepts from one area and extending them to another. A well-known example, mentioned previously, is Lord Rutherford's adoption of the solar system as a possible model for the structure of the hydrogen atom. Although subsequent work in physics demonstrated that the model was not quite right, it still provided a powerful new way to think about atoms. And it stimulated an onslaught of invaluable research and discovery in chemistry and physics. A more recent example of the creative use of analogy from the world of product development is the Reebok Pump. The idea for the design was borrowed from a relatively recent medical marvel, the inflatable splint.[19]

We all employ analogies in understanding the world, but we can also fashion them deliberately to our creative advantage. The *synectics* approach proposed by the noted creativity expert William Gordon makes use of analogies for creative problem solving.[20] Gordon claims that you should exploit many varieties of analogies in creative thinking, such as personal analogies in which you envision yourself as one of the parts of the problem, and direct analogies in which you borrow examples from nature to better understand the problem. For instance, in trying to devise a better mousetrap, you might investigate how different kinds of spiders catch their prey.

The synectics approach is a relatively old one, and we have learned much about what makes a good analogy since it was first introduced. One of the difficulties in using an analogy is knowing which features you should hold onto and which you should discard. When we say that an atom is like the solar system, surely we are not claiming that its nucleus is yellow and has a surface temperature of 5800 degrees Kelvin. What we really mean is that there are smaller entities orbiting around a more massive central entity and that some force prevents them from flying away. But how do you know in advance what are likely to be the most vital similarities?

New research in cognitive psychology tells us that the attributes to keep are those that share similar "higher-order relations," which specify how separate objects are connected.[21] In this case, a higher-order relation might be "revolves around," and thus you might retain the idea that the smaller bodies revolve around the larger ones. The point is, in using analogies to understand something new, do not be misled by pure surface similarities and differences. It is the deeper similarities that are more important. As with the process of abstraction, analogies can help us to narrow down the set of properties that are worth considering.

Later, we will see how creative individuals use analogies in invention, writing, art, and science. Again, knowledge is good because it allows us to map useful properties from one domain to another, particularly if we focus on the higher-order relations that link separate objects.

MENTAL MODELS

Mental models are the most complex cognitive structures we will consider. Just as schemas depict the links among several simple concepts, mental models can consist of several schemas working together.

We actively construct mental models to comprehend complex phenomena, and we use our general knowledge about the workings of the world to do so. We might want to understand the nature of the digestive process in humans, how a clutch or brake system operates, or why the sun, moon, and stars appear and disappear in a consistent sequence. The mental pictures we form of the component parts of these systems and how those parts interact are called mental models.

Let's consider the day/night cycle. As adults in a modern culture, we know the scientific explanation: the Earth is a sphere that rotates on its axis. We also know that the sun and moon are spheres, and that the Earth revolves around the sun and the moon around the Earth. But consider what a young child's model of the system might be like, or that of an adult without the benefit of modern scientific knowledge.

Many first-graders believe that the Earth is flat and motionless, and that the sun disappears at night behind mountains or clouds.[22] Because a flat Earth would not have an "other" side, these children do not think of the sun as being on the other side of the Earth at night. The children's models are similar to those of the earliest astronomers who thought the Earth was flat and motionless, and that the sun hid behind hills or mountains, or went under the Earth at night.

How do children develop more accurate mental models? How do astronomers or other scientists accomplish this? For children, it is a question of how they learn what adults consider to be the right answer, but for scientists, it is a question of how they make the creative leap from an older to a newer way of seeing the world. One way to change a model is by changing, eliminating, or suspending the presuppositions that we use in constructing it. Once again, we see that deliberately examining our most basic assumptions is one of the key paths to change and innovation.

For example, the correct model of the day/night cycle involves a rotating Earth, but it does not make sense to think of a flat Earth as rotating, at least not in a way that plausibly could explain the disappearance of the sun at night. This is especially true if the flat surface is supported by ground going downward indefinitely. So, if we hold the basic assumption that the Earth is flat, it is difficult to construct the appropriate mental model of the day/night cycle.

And a flat, supported Earth seems reasonable because unsupported objects (and people) fall downward. So, intuitively, the Earth needs to have a flat living surface because objects would fall off an underside, and it needs to be supported rather than floating freely in space.

Once we make explicit our flat-Earth theory, we can challenge or reject it in favor of some other shape, such as a sphere. By doing so we then can envision the sun being on the other side of this sphere at night, and ultimately we can envision the change in the sun's relative location as being the result of the rotation of the sphere on its own axis.

This example of discovering a better model for the day/night cycle shows again how creative advances develop from making our assumptions explicit so we can challenge them. Clearly, we can only do this if we are able to identify the very assumptions that should be challenged.

Mental models can also have a profound effect on our ability to develop creative innovations, particularly for complex systems. When we generate and explore them, they allow us to set up hypothetical situations, make predictions about outcomes, and mentally "run" the model to test those predictions. A nephew of one of the authors had a less than complete mental model of digestive processes and wondered why liquids, such as milk, had certain colors entering the body but exited a different color. He came up with the hypothesis that the length of time the liquid was in the body might determine the color change. In his model, more time equaled more change. Being a budding young scientist, he developed the appropriate experiment to test his model: drinking milk while standing in the bathroom. Unfortunately this did not advance the cause of science greatly, but it does show how even young children can use mental models to come up with interesting and creative ideas for experiments.

Mental models can even influence the way we live our lives, right down to our simplest everyday customs. Consider, for instance, what we say when someone sneezes. A typical response is "God bless you," or "Gesundheit," which means "health" in German. Why do we express concern for the person's spiritual or physical health? According to Charles Panati, author of *Extraordinary Origins of Everyday Things*, this custom originated with the idea that the soul or essence resided in the head, and with the related concern that a sneeze might inadvertently expel it.[23] Ancient peoples also had observed that sneezing preceded death from certain diseases, which led them to pray for those who sneezed. Interestingly, around the third century B.C., Romans thought sneezes might expel the "sinister spirits of later illnesses,"[24] which led to the custom of congratulating the sneezer.

The contrast between the customs of praying for and congratulating the one who sneezes is instructive. The customs are based on contrasting views of sneezes being harmful versus helpful, which in turn are based on contrasting naive theories about whether a sneeze is likely to expel one's soul or some harmful spirit. The point is that we use our theories about the workings of the world to construct mental models which, in turn, influence many aspects of our lives, even down to such simple conventions as what to say after someone sneezes.

Most of us no longer believe that people who sneeze risk expelling their souls, but the custom remains. This is an illuminating example of intransigence in changing our patterns even when the original reason for behaving a certain way is lost. The superficial action remains, but the deeper or more abstract reasons are obscured. Changing our customs requires bringing our assumptions into the open so that they may be assessed, altered, or possibly rejected. A recent example is the push to adopt year-round schooling, rather than retaining extended summer vacations which are a throwback to an earlier era in which children were needed to help out on the family farm.

We have examined many varieties of knowledge ranging from simple concepts to elaborate mental models, and considered how they impact on one's ability to behave creatively. Knowledge can inhibit and constrain or invigorate and expand our creative potential. Couching problems in more abstract terms and confronting unquestioned assumptions can help us tease apart which aspects of our knowledge we ought to embrace and which we should exclude. This can, in turn, place us squarely on the path toward greater creativity.

NOTES

1. Eleanor Rosch, Carolyn B. Mervis, Wayne D. Gray, David M. Johnson, & Penny Boyes-Braem, "Basic Objects in Natural Categories," *Cognitive Psychology* 8 (1976), pp. 382–439.
2. Mark H. Ashcraft, "Property Norms for Typical and Atypical Items from 17 Categories: A Description and Discussion," *Memory & Cognition* 6 (1978), pp. 227–232.

3. Thomas B. Ward, "Structured Imagination: The Role of Category Structure in Exemplar Generation," *Cognitive Psychology* 26 (1994), pp. 1–40.

4. Wayne Douglas Barlowe & Ian Summers, *Barlowe's Guide to Extraterrestrials* (New York: Workman Publishing, 1979).

5. Thomas B. Ward, "What's Old about New Ideas," in *The Creative Cognition Approach*, eds. Steven M. Smith, Thomas B. Ward, & Ronald A. Finke (Cambridge, MA: MIT Press, 1995).

6. Barbara Tversky & Kathleen Hemenway, "Objects, Parts, and Categories," *Journal of Experimental Psychology: General* 113 (1984), pp. 169–193.

7. Margaret Boden, *The Creative Mind: Myths and Mechanisms* (New York: Basic Books, 1991), has distinguished between improbable and impossible forms of creative ideas. This distinction is similar to the point we are making here.

8. Eleanor Rosch, "Principles of Categorization," in *Cognition and Categorization*, eds. Eleanor Rosch & Barbara Lloyd (Hillsdale, NJ: Erlbaum, 1978), pp. 27–48.

9. Lawrence W. Barsalou, "Ideals, Central Tendency, and Frequency of Instantiation as Determinants of Graded Structure in Categories," *Journal of Experimental Psychology: Learning, Memory, and Cognition* 11 (1985), pp. 629–654.

10. Francis S. Bellezza, "Reliability of Retrieval from Semantic Memory: Noun Meanings," *Bulletin of the Psychonomic Society* 22 (1984), pp. 377–380.

11. James L. Adams, *Conceptual Blockbusting* (Reading, MA: Addison–Wesley, 1986). Adams and several others have described a number of variations on this same basic procedure. They all involve breaking an object into its components and trying out combinations of changes in those components.

12. Frank C. Keil, *Concepts, Kinds, and Conceptual Development* (Cambridge, MA: MIT Press, 1989).

13. Gregory L. Murphy, "Comprehending Complex Concepts," *Cognitive Science* 12 (1988), pp. 529–562.

14. Edward J. Wisniewski & Dedre Gentner, "On the Combinatorial Semantics of Noun Pairs: Minor and Major Adjustments to Meaning," in *Understanding Word and Sentence*, ed. Greg B. Simpson (Amsterdam: Elsevier Science Publishers, 1991), pp. 241–284.

15. Albert Rothenberg, *The Emerging Goddess: The Creative Process in Art, Science, and Other Fields* (Chicago: University of Chicago Press, 1979).

16. Roger Tourangeau & Lance Rips, "Interpreting and Evaluating Metaphors," *Journal of Memory and Language* 30 (1991), pp. 452–472.

17. Sam Glucksberg & Boaz Keysar, "Understanding Metaphorical Comparisons: Beyond Similarity," *Psychological Review* 97 (1990), pp. 3–18.

18. Roger C. Schank, *The Creative Attitude: Learning to Ask and Answer the Right Questions* (New York: Macmillan Co., 1988).

19. Bruce Nussbaum, "Hot Products: Smart Design is the Common Thread" *Business Week,* June 7, 1993, p. 56.

20. William Gordon, *Synectics: The Development of Creative Capacity* (New York: Harper & Row, 1961).

21. Dedre Gentner, "Structure Mapping: A Theoretical Framework for Analogy," *Cognitive Science* 7 (1983), pp. 155–170.

22. Stella Vosniadou & William F. Brewer, "Mental Models of the Day/Night Cycle," *Cognitive Science* 18 (1994), pp. 123–183.

23. Charles Panati, *Extraordinary Origins of Everyday Things* (New York: Harper & Row, 1987).

24. Panati, *Extraordinary Origins of Everyday Things, p. 10.*

VISUALIZING IN A CREATIVE WAY

We have considered how people can use their concepts to formulate creative ideas. Now we examine how mental imagery can enhance creativity. We will also examine how imagery techniques can sometimes help us avoid the influence of conventional concepts when generating a new idea.

We know that people can imagine creative means to find jobs, win at games, solve problems, or put old ideas together to make new ones. Why is imagery so useful in creative thinking? How can our visualization skills be improved to enhance creativity?

Recent studies in the field of cognitive science have explored the nature of mental imagery and have identified many of its salient features, including the role that imagery plays in mentally synthesizing basic elements and parts into completely novel patterns and forms. The studies yield profound insights into the nature of human thought, and they provide new techniques for improving creative visualization.

59

SOME BASIC PROPERTIES OF IMAGES

We begin by considering some of the most basic properties of images. Imagery can be used to recall useful information, determine directions and other spatial relations from memory, and explore future changes and transformations.

RESOLVING FINE DETAILS

By forming large mental images of objects, we can often detect fine details that would not be noticeable in smaller images. For example, look at the drawing of the elephant in Figure 3.1. Now try to imagine the elephant entirely within the small circle at the top left. You will probably find that your image contains only a few clearly visible features. Next, form your image entirely within the larger circle at the top right, letting it completely fill

FIGURE 3.1. Demonstration of the role of image size in detecting properties.

the circle. Can you now "see" many more details in your image of the elephant? For instance, can you detect its ears, eyes, or the nostrils in its trunk?

This example shows how we can often survey the detailed features of an object by imagining the object at a reasonably large size or close distance. Stephen Kosslyn, a noted imagery researcher at Harvard University, has investigated this phenomenon by asking people to imagine animals and other objects at various sizes. His studies reveal that people require less time to find the features of imagined objects as their images become larger.[1]

As another example, imagine that you were looking at an ant walking along the surface of a table that was three or four feet away. Your image of the ant will probably seem like little more than a tiny speck. Now imagine that you were looking through a magnifying glass at the ant while it was standing on the head of a pin. You can probably now detect many of the ant's features, including its legs, jaws, and antennae.

These properties of image resolution closely resemble those of objects we actually perceive. Just as the features of real objects become easier to resolve as we approach or magnify them, so, too, do the features of imagined objects. This is because imagery and perception seem to share many of the same information-processing mechanisms in the human visual system.[2]

How can detecting features in mental images be advantageous? For one thing, it often allows us to recall information about something that we have never previously committed to memory. For example, consider the following questions: What do a German shepherd's ears look like? Did Thomas Jefferson have a beard? What color is the top stripe on the American flag? Most people report that it is extremely helpful to form mental images when trying to answer such questions.

Why do images help in such cases? Many of the subtle details about our experiences are not stored in our memory as explicit facts, but are stored as visual impressions, which can then be recalled using images. For instance, most of us would not have made a point of remembering that Thomas Jefferson did not have a beard, or that the top stripe on the American flag is red. Such details, however, are available to us when we form mental images, and can then be detected when we enlarge or enrich our images.

Using imagery, we can also compare objects that we may never have directly compared before. For instance, which is larger, a strawberry or an acorn? By imagining each of the objects side by side, it is fairly easy to tell. Again, most of us would not have made an explicit point of remembering that strawberries are larger than acorns. By using imagery to make mental comparisons, we can discover and explore a virtually unlimited number of such relations.

SCANNING MENTAL IMAGES

When recalling various details using images, we often scan across our images, in much the same way that we might move our eyes or shift our attention to scan across actual visual scenes. This scanning process allows us to efficiently "move" our focus from one part of an image to another.

Figure 3.2 is a map of Texas, showing some of its major cities. Briefly study the map, if you are unfamiliar with the state, and then cover it. Now try to visualize the map, focusing first on Austin. Now scan to Dallas, then to Houston, El Paso, and Amarillo. Did you have the impression that you were mentally "traveling" across your image as you were shifting your focus, in the same way that your eyes might travel in scanning a real map?

Experiments on mental image scanning have shown, in fact, that it takes more time to scan greater distances in images.[3] It thus appears that images have a property analogous to the spatial extent of an actual map or figure: The farther away a feature is on an image, the longer it takes to scan to it.

Image scanning can be beneficial when trying to improve your memory. For example, suppose you were going shopping, and wanted to remember a list of items that you were supposed

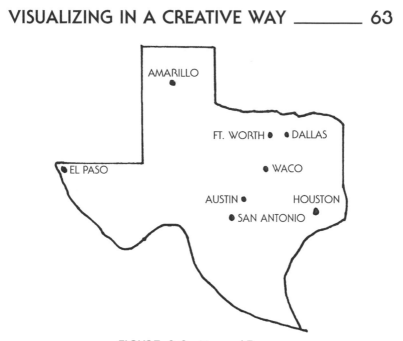

FIGURE 3.2. Map of Texas.

to buy. An image-scanning technique called the "method of loci" could help you to remember the entire list. You might begin by picking out some route that you were familiar with, and that had many familiar, distinctive landmarks along the way. You might then take each of the items on your list and imagine them to be associated in some interesting or creative way with each of the landmarks. Then, when you wanted to recall the items, you could simply imagine walking along the route and looking at the landmarks.

Your familiar route might take you past various landmarks such as a mailbox, a large rock, and a bridge. If your first item was a carton of milk, you might imagine that when you opened the mailbox, milk came gushing out of it. If your second item was orange juice, you might imagine that the rock was painted a bright orange. If your third item was a package of hot dogs, you might imagine looking down from the bridge and seeing an enormous hot dog floating by in the shape of a canoe.

These imagery techniques can often assist us in committing large numbers of items to memory. For instance, people who seem to have phenomenal memories often report that they associate the things they want to remember with salient features along easily recalled pathways. A famous mnemonist in Russia, studied by the psychologist Aleksandr Luria, could remember hundreds of unrelated words in this manner, by forming concrete images of the words and then placing the images at various points along a familiar street in Moscow.[4]

Image scanning can also help us to judge directions and plan travel routes when an actual map is not available. For instance, recall the map of Texas that was used in the earlier example, and imagine that you were looking at San Antonio. With a good mental image, you could indicate the compass direction that you would have to travel along in order to get from San Antonio to Dallas (e.g., north, east, northeast, or northwest). You could also tell whether you would encounter any other cities if you traveled along that particular route.

MENTAL TRANSFORMATIONS

A fascinating aspect of mental images is that most of them are inherently dynamic. Within our imagination, we can turn things around, make objects grow larger or smaller, or even change the shapes of objects. This ability can be extremely useful. It allows us to anticipate how objects might look if rotated, moved, or changed in other ways, so that we could still recognize them and prepare to act. If you walk down a hallway and notice the underside of a flight of stairs, for instance, you can correctly anticipate that continuing around to the other side will allow you to climb up to the next floor. People can even learn to read books that are upside down, by imagining that they are turning the words around.

Many studies on imagery have explored a type of mental transformation known as "mental rotation."[5] In most of these studies, people are shown a rotated pattern and are asked to identify it. For instance, is the rotated letter shown in Figure 3.3 the normal form of the letter "R," or is it the reversed, "mirror image" form of the letter? Most people report that they have to imagine rotating the letter to its upright position in order to tell. These studies have generally found that the time it takes to imagine rotating something increases as the distance it has to be rotated increases. For instance, something that was turned completely upside down would take longer to mentally rotate to the upright position than something that was only slightly tilted. This suggests that the imagined rotations are carried out over time in much the same manner as the way a real object would actually be rotated.

In addition to mental rotation, other types of mental transformations are possible, including imagined changes in the size and shape of something. For instance, suppose you had a ball of pizza dough about the size of baseball. How large of a pizza could you make by rolling the dough out? What other shapes and forms could you make?

The dynamic nature of mental images often enables us to anticipate future actions. For instance, if you were watching a television program and suddenly closed your eyes, you could probably imagine quite easily how the scene would progress for

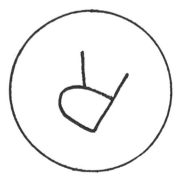

FIGURE 3.3. Type of letter used in mental rotation experiments.

the next few moments. In fact, most dynamic images acquire a kind of mental "momentum," such that their motion automatically continues for a short time along their previous paths.[6]

With practice, we can also imagine changes that might occur over much longer periods of time. For instance, what do you think your best friend would look like twenty years from now? What would cars of the future look like? How would the skyline of a famous city change? A rich variety of future possibilities can be ours to explore when we create and transform our mental images.

Our ability to transform mental images can often stimulate creative insights by giving us fresh perspectives on familiar things. When people imagine three-dimensional objects or scenes, for example, they are often able to visualize how those objects or scenes would look from completely different vantage points.[7] If you were watching a tennis match, you could imagine what the game might look like from each player's perspective, or even from a vantage point directly above the players. As we will see, our ability to imagine things from many different perspectives can lead to surprisingly creative ideas in a wide variety of endeavors, especially when we thoroughly probe all of the creative opportunities those perspectives offer us.

Interestingly, our ability to anticipate can lead to delightful surprises. Thus, because you might expect the opposite side of a piece of pottery or sculpture to resemble the one you see, an artist can catch you off guard to great effect. If you turn the piece around or walk to the other side and find something unexpected, you might laugh, gasp, or stand with mouth agape depending on how big the surprise is.

MAKING NEW DISCOVERIES IN IMAGES

How effectively can we search inside our mental images to unearth worthwhile, innovative mental treasures? Infusing subtle details into mental images, scanning the images to make note of those details, and recasting the images to see things in different perspectives can all inspire original discoveries. In addition, detecting what we will presently call "emergent features" can greatly enhance our ability to uncover something new in our mind's eye.

EMERGENT FEATURES IN IMAGES

On the one hand, it might be hard to understand how mental images could give rise to creative discoveries. Because our images can only be formed according to information that we have already acquired, how could they ever engender new insights? On the other hand, people frequently do report having new insights after having formed and explored their images. Kekule's insight about the circular nature of the benzene molecule, as we have seen, was based on the image of a snake swallowing its own tail.

To resolve this paradox, we must consider emergent features—those properties that become salient when we combine the parts of an image. These properties can come into play in our imagination even though they were not evident initially. At first, an image is constructed from knowledge that we have already acquired. Once assembled, however, an image can bring divergent aspects of our knowledge together. As a result, the image can exhibit novel, emergent features, depending on the way the previous knowledge structures or components were combined. In imagery, as in many other aspects of life, the whole is often more than the sum of the parts.

Imagine, for example, a mythical creature that has the head and legs of an ostrich but the body of a lion. How would this creature walk? How high could it jump? Where would its head be in relation to its tail? Such a creature would have many other types of emergent features that could be discovered in imagination, but which would not have been previously associated with either an ostrich or a lion. It is because of these new and unanticipated properties that we can often use imagery to make genuine discoveries.

Even slight changes in an imagined form can produce emergent features. For instance, imagine a spider that suddenly lost one of its eight legs. By forming and inspecting an image of this modified spider, you could gain insights into how it would walk, or the type of web it might build. Insightful, emergent features can often arise when we remove something from a conventional image.

MENTAL SYNTHESIS AND IMAGE DISCOVERY

Some experiments conducted by one of the authors and his colleagues investigated how mentally combining images can induce emergent features.[8] In one experiment, college students imagined superimposing a pair of familiar patterns, consisting of letters, numbers, or simple shapes, and then reported any new, recognizable forms that emerged. These students were often able to discover emergent forms that were not contained in either of the component patterns. For example, imagine superimposing the letter "X" directly over the letter "H," such that the four corners of each letter coincide. Can you detect any familiar geometric forms, or any other letters or recognizable symbols, that emerge from this synthesis? If you were like most of the students in this study, you probably detected at least some emergent patterns, such as two large triangles, several smaller triangles, other letters (such as an "M" or "W"), and possibly even a "butterfly" or "bow tie." Also, you probably were not thinking about these particular patterns when you first imagined combining the letters; that is, you probably did not intentionally insert them into your images. More likely, they evolved from your use of mental synthesis.

In another set of experiments, we asked students to imagine a sequence of transformations on a pattern, and then to try to identify the final pattern that emerged at the end of the sequence. For example, imagine taking the letter "B" and rotating it by 90 degrees to the left, such that the straight line in the "B" is now horizontal, with the loops pointing up. Now imagine adding an equilateral triangle pointing straight down, and connected to the bottom of the rotated "B" such that its base is the same length as the horizontal line and becomes merged with it. Now imagine erasing the horizontal line. Can you recognize the resulting pattern?

Let's try another example: Imagine the letter "F." Now imagine a "b" attached to the bottom of the vertical stem in the "F," so that there is now one, continuous vertical line connecting the two letters. Now imagine flipping the small loop in the "b" around to the other side, so that it points to the left. Can you recognize the resulting pattern?

Students in these experiments often recognized the emergent patterns in their imagination (which, in the previous examples, were a "heart" and a "musical note"), even though they were rarely able to guess what the patterns would turn out to be prior to having completed the transformation sequences. Many of them, in fact, seemed genuinely surprised by their discoveries.

How do people detect these emergent features? If the features are sufficiently obvious, it may only require a simple scanning of the image to detect them. However, if the features are more subtle or complex, one might need to consider alternative ways of organizing and interpreting the image. For instance, to recognize the "heart" pattern in the example just described, it might have been necessary to rule out competing interpretations such as "a double ice-cream cone."

GENERATING CREATIVE IMAGES

The previous examples reveal that most of us are able to detect emergent patterns in mental images. However, each example contained images and transformations that furnished people with a roadmap to making a particular discovery. Indeed, the room for creativity in the previous studies was rather restricted, in that the image components could only be combined or transformed in certain ways. What if people were given more freedom in forming and manipulating images? Would it then be possible to uncover highly creative emergent patterns?

CREATIVE MENTAL SYNTHESIS

To explore this possibility, one of the authors and a colleague developed an experimental procedure that provided students an opportunity to make genuinely creative discoveries in their imagery.[9] The students were given the names of three of the parts shown in Figure 3.4, which consisted of letters, numbers, lines, and simple geometric forms. These parts were selected at random by a computer, where it was possible for the same part to appear twice or even three times. For example, a person might be given the parts "circle," "square," and "letter C," or "triangle," "triangle," and "letter T." Their task was then to imagine combining all three parts to make a recognizable pattern or symbol. They were allowed to mentally rotate the parts, imagine changing the size of the parts, or imagine superimposing the parts on one another. The only restrictions were that they could not deform the

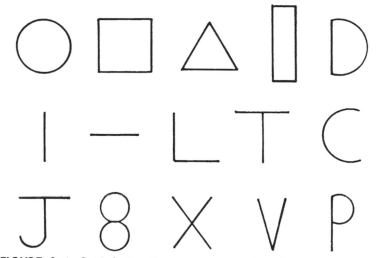

FIGURE 3.4. Set of stimuli used in mental synthesis experiment (from Finke & Slayton, 1988).

shape of the individual parts (for example, compressing the circle to make a narrow ellipse), and that they had to use all three parts. Also, the resulting pattern had to be something that one could easily name, and that another person could easily recognize. The students were given two minutes to perform the task.

Judges then scored the patterns according to how recognizable and creative they were. On average, the students were able to discover a recognizable pattern on about 40% of the trials, and about 10% of the patterns were judged to be highly creative. Examples of these creative, mentally synthesized patterns are presented in Figure 3.5.

You can try this method for yourself. Simply take any three parts shown in Figure 3.4, and imagine combining them in various ways to see if any meaningful patterns emerge. By exploring these various combinations, you can often discover creative symbols and logos. Figure 3.6 presents a logo that might be used to advertize swimwear or a new type of champagne, which was constructed using the circle, triangle, and the letter "T."

When interviewed at the end of these experiments, most of the students reported that, when they first began the task, they had no idea what patterns would emerge. Rather, most said that they had employed an exploratory, imagined synthesis of the parts, simply to try out various engaging and suggestive combinations. In fact, the highly creative patterns were rarely predicted, either by the students or by the experimenters conducting the study.

CREATIVE INVENTIONS AND DESIGNS

Naturally, one would like to do more with creative visualization than simply to generate intriguing patterns and symbols. In fact, similar techniques can also be used to conceive designs for new inventions and other practical devices. In this section, we describe some additional studies that demonstrate not only that this is possible, but that it is a skill that most of us can readily acquire.

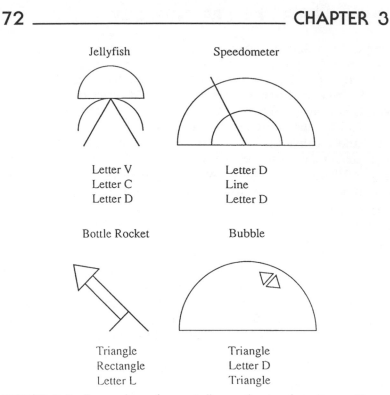

FIGURE 3.5. Examples of mentally synthesized patterns (from Finke, 1990).

IMAGINING POSSIBLE INVENTIONS

Suppose you were given a set of basic object shapes and parts, such as those shown in Figure 3.7. Pick out three parts at random, and then try to imagine combining the parts to make a new, creative type of tool. You can mentally combine the parts in any way, and vary their relative sizes at will. You can imagine putting some of the parts inside of others. Further, the parts can be made out of·any material, such as metal, plastic, wood, rubber, or glass. The only restrictions are that the parts cannot be deformed in shape (with the exception of the wire and the tube,

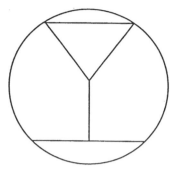

FIGURE 3.6. Logo created by mentally synthesizing components (from Finke, 1990).

which are bendable), and that you must use all three parts in your design.

One of the authors asked college students to do precisely this—to try to imagine practical inventions using sets of randomly chosen parts.[10] The parts were selected by a computer; examples would be "sphere," "cube," "ring," or "cone," "cone," "bracket." The categories for the inventions consisted of furniture, personal items, transportation, scientific instruments, appliances, tools and utensils, weapons, and toys and games. In most of the experiments, these categories were also selected at random by a computer.

The students were given two minutes to imagine a practical object or device within the designated category, at the end of which time they were to draw their invention and describe how it would work. Judges then rated the inventions according to their originality and practicality. Those inventions that were rated highly on each of these dimensions were classified as "creative inventions."

On about half of the trials, the students were able to conceive a practical invention of some kind, and about a third of these were classified as creative. For example, Figure 3.8 shows a "hip exerciser," which was created using the half sphere, wire,

FIGURE 3.7. Component objects and parts used in creative invention experiments (from Finke, 1990).

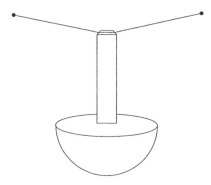

FIGURE 3.8. "Hip exerciser" developed by student in creative visualization experiment (from Finke, 1990).

and rectangular block, for the category "furniture." The device works by standing on the half sphere, holding onto the rectangular block, and shifting one's weight in a circular motion. The wire connects the top of the device to opposite walls in the room to provide stability.

Strictly speaking, the inventions in this study were really invention "concepts," in that they would need to undergo at least some refinements and modifications in order to work exactly as conceived. Even so, it was remarkable that students who had had no previous training in imagining creative inventions were able to come up with so many ingenious ideas.

When interviewed, the students gave provocative accounts of how they had performed the task. Most of them reported that they had started out not by trying to think of a particular invention, but by putting the parts together in suggestive ways, and then exploring various possible interpretations of the resulting forms. For instance, they often imagined how the forms might be handled, put in various positions, or seen in different contexts, as ways of stimulating possible insights into their practical uses.

Ironically, we have also found that when we loosen the restrictions on selecting the parts and the invention categories, allowing people to choose them at will, the resulting inventions are much less creative. Evidently, having the freedom to make these choices allows one to come up with designs that are already quite familiar. By having to use parts and categories that are selected at random, one is often forced to consider less conventional designs.

GENERATING AND INTERPRETING PREINVENTIVE FORMS

There are many cases where people have made important discoveries by shifting their focus away from a particular problem, and by noticing something alluring about an unexpected result. The discovery of safety glass is a good example of the role that serendipity has often played in creative invention. The French chemist Edouard Bénédictus invented safety glass after accidentally knocking down a beaker that had held cellulose nitrate, and noticing that its shattered pieces held together. He had not planned to invent safety glass, but the accident provided him with a fruitful idea to be exploited. Such discoveries can be missed if a person focuses too narrowly on one particular outcome, and ignores significant "accidents" that might give birth to other possibilities.

In light of this, it may sometimes be better to wait before trying to interpret a mentally synthesized form. This might increase the chances of discovering new, inventive possibilities. For instance, when combining parts in imagination, you might start out by creating forms that seemed inviting and important only in a very general sense, before committing yourself to developing a particular type of invention.

The value of delaying the interpretation of imagined forms was explored in additional experiments.[10] Students were instructed to imagine combining three randomly chosen parts, as before, but were not given the interpretive categories at first.

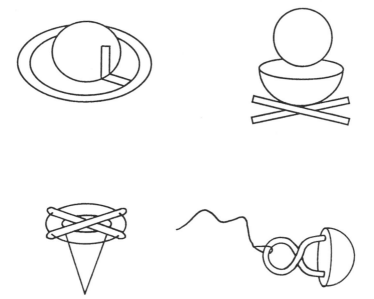

FIGURE 3.9. Examples of preinventive forms (from Finke, 1990).

Instead, they were told to simply try to make their forms seem interesting and potentially meaningful. Examples of these "pre-inventive forms" are shown in Figure 3.9.

Once they had completed imagining their preinventive forms, and had drawn them, they were then given one of the categories, chosen at random, and were told to try to interpret their forms as a practical object or device belonging to that category. What we found was quite intriguing. First, the students were able to discover fewer inventions overall. This is not surprising, because they now had to use forms that were completely uninformed with respect to those categories. However, they were able to discover the greatest number of creative inventions under these conditions. This means that it is some-

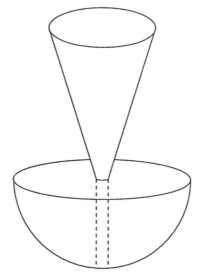

FIGURE 3.10. "Contact lens remover" developed by student in creative visualization experiment (from Finke, 1990).

times better not to know exactly what you are trying to invent when you begin to explore creative ideas.

Examples of some of these creative inventions are shown in the next few figures. In Figure 3.10, the preinventive form was interpreted as a "contact lens remover." This device works by placing the rubber cone against the contact lens, placing a finger over the hole at the back (which seals off the air), and then lifting the lens off the eye.

Figure 3.11 shows a preinventive form that was to be interpreted as a scientific instrument. The student who generated this form came up with the idea of a "tension wind vane." The large, hollow cylinder is made of a lightweight material, and is attached to the base by an array of wires. The base contains a tensiometer that records slight changes in the wire's tension

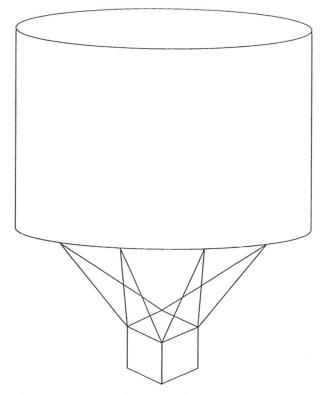

FIGURE 3.11. "Tension wind vane" developed by student in creative visualization experiment (from Finke, 1990).

whenever the wind presses against the cylinder, and thereby provides sensitive information about changes in wind speed and direction.

Overall, the students were able to interpret their preinventive forms as creative inventions on about one of every six trials. This is quite striking, given that none of the students were previously trained in forming and interpreting preinventive forms. Also, in these experiments, they were only given one minute to generate their forms, and one minute to interpret them. When given extended time to explore their preinventive forms, they could almost always discover a creative invention of some kind.

Why were the students so successful in discovering creative inventions under these conditions? Presumably, delaying information about the interpretive categories until after the forms were generated reduced the likelihood that they could simply tailor their forms to fit the categories, which would have resulted in more conventional creations. Instead, not being guided by a particular category evidently encouraged them to generate forms that had a greater, overall potential for creative discovery.

Again, you may wish to try this technique for yourself. First, generate a preinventive form, using three randomly chosen parts. Then pick out one of the categories at random, and try to interpret your form as representing a practical device within that category. It is important not to know, in advance, what the category will be. In this way, you will likely increase your chances of discovering a genuinely creative interpretation of your imagined form.

A common expression holds that "form follows function." For many types of invention, this is certainly true; the final form of the invention is determined by what it is supposed to do. Studies on preinventive forms, however, demonstrate that the opposite rule can also apply: "function follows form." In these experiments, the functions of the inventions were determined by the suggestive, emergent features of the preinventive forms.

In further experiments, we have explored the effects of placing additional restrictions on the interpretive categories. When one imposes categories that pertain to specific types of objects, such as "tables" and "chairs," as opposed to more general categories such as "furniture," people are less likely to arrive at a creative invention, after starting out with preinventive forms. The reason is that it then becomes much harder to find creative ways of fitting the novel forms into these more restrictive categories.

THE ILLUSION OF INTENTIONALITY

There is an interesting illusion that often occurs with creative inventions that are discovered by generating and then exploring preinventive forms. It often seems as if the forms were designed to fit the particular functions of the inventions, rather than vice versa. For example, if you look again at the "tension wind vane" shown in Figure 3.11, it might seem as if the person first decided to try to invent such a device, and then constructed the form with this purpose in mind. In fact, just the opposite occurred.

This "illusion of intentionality" is quite common with preinventive forms. Once the forms are interpreted in a particular way, it often seems to an outside observer that they were designed for that purpose, and that no other interpretations of the forms would have been as meaningful or valid. This may reflect a general tendency to assume that there must be a specific reason behind every creation or design.

It is easy to show, however, that a given preinventive form can be interpreted in any number of interesting and practical ways. For example, Figure 3.12 illustrates how the same preinventive form could be interpreted as a creative invention across all eight of the general object categories used in these studies. Evidently, there is a wide range of interpretive paths that each of us can follow in creative visualization, allowing us multiple opportunities to make new explorations and discoveries.

CREATIVE REFINEMENT OF EXISTING DESIGNS

Another way to use preinventive forms is to take an existing design, add a randomly chosen feature to it, and then probe the potential implications of the modified design. Consider, for example, the implications of adding an L-shaped bracket to the end of a thermometer, as shown in Figure 3.13. The student who visualized this form realized that the bracket could allow one to spin the thermometer to force the mercury down, instead of having to shake it in the usual way.

FIGURE 3.12. Multiple interpretations of same preinventive form (from Finke, 1990).

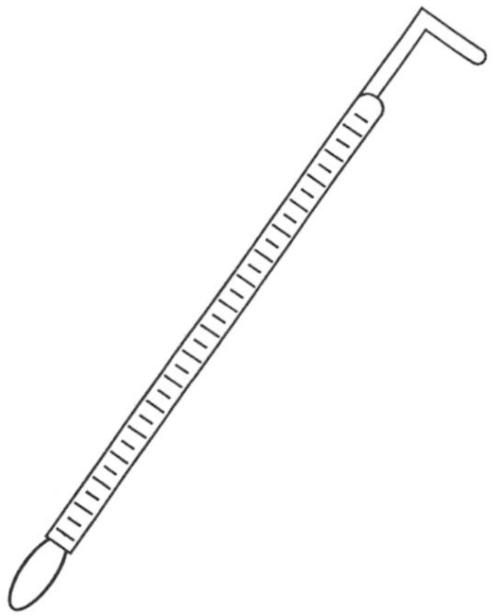

FIGURE 3.13. Thermometer with bracket (from Finke, Ward, & Smith, 1992).

This relatively simple technique opens a door to a world of creative refinements that one could impose on common objects. For instance, try taking the objects shown in Figure 3.14 and imagine adding the designated parts to each object. Again, it is better to do this in such a way as to create forms that are interesting and potentially meaningful in a general sense. Then, once you have completed your mentally synthesized forms, try to interpret them as representing improvements in the original design by considering various ways in which the new features might serve useful functions.

CREATIVE REALISM

In using these techniques to try to improve creative visualization, you might ask the following question: From among the many creative ideas that you might generate, which ones are likely to turn out to be successful? Indeed, there are many

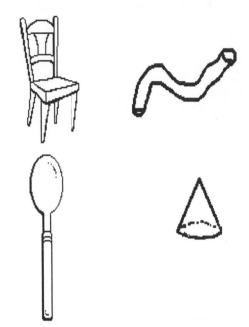

FIGURE 3.14. Sample objects and parts to combine to produce a refinement of an invention. Try adding the tube or cone to either the chair or spoon, and then interpreting the usefulness of the modification.

possible ways of interpreting preinventive forms that would be impractical, nonsensical, or just plain dull. Rather, you would probably want to discover those ideas that are both creative and likely to have an impact on realistic issues and problems. Such ideas would exhibit what we call "creative realism."

STRUCTURAL CONNECTEDNESS

There are two essential properties of creative realism.[11] The first is something called "structural connectedness." Creative designs or ideas that really count are usually connected in meaningful ways to the structure of previous, successful designs or ideas. For example, Edison's original design for the phonograph was structurally connected to earlier designs for devices he had developed for recording telegraph messages. In addition, most important advances in science, even revolutionary ones such as Einstein's theory of relativity, are connected to previously established models and theories. It is extremely rare that an influential, creative design or invention comes from "out of the blue."

When using mental imagery, it is therefore important to try to explore creative possibilities that are tied in at least some ways to existing designs and structures that have proven to be successful in the past. Many of the structural features of established designs exist for important reasons, and should not be ignored or rejected arbitrarily. In addition, as discussed in the previous chapter, the use of established principles and higher-order relations in proven designs can often help to ensure the workability of novel ideas.

IMAGINATIVE DIVERGENCE

A second property of creative realism, called "imaginative divergence," refers to the capacity for new designs or ideas to excite the imagination and encourage the exploration of new possibilities. Consider again the phonograph. Not only was this a novel invention, it also had far-reaching implications. One could now preserve the voices of famous people, great performances, or the sounds of nature. Similarly, the theory of relativity raised many fascinating possibilities, such as time travel. Ideas that display imaginative divergence inspire us to explore and pursue the many new paths that they create.

AVOIDING CREATIVE IDEALISM

New ideas could display imaginative divergence but still fail to exhibit creative realism. Instead, they could result in "creative idealism," which refers to ideas that are creative but are excessively fanciful and impractical. The patent office is filled with examples of inventions that have displayed creative idealism, such as the "spinnet" described in another chapter, which would supposedly assist childbirth by using centrifugal force. Fortunately, there are ways for us to avoid creative idealism, and precipitate creative realism.

There is, of course, never a guarantee that a creative idea will succeed, or become anything more than an idealistic fantasy. Nevertheless, by seeking to develop creative ideas that exhibit both structural connectedness and imaginative divergence, we can improve our chances of achieving at least some degree of creative realism, and hopefully, producing more successful and innovative ideas.

There are also certain illusions that lead to creative idealism, which we can learn to avoid. One is called the "illusion of magical validity." In these instances, an idea that creates imaginative divergence might seem so wonderful and exciting that a person automatically assumes it is valid. The idea that Earth is being visited regularly by intelligent aliens, for instance, might involve one's imagination to the extent that the possibility would seem quite certain, even though it is very remote, at best. Similarly, a person might become so involved in a new invention that he or she loses sight of its true practicality.

Another type of illusion is called the "illusion of synchronicity," the idea that things that occur together by coincidence or chance must be connected in deeper, more meaningful ways. For instance, people often assume that when they think about someone and that person happens to call them on the telephone, there must be some underlying process connecting the two events. Or, if they dream about something that comes true, they might think that the dream was somehow tied to the actual event. This has often led to the development of fanciful theories about paranormal forces and the like, which tend to promote creative idealism.

It is vital to be aware of such illusions when using creative visualization, so that you can guide your imaginative creations in the most realistic and promising directions. Of course, there is nothing wrong with exploring highly idealistic or improbable possibilities—indeed, this is often the best way to overcome rigid thinking—as long as these are kept in perspective and do not blind you to alternative, creative ideas that would have a much greater likelihood of succeeding.

SUMMARY

As we have seen, visualization can be used in many ways to enhance creative thinking. We can create novel images, scan them to explore their emergent properties, transform them to gain new insights and perspectives, and interpret them in a variety of different ways. We can even discover new ideas for creative symbols and inventions, entirely within our imagination.

We have also seen how preinventive forms can often play an important role in creative exploration. The discoveries that preinventive forms often inspire indicate that it is not always necessary to know, in advance, the sort of thing that one is trying to create. Rather, they can often be explored to stimulate new ideas and possibilities, which can then lead one down new and unexpected paths.

We also considered many research studies that have demonstrated the creative potential of mental imagery. But the power of creative visualization is not just restricted to laboratory experiments. Consider, for example, how preinventive forms might be used in many real-life situations. Using their imagination, people could explore creative ways of combining different clothes, adjusting their work schedule, or rearranging their furniture. In each case, preinventive exploration can give rise to unexpected and meaningful insights. And there are many practical uses of generating preinventive forms in art, science, and business, which we will explore in later chapters.

And yet, creative visualization is but one part of the total spectrum of creative cognition. There are many other types of cognitive processes that can also be used to enhance creative thinking, such as creating metaphors, combining old concepts to create new ones, and overcoming mental blocks that often inhibit our ability to take new approaches. Imagery often provides a key for opening the door to creative insight, but it is not the only key that one can use.

NOTES

1. Stephen M. Kosslyn, "Information Representation in Visual Images," *Cognitive Psychology* 7 (1975), pp. 341–370.
2. Ronald A. Finke, "Mental Imagery and the Visual System," *Scientific American* 254 (1986), pp. 88–95.
3. Stephen M. Kosslyn, Thomas M. Ball, & Brian J. Reiser, "Visual Images Preserve Metric Spatial Information: Evidence from Studies of Image Scanning," *Journal of Experimental Psychology: Human Perception and Performance* 4 (1978), pp. 47–60.
4. Alexander R. Luria, *The Mind of a Mnemonist* (New York: Basic Books, 1968).
5. Roger N. Shepard & Lynn A. Cooper, *Mental Images and Their Transformations* (Cambridge, MA: MIT Press, 1982).
6. Jennifer Freyd, "Dynamic Mental Representations," *Psychological Review* 94 (1987), pp. 427–438.
7. Steven Pinker, "Mental Imagery and the Third Dimension," *Journal of Experimental Psychology: General* 109 (1980), pp. 354–371.
8. Ronald A. Finke, Steven Pinker, & Martha J. Farah, "Reinterpreting Visual Patterns in Mental Imagery," *Cognitive Science* 13 (1989), pp. 51–78.
9. Ronald A. Finke & Karen Slayton, "Explorations of Creative Visual Synthesis in Mental Imagery," *Memory & Cognition* 16 (1988), pp. 252–257.
10. Ronald A. Finke, *Creative Imagery: Discoveries and Inventions in Visualization* (Hillsdale, NJ: Erlbaum, 1990).
11. Ronald A. Finke, "Creative Realism," in *The Creative Cognition Approach*, eds. Steven M. Smith, Thomas B. Ward, & Ronald A. Finke (Cambridge, MA: MIT Press, 1995), pp. 303–326.

PROBLEM SOLVING AND REASONING

Jim Crocker was an engineer with a problem that was truly far out—in space. The Hubble telescope, the shining hope of astronomers, just wasn't shining properly, having been outfitted and set into orbit with a flawed primary mirror. At a meeting arranged by NASA, Crocker and his team of engineers floated plan after plan for adjusting the optics on the Hubble, but each idea was ultimately shot down as too complicated or too dangerous for spacewalking astronauts. At an impasse, the team adjourned for a few months before scheduling another meeting in Munich, Germany. At his hotel before the meeting, Crocker, a tall man, reached up to raise the showerhead, which moved with a simple adjustment mechanism. Suddenly, the solution to his engineering problem flashed in his mind. Small optical adjusters could be fitted to correct each beam of information reflected by the Hubble's flawed mirror, with each adjuster manipulated into its proper place by a simple mechanism conceptually related to the showerhead adjustment. And, it worked! Less than a year after Crocker's insight solved the celestial problem, the Hubble telescope had already observed a comet smashing into Jupiter, an immense black hole the size of our solar system, and an ancient galaxy formed near the time of the big bang.

What led the engineers to their initial impasse? What triggered Crocker's unexpected insight? The answers have to do with the ways that people reason and solve problems. How do most people solve problems? How do experts and geniuses do it? How do computers do it? Where do creative solutions come from? To answer these types of questions you must first understand basic cognitive processes. These processes are essential to creativity, and have been the focus of much traditional creativity research.

From the Gestalt psychologists early in this century through contemporary cognitive scientists, researchers have studied problem solving as a means of learning about creativity. Throughout that time, two conflicting positions have dominated theories of problem solving. One position has it that problems are solved incrementally, by applying bits of knowledge piece by piece until all of the components together produce a solution. The other position focuses on the phenomenon of insight, which is a sudden and unexpected realization of a solution to a problem.

To some, the notion of insight seems altogether too magical to be real; how can some unconscious part of the mind come up with fantastic ideas without any work to show for it? On the other hand, others have been dissatisfied with the theory that all creativity comes from slow and steady work at a problem, because it denies the mystery and power of truly novel innovations and discoveries. We will show how creative problem solving requires both the use of knowledge and expertise, as well as insightful thinking.

One of the major issues we will address is what blocks us from solving problems. Impediments to creativity, such as "writer's block" or blindness to basic scientific principles, have been the banes of artists and scientists throughout history. Are there unconscious blocks that impede our creative problem solving? How can we recognize such blocks, and what can we do to conquer them?

To answer some of these questions we must distinguish between different types of problems, and identify the differences between creative and noncreative problem solving. We will also describe the causes of blocks in creative problem solving, demystify insight or "aha!" experiences, and explain the role of various forms of reasoning in creative problem solving.

WHAT IS A PROBLEM?

If we are going to examine problem solving, we should begin by thinking about what a problem is. Consider Lola and her fuel line, an author trying to develop a believable way to get a fictional character out of a jam, a composer searching for a satisfying musical theme, and a scientist trying to develop a vaccine for AIDS. All of these people have problems, but their problems seem so different. What do they have in common?

Remarkably, problems ranging across this broad spectrum do share a crucial feature: They all have a gap. A gap refers to not knowing, at least temporarily, how to get to the solution. The gap represents the difference between what you know and what you need to know, or between the current situation and your goal. To understand problem solving, then, we have to understand how people bridge those gaps.

The best way to span this gap depends on the exact problem confronting us. Some types of problems call for creative solutions, and some do not. We can gain crucial insight into creative problem solving by probing how people approach all sorts of problems whether or not they require truly innovative solutions.

In this chapter we will distinguish among various types of problems that cognitive psychologists have studied. You will see that some of these problems seem artificial and contrived. Solving some of them may not even require an act of genuine creativity. So, how can they help us to understand or enhance creativity?

Consider two analogies. A practice drill is not the same as a great football play in a real game, and a training session for an astronaut in an underwater tank is not the same as an actual space walk. However, some of the important elements of a real football game, and a real space walk are present in doing football drills, and training in a tank. Likewise, some of the important elements of true creative problem solving are present in laboratory problems. Thus, creative thinking can be practiced, strengthened, and studied using artificially created problems, as long as the problems contain critical elements of true creativity.

Some intriguing examples of artificial laboratory problems have lent a great deal of insight into problem solving and will help to illustrate some of those elements.

THE MUTILATED CHECKERBOARD PROBLEM

Imagine an ordinary checkerboard that has 8 squares on each side, alternating black and red. A rectangular domino can cover 2 squares of the checkerboard. The entire board, consisting of 64 squares, can be covered using exactly 32 dominoes. If the bottom-left square and top-right square are removed, leaving 62 squares, can the remaining mutilated checkerboard be covered exactly by 31 dominoes? Why, or why not?

Although some people see the solution to this problem immediately, such people are rare. Most people take a series of steps that correspond to those that characterize real world problem solving. They use *mental imagery*, picturing dominoes covering rows of squares, and mentally counting which squares are covered in various configurations of the dominoes. Many who try the problem at some point find themselves *blocked*, unable to take another step in the problem solution. Using an *analogy*, which will be described in the solutions at the end of the chapter, many realize that they can solve the problem easily. This realization may dawn very suddenly on the problem solver, a phenomenon known as an *insight* experience, which sometimes occurs when people get truly creative ideas. Thus, important elements of creative problems are embodied in this sort of puzzle, which makes them very useful for studying creative thinking.

REPRODUCTIVE VERSUS CREATIVE PROBLEM SOLVING

Before delving too deeply into creative problem solving, however, we should note that creative solutions are not always the best ones. For some types of problems the accepted, standard methods are best. For example, to solve the problem "12 × 12 = ?" you do not need a novel strategy or solution. Similarly, you would not be eager for the pilot of your jetliner to experiment with creative ways of landing your plane.

When you implement known, accepted problem solutions you are using *reproductive* problem solving. That is, you are reproducing a solution or an approach that has been used before. On the other hand, when you find novel solutions to deal with new problems for which known solutions do not apply, you are using *creative* problem solving. By first getting a handle on reproductive problem solving we can gain a better idea of what is so special or different about creative problem solving.

Whether reproductive or creative problem solving is more appropriate depends on the type of problem at hand, and good problem solvers know when to apply each type of approach. To help distinguish which problems demand which type of thinking we can establish the differences between what psychologists have named well-defined versus ill-defined problems, and convergent versus divergent problems.

WELL-DEFINED AND ILL-DEFINED PROBLEMS

Consider the following problems: (1) If Sunday is three days after the day before yesterday, then what day is the day after tomorrow? (2) What is the optimal temperature to have in a school? In the first one, you know where you are starting from, where you are headed, and you have a set of ideas about how to get there. In the second, you have none of these. More formally, the first is a *well-defined problem* in which a starting state, a goal state, and a set of operations that can be used to get to the goal are all clearly expressed. The second is an *ill-defined problem* in which these states and operations are not clear; your understanding of an ill-defined problem or of the type of solution that might be effective is vague or ambiguous.

For the problem of determining the correct day, we utilize information given in the problem about what day today is, as well as knowledge about the days of the week, their cyclic order of occurrence, and the meanings of words such as *tomorrow, yesterday, before,* and *after.* Processing the information in solving the problem involves simple operations such as counting forwards and backwards through the sequence of days. The solution is clearly the name of a weekday. Other examples of well-defined problems are shown in Table 4.1.

When we confront well-defined problems it is usually best to think reproductively, applying knowledge that is directly relevant to the problem. And, the more often you have repro

---

TABLE 4.1. Well-Defined Problems

---

1. If Al is poorer than Betty but richer than Carrie, and Carrie is richer than Dan, then who is second richest?
2. What is one-half the area of a square that is four feet on each side?
3. How many degrees of correction did each information beam on the flawed Hubble telescope require?

---

duced a given type of solution, the more quickly and accurately you can bring your knowledge to bear on a similar well-defined problem. For example, the more you have practiced converting degrees Fahrenheit to degrees centigrade the better you can carry out the conversion.

In contrast, ill-defined problems, such as determining the optimal temperature for a school, cannot be solved in a straightforward way, and they force us to think creatively if we are to have any hope of solving them. In the temperature problem, for instance, there is no clear starting state; you cannot be sure whether the school is a public grade school, a school for Antarctic explorers, or a school of fish. Nor is it obvious whether "optimal" means the most relaxing temperature, the most invigorating one, or the most stressful one. The operations to be used are equally vague. You might compute heat transfer rates or metabolic efficiencies at various temperatures, but it is not clear what type of clothing or climate to consider. The solution might be a single temperature, a range of temperatures, or a variable that depends on other prevailing factors. Other examples of ill-defined problems are shown in Table 4.2.

Creative thinking is the proper prescription for ill-defined problems. The flexibility and variability inherent in such nebulous problems demands thinking that can produce novel variations on ideas. Prior knowledge is as essential for solving ill-defined problems as it is for well-defined problems, but in creative thinking we transform our prior knowledge in some way to produce new types of solutions. When the Hubble telescope was in trouble, NASA needed engineers with vast

TABLE 4.2. Ill-Defined Problems

1. Is vitamin E good for people?
2. How much water does it take to cross the desert?
3. How can spacewalking astronauts repair a flaw in the orbiting Hubble telescope?

expertise to solve the problem, but prior knowledge was not enough; it took a creative mind to transform all that knowledge into a working solution.

CONVERGENT VERSUS DIVERGENT PROBLEMS

Another way to divide up the world of problems is to split it into convergent and divergent varieties. Although many psychologists have used the terms *convergent* and *divergent* to refer to different types of thought processes, the terms can be more clearly understood as types of problems. Convergent problems are those in which thinking converges on a single correct solution, such as finding the square root of 87. They are typically well-defined, and usually call for reproductive thinking. For divergent problems, in contrast, you must hunt for many possible solutions, all of which may vary in their appropriateness.

If we ask you to list as many things as you can that are red, such as tomatoes, roses, and cardinals, we are giving you a divergent problem. The number of different answers is staggeringly large. Although this particular divergent problem has some characteristics of well-defined problems—you can clearly evaluate the adequacy of solutions by determining whether or not they are red—some divergent problems do not even have this characteristic. Some examples are shown in Table 4.3.

Divergent problems encourage creative thinking, they highlight an important aspect of creative problem solving, demanding a great deal of flexibility of thought. Even though no two divergent problems are ever quite the same, you can readily

TABLE 4.3. Divergent Problems

1. What things can you think of that have metal in them?
2. What uses are there for two-liter plastic bottles?
3. What creatures could inhabit an imaginary planet similar to Earth?

increase the flexibility of your thinking, as we will show, if you practice solving divergent problems.

THE ROLE OF MEMORY IN REPRODUCTIVE PROBLEM SOLVING

Reproductive thinking has much to recommend it and examining its strengths will bring to light many useful concepts. Reproductive thinking can move us a long way down the road to many solutions, but it sometimes brings us bumper to barrier with a roadblock. Assessing its limitations we set the stage to see how creative thinking can steer us around the barricades.

When you solve problems reproductively, you apply prior knowledge directly, but that knowledge can take many forms. In the simplest case, you might directly recall an exact solution to a problem you have encountered before. For example, most people have memorized multiplication tables and facts about the number of yards in a mile and so on. When you hear a problem such as "$12 \times 12 = ?$" or "How many miles are there in 1760 yards?," you can simply pull up the relevant fact. In many instances the distinction between memory and problem solving is a fuzzy one. Retrieving a fact furnishes the answer to a problem, and as such must be considered problem solving, albeit of the very simplest sort.

Even when memory does not deliver correct solutions to your door, it can help you get the process moving. For instance, if you must solve the problem "$12 \times 13 = ?$" you may find that your memory does not furnish the final answer directly, but it can get you to within a simple step of the correct solution. Remembering that $12 \times 12 = 144$ is close to the answer for 12×13; if twelve 12s are 144, then one more 12 is equal to "$144 + 12$," or 156. The memory hypothesis is the notion that information in our memory provides material for generating problem solutions.[1]

Stated at a slightly more general level, memory can provide not only final answers, but also strategies or approaches to problem solutions. Two of the most useful types of strategies that people have stored in their memories are algorithms and heuristics.

ALGORITHMS AND HEURISTICS

What is 122 degrees Fahrenheit in degrees centigrade? If you already know the formula for converting from degrees Fahrenheit to degrees centigrade [(degrees Fahrenheit minus 32) × 5/9 = degrees centigrade] you can pluck it from memory, and easily compute the solution to this problem (50 degrees centigrade). This formula is an example of an *algorithm*, a step-by-step method for reaching a solution to a problem. We can reuse algorithms, applying them again and again to new problems, as long as the new problems are appropriate. You may know many other algorithms, not only for conversion formulas, but also for other simple problems that repeat themselves, such as entering commands to withdraw cash at an automatic teller machine, determining whether a number is odd or even, buying a candy bar from a dispenser, or boiling an egg.

You could also construct an algorithm for solving the mutilated checkerboard problem described earlier. Each domino can cover exactly 2 squares on the checkerboard. Therefore, once 2 squares have been removed from the board, the remaining 62 squares should be coverable with one domino per 2 squares. Such an algorithm might be constructed as [number of dominoes needed = number of squares/2].

A fairly simple exercise that illustrates the use of an algorithm will help you see how simple it can be to reuse the same solution again and again. A rope and pulley are set up as in Figure 4.1, with disks that can be attached on the left and right sides. The disks on the left side rest on a scale, and when disks are attached to the right side, they subtract from the weight resting on the scale. For example, in the figure a 10-lb disk rests on the scale on the left side while two 3-lb disks and a 1-lb disk are attached to the right side. This configuration leaves only 3 lb resting on the scale.

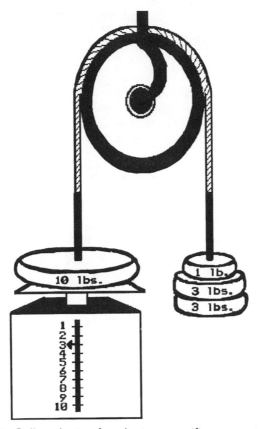

FIGURE 4.1. Pulley device for placing specific amounts of weight on scale.

Some other weight counterbalancing problems are shown in Table 4.4. If disks A, B, and C weigh the given amounts for each problem, determine what disks to attach to measure out the goal weight on the scale. You may use as many A, B, and C type disks as you wish for each problem. To help you get started, we will give you a solution for the first problem. Attach one B disk to the

TABLE 4.4. Counterbalancing Problems

	Disk A	Disk B	Disk C	Measure out this weight
1	5	20	2	11
2	14	163	25	99
3	18	43	10	5
4	21	127	3	100
5	20	59	4	31
6	9	42	6	21
7	23	49	3	20
8	28	76	3	25

left side, and attach an A and two C disks to the right. Because B weighs 20 lb, subtracting an A disk (5 lb) and two C disks (2 × 2 = 4 lb) leaves exactly 11 lb resting on the scale. Now work the rest of the counterbalancing problems as quickly as you can.

If you discovered the algorithm "B minus A minus 2C," then you found that you could quickly solve these problems without going through a lot of lengthy calculations along the way. Often, the reproductive method is the quickest, most efficient way to solve problems.

Another type of problem that can be solved with an algorithm is the anagram (also known as a "word jumble"), which requires you to rearrange the letters in each problem to make one word. Anagrams can be solved with an algorithm and a dictionary. Can you invent a step-by-step strategy that you could use to solve all of the following anagrams?

T B E

U C P

E R D

If your algorithm stated something such as the following, then it could solve not only these three easy anagrams, but any other anagram, as well:

Step 1. Arrange the letters into every possible combination.

Step 2. Look up each letter string in the dictionary to see if it is listed.

Step 3. If a letter string is in the dictionary, then it is a legitimate word.

Although algorithms can be enormously helpful for some problems, we often need other types of problem-solving strategies, even for some simple anagrams. To see this, consider how many letter strings can be produced by the letters in an anagram. For example, try the following seven-letter anagram. As you work on the problem, list some of the strings that come to mind that are not correct solutions.

$$P L E M O R B$$

Of the 5040 possible letter strings that can be made with these seven letters, a few are listed below. There are two columns of strings. Do your incorrect strings of letters look more like those shown in column 1 or in column 2?

Column 1	Column 2
L O M P B E R	B M R P L E O
B L O R E M P	O E L R P B M
P O R M L E B	M B L R O E P

Odds are that your incorrect attempts look more like the strings in column 1. Why? Obviously, the strings in column 2 are not easily pronounceable, and they have letter combinations, such as "BMRPL," that are not typically found in English words.

If you really had been using the simple algorithm noted above, you would have been as likely to write down unpronounceable combinations as pronounceable ones in your letter strings. Yet people rarely try such "illegal" strings before solving the problem (answer: PROBLEM), nor do they generate anywhere near the 5040 possible strings before finding the correct solution.

Without even being explicitly aware that they are doing so, people use _heuristics_, or general rules of thumb, to solve anagrams, and many other problems. One heuristic in solving anagrams is to try pronounceable letter strings. Another is to try commonly experienced letter combinations, such as "BE," "MO," and, hopefully, "PR." A third heuristic is to try common prefixes or suffixes, such as "PRE" or "LER." Using such heuristics can help you find a solution long before you have exhausted all the possible letter strings. Thus, heuristics can provide shortcuts to finding solutions to problems.

Another example of a heuristic is in troubleshooting car problems. If your car would not start in the morning, as a rule of thumb, you might check parts of the electrical system or the fuel system. It would not make much sense to use the algorithm, "In alphabetical order, check the condition of every part of the automobile." Again, heuristics can help you find a shortcut.

Some heuristics may represent what we think of as common wisdom. A cloudy darkening in the sky may well portend a rainstorm. Someone with a camera who is studying a map in a public place may well be a tourist. A flashing light and a siren behind your car may well mean that you have been caught speeding.

Are heuristics always appropriate ways to solve problems? Not at all; rules of thumb can definitely be wrong. We use heuristics because they typically provide shortcuts to solutions, not because they are foolproof. Later, however, we will see how an expert use of heuristics can benefit creative endeavors, such as invention, scientific reasoning, and science fiction writing.

Expertise refers to knowledge that lets you make an informed decision. Because experts have learned about a particular area of knowledge, they can solve problems in that area more quickly and accurately than nonexperts. Expert knowledge consists not only of facts, but also of algorithms and heuristics. Physicians use expert knowledge to diagnose diseases not just once or twice, but again and again. The same is true of experts in any area, whether it is business, sports, or the arts. In short, expertise can be said to consist of knowing when and how to use reproductive problem solving. Unfortunately, reproductive thinking is the wrong cognitive tool for solving creative problems.

LIMITATIONS OF REPRODUCTIVE THINKING AND THE NEED FOR CREATIVE THINKING

You can use algorithms and heuristics to solve problems that no one has ever encountered before, such as finding the square root of 5.834762357. Does using them for such novel problems correspond to creative problem solving? No. Truly creative problem solving refers not simply to solving a new problem, but to solving a new type of problem, one for which existing knowledge cannot yet produce a satisfactory solution. Although creative thinking can involve the use of memories and rules, reproductive thinking alone is insufficient for solving creative problems.

Now, try to solve one more anagram: NEWDOOR. Again, the rules are to rearrange the letters to make one word. As before, do not wait for the correct solution to occur to you before jotting down a few attempts. Typical initial attempts might include DOWNERO, WOODREN, ODORWEN, and REDWOON—strings based on some of the anagram heuristics mentioned earlier. Both NEW DOOR and NEW ODOR use all seven letters, and even represent legitimate English words, but unfortunately neither of these solutions makes one word, as specified in the instructions for solving anagrams.

The solution is, of course, ONE WORD. Now wait a minute, you are no doubt objecting; that cannot be the correct solution because it is two words. On the contrary, this solution is not two words; it is ONE WORD.

Most people have difficulty with the ONE WORD problem because they get stuck on the idea that their solution must take the form of a single word. Without giving up this assumption, you cannot solve the problem.

What this example shows is that there are times when expertise in the form of algorithms and heuristics cannot solve certain problems, even though the problems do not appear to be different from other problems in any obvious way. In such cases you need to reject your expertise, or at least temporarily suspend its use, and instead use creative problem solving. Let's consider some other ways of getting stuck on old knowledge as well as procedures for getting unstuck.

FIXATION AND MENTAL SET

The ONE WORD problem provides an example of being fixated on an inappropriate idea. Fixation, or a block to successful problem solving, is most troublesome if you do not know what is causing the block, or, worse yet, if you do not even know that you are blocked. An example of a subtle source of fixation can be seen in the following problem.

The Parent Trap: Version 1. Disappointed with his son's calculus grades, a man went with his son to see the math professor. The secretary for the math department at the university asked the father and son to wait, and went to get the professor. The professor was hunched over a computer terminal that was partially obscured by pipe smoke when the secretary knocked on the office door. "Some kid is here with his father to see you," said the secretary to the graying professor. Looking out the office door, the surprised professor replied, "That's not just 'some kid'—That's my son!" How is this possible?

The solution to this problem may be very obvious to some, but many will be stumped. Did the professor's pipe smoke somehow obscure his vision? Was he blind? When he said, "That's my son!" was he referring to the man in the waiting room rather than to the boy? Was one of the fathers a stepfather, a grandfather, or a priest? These clues seem suggestive, but none leads to a very satisfactory answer.

If the solution is not obvious, it is likely that your thinking is blocked. When you are blocked, you may not be aware of exactly what is causing the block. You may try all of the strategies that you have determined are relevant to the problem, to no avail. The block that people are likely to encounter in the above problem has to do with a sex role stereotype. In case you still do not see the solution to the problem, try version 2 of the problem.

The Parent Trap: Version 2. Disappointed with her son's calculus grades, a woman went with her son to see the math professor. The secretary for the math department at the university asked the mother and son to wait, and went to get the professor. The professor was hunched over a computer terminal that was partially obscured by pipe smoke when the secretary knocked on the office door. "Some kid is here with his mother to see you," said the secretary to the graying professor. Looking out the office door, the surprised professor replied, "That's not just 'some kid'—That's my son!"

People are not likely to even see this version as a problem, because there are no gaps in the situation when the professor is automatically pictured as a man. The first version of the problem, however, contains a gap if unconscious sex role stereotyping biases you to see the professor as male, because the boy cannot have two fathers. If you were able to see the pipe-smoking professor as a woman, however, then you either avoided the block or overcame it with creative thinking.

REMEMBERING THE WRONG THINGS

Fixation refers to a block that obstructs successful problem solving, such as the sex role stereotype illustrated in the above problem. Fixation can take many different forms. In every case, however, fixation is an unfortunate by-product that sometimes results from using prior knowledge blindly when you are trying to solve a problem.

The simplest way to think of fixation is in terms of interference, a term taken from theories of human memory. Interference occurs when your mind has hooked up a stimulus with more than one response, and the wrong response gets pulled up when you encounter the stimulus. For example, if we ask you what country has Moscow as its capital city, you might accidentally answer the Soviet Union rather than the correct answer, Russia. Here, the stimulus, "Moscow," has been associated with two different responses, "Soviet Union" and "Russia." Remembering the inappropriate response blocks or interferes with memory of the correct response. Fixation, then, is tantamount to drawing inappropriate responses from your memory.

Ordinarily, we think of memory as a positive thing. When you forget where you left your keys or your wallet, you are frustrated and angry, and when you find them, you are relieved. When relatives begin to lose their memories, you worry. What you may not realize is how useful forgetting can be. Just consider trying to remember where you parked your car at the mall; that is, where you parked today, not where you parked all of the other times you have been there. To be able to do this, it would probably help to forget where you parked all of the other times. Because you can only recall so many things at one time, it is easier to focus on the proper memory if irrelevant ones do not intrude.

Another example of how forgetting can be useful can be seen in the tip-of-the-tongue (TOT) phenomenon, in which you know a word, a person's name, a song lyric, but can't quite get your mental hands on it. You will recognize it if you hear it, but you just can't drag it out into the open at the moment. The TOT state has been likened to the feeling you get when you need to sneeze but, for the moment, cannot.

In some of our research studies we have actually been able to produce these TOT memory blocks by causing people to initially remember the wrong things.[2] For example, given the blocker words TRANSPARENT and TRANSLUCENT, people often find it difficult to think of the word that means "impenetrable by light." Some other examples of words that may block memory and cause TOT states are shown in Table 4.5. For the best effect, read the four blocker words first before trying to think of the answers to the definitions. If you remain blocked on any of the answers, check the end of this chapter.

What you are currently remembering can block your access to other things you want to recall. If your next-to-last parking place keeps popping into your mind, it may be harder for you think of the current one. Recalling an inappropriate word or name can block the one you are really searching for in your memory. So it is with having innovative and insightful ideas. It may be necessary to put old ideas out of your mind to allow new ideas to emerge. We saw this earlier in the case of people trying to develop interesting extraterrestrials, and yet being blocked by recalling and conforming to typical Earth animals. And we will later encounter how scientists and artists have escaped from such mental ruts to achieve compelling insights.

As we have seen, our basic mental processes, such as remembering and forgetting, are inextricably linked to creativity. You should also see that to be creative, you may need to use these processes in odd or unusual ways. Most of the time you concentrate more on remembering, but to be creative you may

TABLE 4.5. Tip-of-the-Tongue Cues

Blockers	Definitions
1. *Surgeon, chiropractor, psychiatrist, cardiologist*	Expert in children's diseases
2. *Cyanide, venom, strychnine, arsenic*	The poison that Socrates took
3. *Riddle, question, dilemma, puzzle*	When contradictory statements are nonetheless true
4. *Dishonesty, counterfeit, lying, fabrication*	Not telling the truth under oath

want to deliberately try to forget about old approaches, at least temporarily, especially when the old methods are not working.

FIXATION IN PROBLEM SOLVING

In some of the classic problems discussed in the creativity literature, people often become fixated on old solutions or ideas before they realize a better way. That is, they have a hard time preventing the old patterns of thinking from automatically taking over. Fixation can assume many forms, but one of the most common in everyday situations is getting hung up on the standard functions of objects.

Many early studies of creativity examined this kind of functional fixation. In one classic problem, subjects were supplied with a box of matches, some thumbtacks, and two candles. The subjects had to mount the candles on the wall so that they could be lit without burning the wall. After some effort, people realize that the matchbox can be emptied and tacked to the wall to create a makeshift stand for the candles. The typical use of the box, to hold matches, interferes with achieving this solution. This notion of functional fixation is such a basic part of early approaches to creativity that one test of creativity, the Alternate Uses Test, explicitly measures our ability to think of new uses for common objects, such as a shoe or a button.

We saw an everyday example of overcoming fixation earlier when Lola Lopes needed something to plug her troublesome fuel line. Recall that she initially tried to find something that would plug up the fuel line by fitting inside it. Lola dodged that functional fixation as well as fixation on the typical uses of potatoes in achieving her solution.

Fixation can also take the form of counterproductive adherence to rules, such as algorithms or heuristics. Turn back for a moment to the weight counterbalancing problems shown in Table 4.4. In that exercise you were supposed to have learned of the repeated usefulness of an algorithm, B − A − 2C = Goal weight to be measured. Reproductive reapplication of this algorithm can solve problem after problem. But, look carefully at problems 7 and 8 in that series. A much simpler solution, A − C, is possible for those problems. Furthermore, the old algorithm B − A − 2C does not even work for the last problem! Although a much simpler solution seems obvious, most people simply continue blindly with the old solution, even when it does not produce the correct solution.

What these tasks show is that people tend to develop rules that they then apply rigidly, even when the old rules no longer work, and even when simpler solutions are staring them in the face. Anyone who has been hassled by bureaucracies understands the slavish devotion to rules that can occur in the real world, even when the consequences of that devotion are truly idiotic.

INCUBATION: AN ESCAPE FROM FIXATION

To foster creativity you often need to escape from interfering ideas and rules. In some of our studies, we purposely gave people interfering information and tested ways to get them to forget it so that new, creative solutions might emerge. Figure 4.2 shows some of the picture–word problems we used, called *rebuses*. For each rebus you should try to determine the common expression the figure captures. For example, the first one represents "search high and low." Before trying to solve them, read the clues listed below each one. For example, the clue listed for number 2 is "dumb bear," and the clue for number 3 is "chemical."

What is likely to happen is that the clues will make it more difficult for you to find the correct solutions to the problems, because we purposely devised them to be misleading. What this means is that trying to forget the clues, or at least the kinds of solutions they suggest, should now help you. To do this, you

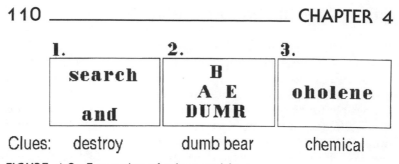

FIGURE 4.2. Examples of rebus problems.

might want to temporarily put these problems aside and come back to them later. If you do so, remember not to look at the misleading clues.

Our experiments have found that people are more successful if we force them to move away from the problems or distract them temporarily. This distraction allows them to forget the wrong information and remember more useful information.[3] (The solutions are given at the end of this chapter.)

Getting away from the problem temporarily has been said to cause an "incubation effect," because it seems that unformed ideas must be developing out of sight. Rather than actively working on a problem, we may do better by putting it aside for a time. In psychology textbooks incubation has been noted often as an important stage in creative problem solving. Until recently, however, no one has been quite sure why or how it works. Our research findings in creative cognition tell us that one reason it works is that it gives you time to forget whatever information was keeping you from getting at the correct solution. Incubation time not only helps you to resolve problems that have you stuck, it also weakens memory blocks. That means that when you are in one of those frustrating tip-of-the-tongue states and cannot think of the right name or the right word, continuing to search memory is like banging your head against the wall; take a break and it will come to you later.

Incubation may also lead to insights because, in taking a vacation from the problem, you change the whole context in which your ideas occur. People forget more when they try to remember information in a place that is different from where they first learned it.[4] So, when you change your context by going away from a problem, it is easier to forget the interfering details and to think about other potential solutions. When you are stumped on a problem you can increase your potential for having creative insights by deliberately shifting your context, either physically, by getting up and going somewhere else, or mentally, by simply imagining some new setting. In fact, this pattern of getting fixated, leaving the problem context, and getting an insight, describes very well the circumstances that led to a solution for fixing the Hubble space telescope, described earlier in this chapter. The pattern of fixation, context shifting, and insight also describes a number of other important inventions and scientific discoveries that we will relate in the Science and Art chapter.

DIVERGENT THINKING AND REMOTE ASSOCIATION: RANGING FAR AND WIDE IN YOUR THINKING

What are the first five words that come to mind when you read the word *book?* Write them down. If you wrote, for example, *page, read, cover, mark,* and *library,* you would be giving common associates. If, however, you thought of *flip, worm, arrest, reservation,* and *keeping,* then you would be giving more unusual or remote associations. Notice that the common associates all refer to essentially the same object, namely, the type of thing you are reading right now. There are, however, many other meanings and uses of the word *book.*

The remote associates above come from different categories of ideas: simple animation, readers, legal accusation (e.g., "Book 'em, Dano!"), arranging events (such as hotel rooms), and accounting. Because the second set of responses are so varied, they are called divergent. Remote association and divergent thinking are important for creative problem solving, and are particularly useful for overcoming fixation.

Common associations are the first and most likely things that you think of when you are solving problems. Normally, common ideas are the most useful ideas for finding solutions—otherwise they would not be normal. But, when you are searching for creative solutions, divergent ideas are most helpful. Remote associations are more productive in creative thinking because they represent new directions for thinking. Such thinking is crucial when old solutions do not work.

One way to study creative associations is by using the Remote Associates Test (RAT). Although the problems contained in the test by no means measure overall creative ability, they do tap one's ability to think of unusual but appropriate responses—an important aspect of creative cognition. The instructions are to find a single word that is related to each of three test words. For example, given the words *apple, house, family*, we can think of a word *tree*, that is associated with each test word (*apple tree, tree-house,* and *family tree*). Examples of RAT problems are shown in Table 4.6.

Earlier, we saw how we might develop more innovative ideas by avoiding the most typical instances of a concept, those that come to mind first when developing new ideas. Practice at generating remote associates is a wonderful tool to help you to

TABLE 4.6. Remote Associates Test Problems

1. Blue	Cake	Cottage
2. News	Doll	Tiger
3. Surprise	Line	Birthday
4. Wheel	Electric	High
5. Weight	Wave	House

develop the habit of getting past the first, and most obvious, ideas in a given situation.

INSIGHT

If your kitchen fuse kept burning out, before calling the electrician you might suddenly recall seeing a bare wire in the light fixture the last time you changed a bulb. In a trice, your idea could lead you to a quick and inexpensive repair job. Insight, also known as illumination, epiphany, and the "aha!" experience, refers to the sudden realization of an idea. Insight experiences may occur to you in perfectly mundane situations, such as the fuse problem, and are not restricted to historically important realizations. The phenomenon is somewhat controversial because its causes are not at all apparent. Insight is nonetheless

TABLE 4.7. Some Insight Problems

1. A man who lives on the 65th floor of his apartment building rides the elevator from his floor to the ground floor every morning when he leaves for work. When he returns in the evening he rides only to the 60th floor, and walks up the stairs to his apartment. The elevator works properly, and in fact he rides all the way to the 65th floor if it is raining, or if there are other people on the elevator. Explain his strange behavior.
2. A lily pad grows happily on a pond, doubling the total surface area of its pads every day. If the pond is covered with pads in exactly 24 days, how many days does it take before the pond is covered halfway?
3. A woman goes into a bar and asks for a glass of water. The bartender reaches behind the bar, but instead of water, he whips out a shotgun and aims it at the woman. She screams, then thanks the bartender, gives him a tip, and leaves. Explain this sequence of events.

recognized as one of the most important psychological phenomena in creative cognition.

Cognitive researchers have produced insight experiences in controlled laboratory settings with the use of insight problems. These are brain teasers with twists or tricks that make solutions nonobvious. People typically begin insight problems by using strategies that seem reasonable at first, but which lead down blind alleys. Some examples are shown in Table 4.7.

Insight problems show us that solutions can sometimes arrive in what appear to be great leaps. This contrasts with the apparently slow, step-by-step progress often associated with reproductive problem solving. As we will describe below, even these sudden insights may often be the result of incremental progress that goes on outside our awareness.

UNCONSCIOUS ACTIVATION OF IDEAS: INTUITION AND INCUBATION

Many theories of memory picture our permanent knowledge as information mapped out in a giant interconnected network. Each bit of information is referred to as a node, and each connection is an association. To use information in this vast network you must move from node to node along the connections. The more closely related two pieces of information are, the closer together and more directly linked the nodes will be.

When you use information in this network you become consciously aware of it only if it gets enough mental energy, or activation. According to some theories, information can have such a small amount of activation that it is not enough to reach your conscious awareness. Such a situation is referred to as unconscious activation, and has been suggested as a possible cause of intuition (a hunch) and incubation (unconscious problem solving), both of which bear directly on the issue of insight.[5]

Earlier, we noted that forgetting is important in incubation, a break from a problem that results in an insight experience. However, other memory factors may also contribute. For example, even after you put aside a problem, some amount of mental activation may persist below the level of your conscious awareness. The material in your memory that you initially bring to bear on a problem is then said to be sensitized; that is, you become sensitive to information or ideas that relate to the problem. Once away from the problem, you may stumble across some clues that are relevant to your initial work. Because the problem has remained sensitized, the clues cause the initial work to be brought back into consciousness. Now, with the new relevant clues, the problem can be solved. This may explain why inventors and scientists often report that unusual clues (such as the showerhead clue for repairing the Hubble telescope) led them to insights after they temporarily put the problems aside.

This unconscious activation can prepare you to make use of helpful clues when you later encounter them. To use a metaphor from chemistry, the activation that goes on below the surface may produce something like a supersaturated solution. When a seed crystal is added, there is a sudden change in the structure of the mixture. Likewise, if your mind is sufficiently prepared, a clue that might have gone unnoticed before can produce a dramatic change in your understanding of the problem.

Intuition may be another result of unconscious activation. Intuition and insight are similar in that you are not consciously aware of the mental steps leading to either one; they are experiences that seem to erupt suddenly into your mind without forewarning. The two differ, however, in that insight is considered to be the production of a relatively full-blown idea, whereas intuition is better regarded as a lead or a hunch. For example, you might have an intuitive hunch that someone has been embezzling from your business, whereas an insight would be more complete, telling you who was stealing and why. That is, when your work on a problem reaches a point at which your thinking might go in a number of possible directions, an intuitive hunch can lead you in the more promising directions.

Just as with insights, intuition can be described as unconscious activation of knowledge relevant to a solution to a problem. According to this theory, when you first attempt a problem, some of your knowledge is activated, including the correct solution to a problem. If the activation is strong enough, you become aware of the solution. If it is unconscious activation, it can still be strong enough to give you a good hunch that can lead you to the solution.

Research has shown that even before people have finished solving a problem, they can guess at a better than chance rate which unsolved problems are solvable, and which are not. They can also guess which hypotheses are more promising leads, even before they are given a chance to find out which hypothesis is correct. You cannot be certain about your hunches before going through a verification process, but there are times when a hunch might well pay off.

ARTIFICIAL THINKING

Throughout this book we focus mostly on human creativity. However, many cognitive scientists have begun to study both creative and noncreative cognition through computer models. Some even claim that their computer programs exhibit true creativity.

If thought is the manipulation of information with various rules, then the human brain is not the only entity capable of thinking; computers, after all, are information-processing machines. Furthermore, if we can specify the operations carried out when you go through a sequence of thoughts, then we can program a computer to go through the same sequence of processes. This idea is at the basis of artificial intelligence. The potential usefulness of artificial intelligence systems is twofold: (1) to help machines behave more intelligently and (2) to serve as a model for human cognition. The latter of these uses, a model or theory of thinking, can help us understand the mind, and will be briefly considered here.

Computer models of the mind are called computational models because of the mathematical and logical operations carried out by a computer program. In computational models information can be represented by different formats, such as lines of programming codes, magnetic fluctuations on an electronic recording device, or flowcharts. In many ways, it is useful to think of cognition as if it were a computer program or a flowchart. Although these models are not completely accurate, they can provide enlightening ways of thinking about the subject of interest, explaining known phenomena, and predicting new ones.

Most models of cognition represent information as existing in an imaginary space. When thought goes from one idea to another, this is represented as information moving within this theoretical place. In the theory, information moves in specified operations, called information processes.

One of the best known and most ambitious computational approaches to cognition is the one developed by Alan Newell and Herbert Simon, along with their colleagues. The theory begins with a symbolic representation of a problem, which is called the problem space. The problem space graphically represents the information that you have when the problem is given, as well as every possible idea that you could go through on your way toward solving the problem. In this model, you can get from one place in the problem space to another using operators, or rules. You begin problem solving at one point in the problem space, and by applying the rules you work your way step by step through the space until you find the solution, which is also known as the goal situation.[6]

A simple example is the solution of a four-letter anagram, such as "ALGO." The initial problem information includes the four letters, "A," "L," "G," and "O," the allowable operation is to rearrange the order of the letters, and the goal is to find a string that represents a word. This problem space is depicted in Figure 4.3. There are 40 possible knowledge states that can occur in working this problem, and 24 possible four-letter solutions. A

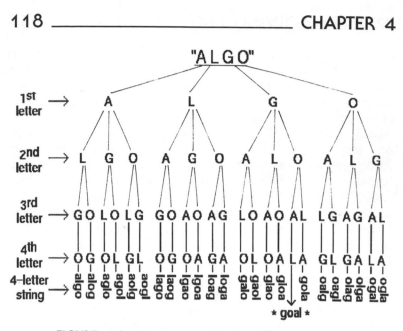

FIGURE 4.3. Solution tree for "goal" anagram.

complete search through this problem space will produce the correct answer.

As problems become more complex, the problem spaces needed to represent the problems become immense and unwieldy. Just imagine the space for a 20-letter anagram! Or, imagine the number of possible configurations in which you might be able to lay out 31 dominoes on the mutilated checkerboard. The number of possible combinations that a safecracker might try defies our understanding of big numbers. For complex problems, most of which are far more complicated than these examples, this computational scheme seems impractical, if not impossible. Although a computer might eventually crank out the answers by searching through gigantic problem spaces, you might have something better to do with your time than billions of mindless computations.

Fortunately, there are ways you can limit the search for a solution using heuristic strategies. One such method is subgoal analysis. If you know that certain specific subgoals must be achieved before getting to the solution to a problem, then at any given time during your search you can focus on those operations needed to get to the next subgoal. For example, if you had the problem of getting from your present location to the Statue of Liberty in New York, then every step presents another of a seemingly infinite number of decisions. If, however, you consider that a New York airport and a cab are necessary subgoals, then there are a great number of possibilities that you can eliminate from consideration. Identifying and putting to work subgoals is an important problem-solving technique used both by computer programmers and by our own minds. The subgoal analysis is only one of the heuristic strategies that can be used as a shortcut through an unwieldy problem space.

These types of computational programs have proven surprisingly creative, having been used to get computers to make scientific discoveries, draw interesting sketches, and compose music.[7] The hope is that if we can understand every step that a computer carries out in the course of creative computing, then we can also understand all of the steps in creative problem solving in people.

SOLUTIONS TO PROBLEMS IN CHAPTER 4

Mutilated Checkerboard: If you think of an analogy to almost anything that involves alternation, such as a set of lights that alternate on and off, the solution becomes easier. This focuses attention on the fact that the squares of the board alternate red and black, and on the idea that each domino will cover one red and one black square. Since the cutting procedure removes two squares of the same color, we are left with 32 squares of one color and 30 of the other. Thus, 31 dominoes cannot cover all of the squares.

Rebuses: 1, search high and low; 2, Bermuda Triangle; 3, hole in one.

The Parent Trap: In version 1 the professor is the boy's mother. In version 2 the professor is the father.

Tip-of-the-Tongue: impenetrable by light = opaque; 1, pediatrician; 2, hemlock; 3, paradox; 4, perjury.

Insight Problems: 1, the man is too short and can only reach the elevator button for the 60th floor—on rainy days he has an umbrella, which he uses to reach the button for the 65th floor; 2, 23 days; 3, the woman wanted the drink of water to cure her hiccups, but the bartender's scare with the gun cured them instead.

NOTES

1. Robert W. Weisberg, *Creativity: Genius and Other Myths* (San Francisco: Freeman, 1986).
2. Steven M. Smith, "Frustrated Feelings of Imminence: On the Tip-of-the-Tongue," in *Metacognition: Knowing about Knowing,* eds. Janet Metcalfe & Arthur Shimamura (Cambridge, MA: MIT Press, 1994), pp. 27–45.
3. Steven M. Smith, "Getting Into and Out of Mental Ruts," in *The Nature of Insight,* eds. Robert J. Sternberg & Janet Davidson (Cambridge, MA: MIT Press, 1994), pp. 121–149.
4. Steven M. Smith, "Theoretical Principles of Context-Dependent Memory," in *Aspects of Memory (2nd edition): Theoretical Aspects,* eds. Peter Morris & Michael Gruneberg (London: Routledge Press, 1994), pp. 168–195.
5. Kenneth S. Bowers, Peter Farvolden, & Lambros Mermigis, "Intuitive Antecedents of Insight," in *The Creative Cognition Approach,* eds. Steven M. Smith, Thomas B. Ward, & Ronald A. Finke (Cambridge, MA: MIT Press, 1995), pp. 27–51.
6. Allan Newell & Herbert A. Simon, *Human Problem Solving* (Englewood Cliffs, NJ: Prentice–Hall, 1972).
7. Margaret Boden, *The Creative Mind: Myths and Mechanisms* (New York: Basic Books, 1991).

INVENTION
AND
PRODUCT
DEVELOPMENT

We have seen that people often rely heavily on old ideas when they formulate new ones. In this chapter we will examine how existing knowledge influences the artifacts that humans produce. We will see that innovation is basically a conservative process, but also one that allows a flowering of useful new ideas.

INVENTION AS AN INCREMENTAL PROCESS

In history classrooms throughout the United States, children are instilled with accounts of great American inventors and their accomplishments. Few children complete their education without hearing about dramatic breakthroughs, such as the cotton gin, light bulb, telephone, and airplane, that shaped the American experience, opened new paths to economic progress, and drastically altered the way we live our lives.

Every schoolchild is taught that Thomas Edison invented the incandescent light bulb in 1879. But let's consider the statement a little further. What does it really mean? Does it mean that Edison was the first person to think of using electricity to heat an element to the point of glowing? No. Sir Humphry Davy demonstrated that phenomenon as early as 1808. Was Edison the first to try to isolate the element in a small glass enclosure? Again, no. Edison was the first to bring the world a practical version of the light bulb, but more than 20 other determined tinkerers preceded him with similar, though less successful designs.[1]

Edison's momentous advance actually resulted from a series of small steps that came before. Many prominent inventions, including the cotton gin, the steam engine, the automobile, the airplane, and the transistor, followed this same pattern.

Eli Whitney's cotton gin stands as the classic case of ingenuity at work. The gin revolutionized the cotton industry in the United States by making it possible to separate the fiber from the seeds of the Inland cotton plant that grew well in the southern states. Much is made of how rapidly Whitney completed his gin, in only ten days, after he learned of the need for such an implement. But, the idea for the cotton gin did not simply spring full-blown into Whitney's mind with no antecedents. It was primarily an improvement on the Indian _charka_, a device that Whitney was familiar with, and that had been used for centuries to clean a different variety of cotton whose fiber and seeds were more easily separated than those of Inland cotton.[2]

We are not minimizing Edison's or Whitney's impressive technical achievements. Among other things Edison was able to produce and maintain a high vacuum, which was needed to prevent the element from burning itself up. Likewise, Whitney saw how to improve on the charka, whereas others before him had not. But, like other new marvels, Edison's light bulb was not conceived in a vacuum, and Whitney's gin was connected by a thread to others before it.

The notion that inventions are based closely on old products conflicts with popular stereotypes. We tend to romanticize invention as a process that breaks sharply with the past and moves us in great leaps toward better ways of meeting our needs. And we tend to think of inventors as highly gifted, possibly eccentric individuals whose minds work differently from ours, by conceiving new miracles "out of thin air."

We hold this stereotype, in part, because we readily call to mind creations, such as the light bulb, that have significantly changed our world. It is easy to mix up their degree of impact on our lives with their degree of novelty. But even these phenomenally influential wonders often arise when diligent workers impart small, incremental changes to existing concepts; they derive from the ordinary cognitive processes of consulting existing knowledge as a jumping off point.

To be sure, it is worthwhile to consider how new ideas arise, but it is equally valuable to focus on what came before. Without very specific existing objects and ideas, the inventions noted earlier would have been impossible.

To claim that new concepts always build on old ones, however, raises an interesting question. We are compelled to ask where those older ideas came from, and we can fall into the trap of an infinite regress. At some point there must have been an original idea, a kind of primitive foundation on which all other inventions were built. By definition, such a concept would not have grown out of a previous invention.

One way to circumvent this problem is to note that the earliest building blocks of our creations came, not from anything we decided to make, but from objects we discovered in nature that could meet certain needs, what Basalla called *naturfacts*.[2] Nonhuman primates recognize useful objects, such as sticks they can wield to feed on ants, and even the humble sea otter places a flat stone on its belly to crack open its shellfish dinner. Surely, then, the earliest humans would have recognized a good stone tool when they saw it.

The earliest human tool users almost certainly did not begin by making their own stone knives. Rather, they discovered that the sharp rocks they found all around them could be used to cut or scrape meat from bones. Only later did they realize that they could fashion their own sharp stones by chipping at dull ones to form a primitive blade. Still later they realized that they could improve on those first primitive designs by crafting points, and handles of increasing sophistication. A hypothetical sequence, adapted from Robert Weber, a noted expert on the psychology of invention, is shown in Figure 5.1.[3]

A DOUBLE-EDGED SWORD

Because people apply knowledge about existing artifacts in giving birth to new ones, many of the central properties of those old objects are bequeathed to the new ones. This can be helpful because we do not have to begin anew each time we want to fabricate a new product. We can bring to bear our knowledge of what has come before to guide the development of the new concept.

When the descendants of *Homo habilis* chipped out ever more sophisticated stone tools, for instance, they were relying on the earlier concept of shaping stone to meet a particular need. They did not have to discover that possibility anew. When people formed the first copper knives, even double-edged ones, they did not have to dream up the concepts of a blade and handle. Those properties were already embedded in the stone predecessors. When Whitney wanted to build the cotton gin, he did not have to conceive of drawing the cotton fiber between two rollers. A working model already existed in the charka.

Starting with a basic object and introducing minor variations also allows for the astonishing number and variety of artifacts that surround us. It is relatively easy to compose variations on a theme, and this allows an enormous degree of

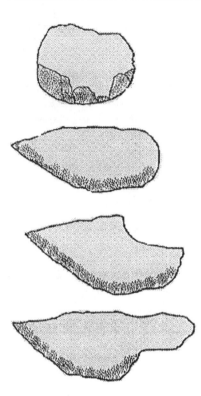

FIGURE 5.1. Possible progression in sophistication of stone knives (adapted from Weber, 1992).

specialization. If you have recently purchased a computer or other electronic gadget, a major appliance, or a car, you are familiar with the overwhelming range of choices available. And the same holds true for much simpler objects, such as athletic shoes and hand tools.

On the negative side, however, carrying over the properties of old products into new ones can sometimes put people at risk, complicate the development of the new contrivance, and lead to a less than optimal design. We have already seen how conductors were put at risk by the design of the earliest train cars. Below we will see how Edison's reliance on earlier ideas complicated the construction of his electric light distribution system.

Real-world examples and controlled laboratory experiments also disclose how older ideas can impose unnecessary limits and block innovation. A recent case in point will be familiar to readers who use personal computers, particularly those who rely on MS-DOS or who plug their lifelines into a mainframe computer.

You are diligently writing your term paper, research report, the family Christmas letter, or the Great American Novel. Your verbosity has gotten you into trouble again, and turned your text into a rambling monster that will gobble up more paper than you had in mind. So you want to squish it back into fewer pages.

Rather than edit and lose your precious gems, however, you change to a smaller font size, kidding yourself that you can fool your readers into thinking it's shorter. And what happens? Instead of seeing more words on the screen, the end of each line runs out beyond the edges of the screen as if it's trying to tell you to lose it. To see those words again you have to move the cursor all the way to the right, at which point the screen shifts, and the words on the left jump into hiding. No matter what you do, you cannot get your screen to show more than 80 characters per line. Why is this so? Why not 50 or 100? Why not an adjustable range between 5 and 500? The major reason is that the property of 80 columns descended directly from earlier modes of interacting with computers.

The authors, and many readers, are old enough to remember writing their first computer programs on punch cards. Each line of a program required a separate card, and each card allowed exactly 80 characters per line. This was a physical limitation imposed by the size of the cards, the fact that different characters were represented by different sets of punched holes in a given column on the card, and the nature of the machines used to punch the holes and read the cards. Interestingly, the 80-column format made its way, first to magnetic tape, where there was no longer the same physical limitation, and ultimately into the programs for displaying text on computer monitors.

An operating system for a personal computer is an enormously creative invention that would not have been possible without many devices and concepts that came before. Prior knowledge was essential. But the 80-column limit supports our point that existing knowledge also can constrain even the most imaginative ideas.

The jump from punch cards to magnetic tape is a specific case of a more general phenomenon. Innovators often inject unnecessary properties from the past into new objects when they change the materials from which the objects are made. For example, when people first made tools of copper and bronze, they simply copied the shape of existing stone tools, even though a much wider variety of shapes was possible with those new metals. Only later did people begin to hammer out new forms and new types of tools. A similar pattern occurred when craftsmen shifted from wood to masonry in architecture, and from wood to iron in bridge construction.[2]

In each of these cases, a change in materials eventually liberated designers from previous constraints. This leads us to suggest the *new materials* heuristic. Whenever new materials become available, would-be innovators should consider not just how those materials could be used to do the same things better, but also what new things might be done with those materials.

The results of laboratory studies complement these historical observations. Subjects in experiments often project properties of old ideas onto new ones, even when doing so gives rise to inferior designs for new objects. In one experiment, for example, David Jansson, then of Texas A&M University, and one of the authors asked mechanical engineering students and professional engineers to design new objects, such as bicycle racks, spillproof coffee cups, and measuring devices for the blind.[4] Some of the participants saw examples of flawed designs, such as a coffee cup with a straw, prior to concocting their own plans.[5] These people tended to include the same flaws in their own designs, even when they were instructed not to.

Similarly, when nonengineering students were asked to design new toys for an imaginary setting, they included many features of the examples we showed them, even when instructed not to do so.[6] Because the setting was an imaginary one, we cannot judge whether the designs were optimal, but it is clear that they were less innovative than those devised by students who saw no examples.

Because some of the properties of existing ideas might be helpful and some might be harmful, it is difficult to know what to keep and what to discard. One method that might help in making that determination is abstraction.

ABSTRACTION

Earlier we spelled out the claim that bringing to mind specific objects can inhibit creativity: the central properties of those objects set up roadblocks on the routes to innovation. One way to dodge that inhibition and clearly home in on the goals we want to reach is to cast the problem more abstractly. In mounting a more abstract assault on a problem we still deliberately apply knowledge, but we marshal it differently.

In fact, some mechanical engineering programs are beginning to teach promising new techniques that encourage students to think first about highly abstract principles, rather than about specific, earlier designs. One example of this approach, called *function–structure development*, encourages students to represent their design problems at the highest possible level, that is, in terms of fundamental physical principles.[7]

For example, consider the task of designing a brake system for a new type of vehicle. You could tackle the job directly by patterning the new system after one of the two most traditional specific brake systems: disc or drum brakes. Alternatively, you could begin by posing a fundamental question: What is a brake system designed to do? The answer that pops to mind first, "to stop the vehicle," is accurate, but not abstract enough to be helpful. In its most abstract sense, a brake system transforms the kinetic energy of a vehicle into some other form. To stop a car you have to somehow take the energy of its movement and change it into something else.

There are plenty of ways to transform the kinetic energy of a vehicle, such as popping open a parachute or extending broad fins to increase wind resistance. Some of these would beget extravagantly impractical designs, but others might provoke clever new solutions to the old problem of bringing a vehicle to a halt.

If an engineer decided from the start to approach a design task as a "disc brake problem," he might never envision any of those other ways to stop the vehicle. Based on the "disc brake" model he would also infuse his new design with the specific details of disc brake systems that may not even be the best ones for the new situation. By settling for the expedient method of relying on the past, the designer might miss a great opportunity to move into the future and come up with a truly revolutionary new system.

By first formulating the problem at an abstract level, designers can discover exactly what goals they need to accomplish without having to commit themselves to any of the standard ways of reaching those goals. By then exploring the greatest possible range of means to those ends, designers can move beyond the narrow thinking that comes along with considering only the small set of existing solutions. In attacking the problem this way, they may discover innovative solutions that would not otherwise have occurred to them. And if they ultimately decide that a disc or drum system is appropriate, at least the decision will be based on the fact that the system is the very best one for getting the job done.

This abstraction approach can also encourage truly ingenious breakthroughs. For example, what happens to the kinetic energy of your car when you step on the brake? It is dissipated in the form of heat. Is that the only possibility? If you are not locked into the details of existing systems, you might consider other possibilities such as storing the transformed energy for later use. This type of innovation may be advantageous in a new situation, such as coping with an energy shortage, or designing an ecologically sound vehicle, and would be very unlikely to emerge in more conventional approaches to design.

Because these training programs are relatively new, they have not been tested rigorously to determine if they really do help students think more imaginatively than do other, more traditional programs. It is therefore premature to claim that engineering departments across the land should adopt this type of teaching procedure. However, professional engineers have praised the student designs that evolve out of this abstraction approach, which convinces us that it holds a great deal of promise.[7]

Not all design problems call for truly innovative solutions, and so abstraction may not always be the best strategy to pursue. Sometimes it is more efficient simply to reuse specific old ideas. This would be particularly true if there were nothing radically different about the new design problem. If you're just designing another in a long series of ordinary cars, disc brakes are a perfectly acceptable, indeed preferred, solution. Why bother racking your brains to come up with some wild new system when the old one works so well? If it ain't broke, don't fix it, so to speak.

However, the *new situation* heuristic states that abstraction would be the method to choose when designing for new tasks and new environments. For instance, trains have their movement constrained by a pair of parallel iron bars that guide a set of cars strung together along a sometimes tortuously curving path. The situation is different enough from that of stagecoach travel that it might have warranted an abstraction approach.

Perhaps early railcar designers would have done well to think more about the basic goals of transportation and less about stagecoaches.

Hindsight is, of course, 20/20, while foresight is legally blind. It is easy to look back and see how previous designers might have done better, and much harder to know where to go from here. But, as we begin to explore a broader range of environments—other planets, the deepest recesses of our planet, the bottommost floor of immense ocean trenches—we might be better off dreaming up entirely new systems than adapting old ones.

We have seen the wilder side of abstraction, but paradoxically we can also use it to take smaller steps, add incremental changes to existing devices, and fill niches for desirable new tools not so different from current ones. Other authors also have extolled the creative virtues of abstraction, and have proposed special techniques to help people construct abstract descriptions. Robert Weber of Oklahoma State University, an expert on the psychology of invention, advocates building an abstract frame, or outline to describe an existing invention, and then working within that description to get new ideas.[3]

The frame would state the purpose of the invention, elucidate the physical principle by which it accomplishes that purpose, and describe its physical parts and attributes such as its size, material composition, and so on. Ordinarily, a fork is just a fork. But we can tease it apart into a more abstract description— an implement for eating usually made of metal or plastic and composed of a handle and a set of four tines approximately one-third the length of the handle. By generating this type of abstract description, we let ourselves see the fork in a new way. We know it has those properties, otherwise we couldn't construct the frame, but we don't ordinarily bring them to mind. Once we bring this existing knowledge out of hiding, we can probe it to determine which attributes could be varied, and in what way to develop new inventions.

Weber also exhorts inventors to note down in the abstract description the family of inventions from which an object comes.

Forks, of course, are in the "eating implement" family along with spoons, knives, and chopsticks. By taking a snapshot of the whole family, an inventor might be able to notice "gaps"— possible offspring that haven't yet been born—and thereby grasp an idea for a new invention. Weber mentions exactly such an implement: the spork, which is a cross between a spoon and a fork. The spork is not so wildly different from either of its parents, but it may nevertheless fill a useful niche. It certainly seems ideal for eating stew, having a small indentation for broth and sharp tines for stabbing chunks.

William Middendorf has also directed design engineers down a similar path. He has prodded them to identify the basic functions of existing implements and the ways those functions are satisfied.[8] This sometimes involves breaking the invention into subunits that perform different tasks. For example, a simple hand-operated can opener has one subunit to separate metal, and one to apply power. The first unit typically uses shearing to achieve its purpose, and the second uses hand power. By highlighting what each subunit does, we can test out alternate ways of satisfying the same needs, which could spur a fresh invention. For instance, perhaps we could melt the metal of the lid with a laser, or erode it through some chemical reaction.

As an exercise, consider some other simple objects that you use everyday, such as a toothbrush, faucet, deodorant dispenser, or salad spinner. What do they do and how do they do it? Try to generate an abstract description of each and then think of other ways a different sort of object might meet the same needs.

Abstraction also harkens back to traditional advice about how to be more creative, that is, to try to "restructure" a problem. Unfortunately, this is usually a vague suggestion that means something like "think about the problem differently." But how are you to do this? Abstraction is one principle you can use. State the problem in its most abstract form. What is the *essence* of what you are trying to accomplish? Are you trying to build a better mousetrap, or are you trying to make sure that you do not have to share your living space with undesirable vermin? (If this process of abstraction leads you beyond mice to consider ways to eliminate your in-laws as well, perhaps your restructuring has gone too far.)

Abstraction may help to identify the goals of the problem, but by itself, it does not provide the ways of meeting those goals. We now turn to analogy and conceptual combination as possible sources of ideas for meeting goals.

ANALOGY

Analogies can provide clues to help us achieve certain ends. By pondering how needs are met in a different arena, we may see more clearly how to do something similar for the problem we are confronting.

From their own reports, and from the historical record, we see that inventors often use analogies in developing new ideas. Thomas Edison devised the light bulb as part of a large system for distributing electric light to individual households. He patterned his system, by analogy, directly on the existing gas lighting distribution system, which in turn had been based on urban water distribution systems.[1,2]

The parallels between the systems are striking. Gas was distributed from a central facility, through underground mains, to individually controlled lights at each household, and its use was metered. Likewise, Edison wanted a system in which electricity was sent out from a central generating station, through underground wires, to individually controlled lights whose use would be metered.

The components of each system, such as the mains and wires, obviously differ in superficial ways, but they are connected by similar higher-order relations, such as "path from central facility to individual units." This makes for a complete and compelling analogy.

CHAPTER 5

Edison certainly knew about other types of distribution systems, including the telegraph and arc lighting systems, which relied on aboveground wires, but he adhered steadfastly to the gas distribution analogy, for better and for worse. For example, he insisted on laying wires underground even though it was a costly and technically difficult alternative to stringing them between poles above ground. At the time, there was also no practical system for monitoring individual use of electric lights. But he was ultimately able to craft a working system.

The Wright brothers also exploited analogies as they fulfilled humankind's long-standing desire to fly. Theirs is a particularly informative case, because it highlights the importance of choosing the right analogy, and of having extensive knowledge. Rather than patterning their airplane propeller on a ship's propeller, which was the predominant approach of others in their day, the Wright brothers used the wing as their analogy. They knew almost nothing about propellers for boats, but they had learned a great deal about the lift of wings through experiments in a wind tunnel. The genius of their approach was to conceptualize an airplane propeller as a rotating wing. This allowed them to craft an efficient design relatively quickly.[9]

Velcro is a more recent example of how analogies can spawn new creations. Velcro was conceived when its inventor, George de Mestral, returned from a walk in the woods with many burrs attached to his clothing. On examining the burrs under a microscope, he was amazed to discover that they were collections of miniature "hooks" that had attached themselves to the "eyes" in the cloth of his pants and socks.

Mestral realized that a similar hook-and-eye system could be pressed into service as a fastener. All that would be required would be to manufacture separate pieces of material that had surfaces of tiny hooks or eyes. When the two surfaces were pressed together, they would cling to one another. When pulled apart they would release with only modest reluctance. As simple as this sounds, however, it took nearly a decade to bring it to fruition.

Velcro grew out of an analogy borrowed from nature, and it stands as a clear reminder that nature holds a rich bounty of solutions that can be brought to bear on practical problems. Materials scientists currently are probing the mysteries of other natural substances to assess their potential applications. As one example, spider silk is stretchy, yet stronger than Kevlar, the material from which bulletproof vests are made. Perhaps it can serve as an analogue for an artificial material that would have those same properties and meet some human need.[10]

Now for the fine print. It is one thing to claim we should use analogies to provoke ingenious ideas. It is quite another to find and exploit good analogies when we need them. Parallels between concepts are easy to recognize after the fact, but much harder to generate.

One difficulty is that there may be a nearly infinite number of possible topics to relate to the problem you want to solve. What are some heuristics you can use to narrow the range of possibilities? We will explore three that are most central to invention and product development: *relevance, prior success*, and *abstraction*.

Consider why Edison held fast to the gas distribution system as an analogy. At the time it was the relevant competitor for electricity, and was already successfully supplying lighting to individual households. Edison was keenly aware that if electric lighting was to be viable it would have to be economically competitive with gas.[1] So he chose a relevant and successful model with the belief that his system could do the same job better.

The analogy to the gas system provided not just a model to copy, but also a *relevant* yardstick to measure *relative* success. It did not matter in absolute terms how much it would cost Edison to build and operate his system. It mattered whether he could do it better or more cheaply than with gas. In the world of creativity where yardsticks are hard to come by, the relevance heuristic can provide guidance, particularly in business settings.

As is true of heuristics in general, the relevance heuristic does not guarantee you will find the best or the easiest path to a new product. Note, for instance, how it compelled Edison to stick with the difficult process of laying wires underground. At best, any heuristic will only point in a generally helpful direction.

The *prior success* heuristic tells us why using analogies from nature may be so desirable. Over billions of years, life forms have evolved and fine-tuned exquisitely successful means of performing certain tasks. By considering the goals we want to accomplish, and how various living things reach them, creative solutions might emerge. Once again, we return to our theme that the more knowledge you gather, and the further afield you explore, the better able you will be to see novel solutions to problems.

In the case of engineering design and invention, it may seem odd that knowledge about living things would come in so handy. After all, engineers design cold, hard, mechanical systems, and life forms tend to be warm, soft, and a bit squishy. But living organisms are nevertheless complex and remarkably adaptive systems that may hold the secrets to success in the world of mechanical artifacts.

The *abstraction* heuristic tells us to pose our problems in as abstract a fashion as possible. When casting about for an analogy that may provide a solution to an engineering design problem, we must also think abstractly about the other domains of knowledge, such as nature, politics, or human relations, that might apply.

To return to our example of designing a new brake system, we noted that abstraction could help in posing the problem, but we did not say how you could find ways of meeting the abstract goals. Seeking an abstract analogy might help. Are there successful examples in nature of how to transform energy? A possible analogy might take the following form: "X is a successful energy transform in nature, can it be used for transforming the kinetic energy of a vehicle?" Of course this would only provide a way to coax an initial idea out of hiding. You would still have to thoroughly explore the newly uncovered analogy to see if it would work. But, at least the combination of the abstraction and prior success heuristics suggests a place to begin.

The abstraction heuristic prods us to seek out and store abstractions from a wide range of domains. We should keep in mind what our most abstract goals are, and constantly stand on the lookout for examples of systems that meet those goals. If our job is designing brake systems, we should continually search for systems that transform kinetic energy. How do birds, or fish, or elephants, or cheetahs stop themselves? Many animate creatures rely on opposing muscle groups. Would a similar system be useful in a vehicle? What about a vehicle operating in low-friction or low-gravity environments in outer space?

CONCEPTUAL COMBINATION IN INVENTION

We know that when people combine two existing concepts, new ideas can spring forth that are quite different from either of the concepts alone. Does the same thing happen when we actually piece together two physical objects? As it turns out, although completely new ideas and possibilities can crop up when people fabricate new products, this does not always occur. Consider, for example, two separate tools, one for pounding in nails and one for prying them out. When we combine them in the same tool, we have the familiar claw hammer. The combination may allow us to work more efficiently, because we do not have to find and grasp a different tool when we want to switch from hammering to prying. However, combining a head and claw into the same tool does not alter the basic function of either one. A similar case can be made for many familiar combinations such as a lead pencil with an attached eraser.

A less well-known example of a combination is the mirror attachment for table implements (U.S. Patent No. 886,746—1908), which is a mirror set in the handle of a knife or fork to allow people to check for food between their teeth. Another is a combined clothes brush, flask, and drinking cup (U.S. Patent No. 490,964—1893), which is simply a flask in the handle of a brush that has a detachable lid to serve as a cup.[11] Although these inventions were considered novel and useful enough to be patented, nothing emerged from either one that changed the basic function of the knife, mirror, flask, or brush.

Why is it that nothing truly novel blossoms forth from these combinations? Is it just that we have not yet combined enough objects? Consider one of the most elaborate combinations of simple implements: the Swiss Army Knife. Even the most basic models of this knife sport several blades, a corkscrew, and other attachments. What happens when we combine these multiple elements into a single object? One obvious advantage is that the combination is compact and portable. Rather than carrying several separate knives and a corkscrew, you can carry a single compact device. But does anything truly new or different jump out at us from the combination? Can you do anything with a knife blade and corkscrew attached together in the same contraption that you cannot do with those objects as separate entities? Generally, the answer is no.

Do combinations of artifacts ever summon up new properties? Consider what happens if we combine a pointed awl, used for boring holes, and a rounded blade, used for scraping or cutting, into a single, pointed blade. The result is that we can now perform a new function, etching, which requires the point and blade to be used simultaneously.[3]

Perhaps we can discover emergent functions for the Swiss Army Knife by envisioning how we might use its parts simultaneously. Suppose, for example, you needed to have both hands free, but still wanted to use a blade to cut something. You could embed the corkscrew in a tree to attach the body of the knife. You could then use both hands to drag whatever needed to be cut across an open blade. In this case, the corkscrew would perform a very different function than it was originally intended to serve. What this exercise reveals is that sometimes new properties emerge only when we scrutinize the potential of a new object.

As another example of this brand of emergence, start with one wheel attached near the front of a platform and then add two more near the back. With one wheel, the cart is unsteady, and unlevel. Once we have at least three wheels attached to the platform, the properties of stability and levelness emerge. They are properties of the combination, not of any one component. This is an example of using Weber's *repeated-element* heuristic to guide how we combine objects. When an element has an interesting function, try repeating it.[3]

Even these types of emergence do not seem as dramatic as the computer dog example we mentioned earlier, however. What is different? One major factor is that now we are talking about combining artifacts, whereas earlier, we were combining concepts. The Swiss Army Knife combines real blades and a real corkscrew, but the computer dog does not literally combine a computer and a dog.

As we saw in Chapter 2, the essence of an artifact is its function. Thus, an artifact will naturally resist having its function changed in a combination. The blades of the Swiss Army Knife retain their essence, which is to cut, even when they are combined with a corkscrew. Combining concepts allows more flexibility, because concepts can readily be interpreted differently.

The limited emergence that occurs when we combine artifacts is not a cause for concern. On the contrary, this resistance to radical change supports one of the key goals of invention, which is to supply novel yet practical products. It does not matter that no new functions emerge for a claw hammer or a Swiss Army Knife. What does matter is that we now have more efficient tools than we had before.

Robert Weber has provided an excellent set of heuristics to guide how we can combine artifacts to develop practical new inventions. For instance, he introduced the inverse heuristic, which states that if an object performs one function, a new artifact might be realized by combining it with an object that performs the opposite function. The claw hammer is a good example of this heuristic. So is a pencil with an eraser.

As an exercise, try to contrive some new ideas for inventions using the inverse heuristic. Perhaps a small cap for tightly sealing a soda can could be attached to the lever of the pop-top device. Continuing the motion of the lever beyond the point needed for opening the can would drive the seal into the hole. Try to cultivate some additional possibilities using relatively simple implements.

MENTAL MODELS AND VISUALIZATION

Many important inventions, such as the airplane and automobile, are comprised of a multitude of components organized into an elaborate and dynamic system. To envision and refine such systems, a person must be able to generate a complex mental representation of the components and how they interact. To get a sense of how such a system would operate, the designer must be able to run and test a mental model.

Earlier we noted that the Wright brothers designed their propeller by using the wing as an analogy. They actually employed many other analogies in visualizing an elaborate mental model of the process of flight. Other designers of their day had assumed that the pilot would not be able to control the roll of the plane, that is, its rotation about the long axis. Rather the plane would remain stable in flight just as most land vehicles are stable along that axis. In contrast, the Wrights used an analogy to the bicycle, on which a rider controls the roll by shifting his or her weight. The Wrights assumed that if a rider could stay balanced on a bicycle while negotiating a sharp turn, a pilot could do the same in a plane. However, they did not want to force pilots to shift their weight to control the roll. So, the Wrights spent many hours watching birds to extract yet another analogy: a pilot could control roll by adjusting the angle of the wing tips.

As Tom Crouch puts it, "The Wrights had taken a set of graphic images—a bicycle speeding around a corner, a bird soaring through the air. . .—turned them into thought problems, and reassembled the lessons learned into a mechanical system for controlling an airplane in the roll axis."[9] The resulting mental model allowed them to achieve solutions to problems that had eluded others.

This example shows the important link between visualization and mental models. When we forge and test a mental model we usually get a mental picture of a system and can envision how it operates. Other famous putterers, such as Bell and Edison, clearly used similarly elaborate mental models in hatching their inventions.[12]

Mental models can also be useful in anticipating how readily a new contrivance will be accepted. We have been focusing on practical and important inventions, but thinking about impractical ones can help us see this broader role for mental models. One such creation is the *spinnet* shown in Figure 5.2. The spinnet is an inclined stretcher on a rotating platform, designed to aid childbirth by centrifugal force. As an expectant mother you would lie down on the stretcher and be whirled around until the baby dropped out. Your baby's arrival would, hopefully, stop the rotation and set off an alarm.

The spinnet does involve abstraction. Note the focus on centrifugal force, an abstract principle. But abstraction alone

FIGURE 5.2. Spinnet device to aid childbirth through centrifugal force (adapted from Richardson, 1990).

does not help because the apparatus misses the bigger picture that could be gotten by constructing and running a mental model of the birth process.

As anyone who has given birth or seen it happen can attest, it is a painful, messy process. Just briefly conjure up a mental image of a woman, experiencing frequent, intense contractions, and nauseated from the pain. Now envision her strapped to a whirling, inclined stretcher, alone and waiting for her baby to arrive and trigger an alarm. This short test of the mental model reveals that not many women will opt for using this mechanism.

Inventions are used by people in particular contexts. So, to be valuable, they must be more than just novel, and physically capable of accomplishing their stated goal. They must fit with the workings of the world in a broader sense, and with human needs and desires. Even if centrifugal force would help to move a baby through the birth canal, you would not choose to have your baby on a spinnet. It would have to seem sensible or inviting in some way.

Returning to our novel can openers for another example, it might be possible to manufacture a gizmo that would dissolve the lid of the can by dripping acid on it. But not many people would be happy about eating the food from the can.

An inventor can get a clearer sense of the true utility of an object by assembling and evaluating a mental model of the whole situation in which the device will be used. Adopting the perspective of a potential user can improve the design process by leading to a mental model consistent with the user's view of the situation.[13]

Let's try another exercise using a mental model and the Swiss Army Knife. As we saw, the blades do not take on any new functions simply because a corkscrew is added. Perhaps the new gadget can be thought of differently, however, as a "picnic in a pocket." That is, you can cut bread, cheese, and fruit with one blade, spread butter with another, and open wine with the corkscrew. By creating a kind of mental model of a picnic and noting what's missing as you test the model, you might think of other useful additions, such as a toothpick (which many army knives have), a mirror embedded in the handle to check for food between your teeth, a refillable compartment in the handle to hold ant repellent, and so on. We could dream up and play with a wonderful array of variations on this theme.

GENERATING IDEAS FOR NEW PRODUCTS USING MENTAL SYNTHESIS

In the chapter on improving creative visualization, we discussed various methods for generating new ideas for inventions by combining mental images. Let's consider a few examples of how some of these methods might be used in actual practice. First, take the following three parts, and imagine combining them to make a preinventive form: two cones and a half sphere. Now try to think of ways in which your form could be turned into a marketable product.

FIGURE 5.3. Preinventive form interpreted as a "squeaker."

An example of a preinventive form using these parts is shown in Figure 5.3. While exploring the possibilities of this form, Ronald Finke envisioned a new product called a "squeaker." The squeaker is made of rubber, and a person wears it around his or her neck. Each squeaker has a distinctive squeak, and they come in different shapes and colors, to reflect different types of personalities. Although the squeaker is a bit fanciful, we use it here simply as an imaginative example to illustrate the preinventive form technique.

The squeaker could be used in a variety of social settings. It might help shy people break the ice with strangers, for instance. Often, shy people want to meet others, but are too reserved or self-conscious to speak. Such a person might initially "squeak" at a stranger. If the squeak is returned, the person would know that the feeling was mutual, and could then start a conversation with more confidence. Readers might envision other ways squeakers could be used to send messages to people without having to use words. Perhaps codes would arise, with different numbers or types of squeaks taking on special significance. People might even learn to control their squeaks artfully to convey complex or subtle messages.

There would be at least some potential for the squeaker to catch on as a new fad. One of the reasons why products based on preinventive forms often hold the promise of becoming successful is that the forms have a natural appeal. They are novel, and yet meaningful in a general, abstract way. When shown examples of ideas such as the squeaker that were developed using preinventive forms, people often comment on how they wish they could obtain such a "neat," creative product.

One can also try to concoct new ideas by taking an existing product and attaching an abstract part to it. For example, Figure 5.4 shows a television set with an inverted cone attached at the top. How could this be useful? The cone could be (1) a dish for mints or snacks, (2) a holder for flowers, decorations, dust cloths, static cloths, remote controls, or other objects, (3) some new type of antenna, (4) an instrument to measure external sounds or

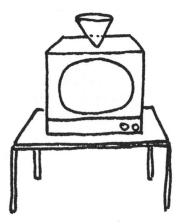

FIGURE 5.4. Television with inverted cone serving to stimulate ideas for inventions.

other room conditions and adjust the TV's volume accordingly, or (5) a symbolic reminder to recovering couch potatoes that they all too easily get sucked into programs when they ought to be doing something else. Perhaps you can think of other potential applications of this novel feature.

It may be a telling comment on the goal-oriented focus of our world that few inventors report using this preinventive form procedure. The more typical approaches are to discover a need and craft a product to fill it, or to take a specific existing invention and tweak it to make something modestly new. As experimental research shows, however, there is much potential in being more playful. Inventors would do well to occasionally get out their mental sketch pads and imaginatively doodle on them with no particular goal in mind. Later they can scrutinize their efforts, bringing the harsh light of practical reality to bear to see if their images spark useful inventions. In addition to letting the needed function drive the form of every invention, it may be helpful sometimes to let preinventive forms suggest possible functions.

INCUBATION AND INSIGHT

Earlier, we noted that creative new ideas can sometimes emerge if people step away from their problems temporarily. Gutenberg's realization about how to build a workable printing press illustrates the power of this process called incubation.

Gutenberg understood that an essential component of a printing press would be some mechanism to propagate the force needed to press an inked surface against a sheet of paper. The solution came to him while he was incubating at a wine festival. He observed a wine press and recognized that the device could be adapted to press inked surfaces as well.

There are two important lessons to take from this example. The first is that pulling back from a difficult problem can sometimes help. By relaxing or shifting to a new context we may forget unworkable ideas that may be clouding our view of a better path to a solution. We also may notice new clues that will guide us to that path.

The second lesson, however, is that simply avoiding problems will not, by itself, help us solve them. Gutenberg would not have noted the relevance of the wine press for the printing press if he had not been so intimately familiar with the problem. Hard work, possibly in the form of generating an abstract characterization of the problem, can prepare our minds to appreciate the significance of cues.

SUMMARY

We have seen how our knowledge both fosters and inhibits innovation, how new situations and new materials can signal invaluable opportunities to break with the past, and how abstraction can help people avoid fixation while also preserving the best of what has come before. We also described how analogy and conceptual combination can serve as the wellspring of new ideas, and how incubation and imagery might help people simultaneously evade thoughts that inhibit and notice clues that can lead to ingenious solutions. The principles of creative cognition are surely evident in the arena of invention. With deliberate attention to those principles, they might be applied even more effectively. The most successful inventors throughout human history have used some of these techniques to move us forward in small steps and great leaps. Noting what they've done, where they've been successful, and where they've stumbled can help direct us more surely along the path to a better future.

NOTES

1. Robert Friedel & Paul Israel, *Edison's Electric Light: Biography of an Invention* (New Brunswick, NJ: Rutgers University Press, 1986).
2. George Basalla, *The Evolution of Technology* (London: Cambridge University Press, 1988).
3. Robert J. Weber, *Forks, Phonographs, and Hot Air Balloons* (London: Oxford University Press, 1992).
4. David G. Jansson & Steven M. Smith, "Design Fixation," *Design Studies* 12 (1991), pp. 3–11.
5. The problem with a straw is that it does not allow air to circulate around and cool the liquid while it is being consumed. Thus, the coffee would be too hot to drink.
6. Steven M. Smith, Thomas B. Ward, & Jay S. Schumacher, "Constraining Effects of Examples in a Creative Generation Task," *Memory & Cognition* 21 (1993), pp. 837–845.
7. Sridhar S. Condoor, Harvey R. Brock, & Christian P. Burger, "Innovation Through Early Recognition of Critical Design Parameters," Paper presented at the meeting of the ASEE, Urbana, IL (June, 1993).
8. William H. Middendorf, *What Every Engineer Should Know About Inventing* (New York: Marcel Dekker, 1981).
9. Tom D. Crouch, "Why Wilbur and Orville? Some Thoughts on the Wright Brothers and the Process of Invention," in *Inventive Minds,*

eds. Robert J. Weber & David N. Perkins (London: Oxford University Press, 1992), pp. 80–92.

10. Madeleine Nash, "Copying What Comes Naturally," *Time*, March 8, 1993.

11. Robert O. Richardson, *The Weird and Wondrous World of Patents* (New York: Sterling Publishing Co., 1990), pp. 57–58.

12. W. Bernard Carlson & Michael E. Gorman, "A Cognitive Framework to Understand Technological Creativity: Bell, Edison, and the Telephone" in *Inventive Minds*, eds. Robert J. Weber & David N. Perkins (London: Oxford University Press, 1992), pp. 48–79.

13. Donald A. Norman, *The Psychology of Everyday Things* (New York: Basic Books, 1988).

BUSINESS APPLICATIONS

The Dallas Cowboys have just intercepted a pass in New York Giant territory. Coverage of the game is about to yield to a commercial break. Time to pull away from the television, and go forage in the refrigerator. But wait. What's this? In a bizarre twist on reality it's a television advertisement about people watching television. A group of attractive young men and women are arguing about which program to watch. Some argue for a beauty pageant, and others want to watch hockey.

One of the viewers settles the argument. "Let's watch both." He taps the television with a bottle of Miller Lite. The screen flickers momentarily, and then we suddenly see women dressed in formal gowns playing ice hockey. They skate around carrying hockey sticks, and check each other hard into the boards. One of them smiles to reveal a gap where her front teeth ought to be.

You have just been captured by one in a series of clever commercials developed by Leo Burnett Company for Lite beer.

Others in the set include "full-contact golf" in which a frail-looking golfer is tackled by brawny, fully uniformed football players, and "luge bowling" in which a luger is pursued down the course by an enormous bowling ball.

These commercials show us yet another use of conceptual combination. It can foster creatively captivating ways to market products.

Advertisers must persuade you to buy things, and they must leap two critical barriers to do so. First, they must capture your attention. If you trek to the refrigerator rather than vegetating in front of the TV during a commercial, all the clever script writers and attractive models will be unable to reach you. Having roped you into watching, they must also penetrate your defenses deeply enough that you will remember their product and pick it up when you shop. So, the ad must be engaging and memorable.

The humor that ensues from combining the wildly discrepant concepts of beauty contests and ice hockey arouses interest and keeps viewers watching. Humor is not a key feature of hockey or pageants alone. It emerges when they are joined together.

The ads are also memorable because the idea of combining discrepant concepts reinforces an earlier Lite beer theme. Previous commercials had emphasized that the beer tastes great, but is less filling. The more recent series secures the link more tightly by noting that "If you can combine great taste, and less filling, you can combine anything."

CONCEPTUAL COMBINATION IN PRODUCT EXTENSION AND POSITIONING

There are many other solid business uses of conceptual combination, not the least of which are product extension and positioning. Most products follow a characteristic life cycle. When first introduced, their relative anonymity limits sales and constrains profits. As they become better known, sales and profits increase dramatically. Then the rate of increase slows, and finally, sales and profits decline. To remain competitive, businesses constantly introduce new products, either by adapting old ones or by developing new ones. Conceptual combination can aid these efforts by suggesting new products and new ways to position a product in the marketplace.

Sometimes forming new combinations is as simple as taking two or more existing products and melding them together. The Swiss Army Knife discussed in the previous chapter is a good example of such a product. A more personally tempting one is the inspired and delightful merging of chocolate and peanut butter to form peanut butter cups. A recent high-tech version is the marriage of a color television screen to a camcorder in a product that treats proud parents and awed tourists to immediate feedback on how well they've captured the moment.

It's relatively easy to think of additional blends. What if we brought together a recliner—possibly built for two—with a VCR, a CD, a large surrounding screen, and a killer sound system to construct the ultimate in self-indulgent home entertainment devices? What about coupling a sound chip and a zipper so that a discrete alarm would sound if you've forgotten to secure your pants? What about merging an exercise bicycle and a manually operated generator so that power would go to a radio or TV only as long as a person continued to work out?

Random pairings might evoke marvelous new creative ideas, but they may also lead nowhere. The competitive nature of the business world means that companies can only afford to attempt just so many innovations. So a more targeted approach to finding promising combinations is called for. A good place to start is with observations of how people think and behave. What separate items do they combine for themselves?

Health-conscious partiers often mix wine with soda to concoct a refreshing drink that's low in calories and only mildly alcoholic. So it was only natural for beverage makers to blend wine and carbonated soft drinks to formulate ready-to-drink wine coolers. Snackers love to dip chips, but may not like the potential embarrassment of dropping globs of dip on their party clothes. One solution put forth by several food companies: spread a sour cream and onion-flavored coating directly onto chips. Children devour millions of peanut butter and jelly sandwiches every year. This led naturally to swirling peanut butter and jelly together in the same jar.

Sometimes product extension is just a matter of probing what else an existing product can do. Church & Dwight Company, maker of Arm & Hammer baking soda, for instance, has often touted the fact that baking soda absorbs odors. They have encouraged people to put a box in the refrigerator, freezer, or any other location where odors might crop up. Now they have taken this basic concept and extended it to specific new products, including their own brand of deodorant, cat litter deodorizer, laundry detergent, and toothpaste.

Sometimes the merger is between abstract concepts rather than physical objects. These blends can lead not only to new products but also to new ideas for positioning or promoting a product.

A classic example of combining opposing concepts to position a product in the marketplace is the Nissan Altima. It is pitched as providing affordable luxury. It appeals to the market segment that may desire an expensive luxury car but not have the resources to purchase one. The Buick Park Avenue evokes a similar theme by claiming to be "the best luxury car buy in America." Hyundai recently joined the same chorus by pitching the Accent as embodying state-of-the-art technology in an affordable car. Other automobile manufacturers have emphasized affordable safety. You don't have to be rich to feel safe. You don't have to pay an exorbitant price to obtain the security of antilock brakes and dual airbags.

In fact, almost any valued trait that normally comes at a high price could be combined with the concept of affordability to pitch a good or service. Consider, for instance, the long-distance phone wars with their competing messages about quality phone service at a lower price.

By combining opposing traits, manufacturers can carve out special niches in the world of products. If we think of products as existing in some vast space, we can see that some parts of that space are empty, just waiting to be filled by a successful offering. Combinations bring out unique ways of filling those gaps. Of course, the space must be a desirable one. Some gaps are there for a good reason. Combining an exorbitant price with a low-quality product may plug a whole in the space of possible products, but people are unlikely to rush out and buy an "expensive economy car" or a "bland but fattening snack."

Affordability is obviously critical to many products, but it need not be included in every combination. How many foods beckon dieters with the combination of scandalously delicious fare but a minimum of fat and calories? What new products or sales pitches would emanate from rugged comfort or rugged elegance—perhaps the sort of pickup truck you could bounce around the ranch in and then later use to escort your date to the ballet? What about toys for people who take their fun seriously; financial services that promise growth and security; personal products for the tender yet virile man or the competently assertive yet softly sensuous woman; or living spaces or transportation services for those who seek rural solitude combined with urban convenience? It's easy to see how a melding of concepts that seem to be incompatible can open a world of possibilities.

Putting abstraction to work also can boost your efforts to position products. You can use it to rationally assess which consumers you want to pitch to, and which competitors you want to target. We saw earlier that moving to the highest level of abstraction can help people avoid getting hung up on specific details from the past, and we noted how important that might be in spurring an initial idea for an invention. For positioning an existing product, however, the act of formulating an abstract hierarchy is more important than moving to its highest level. It may actually be better to position a product at a very specific level, where there would be a smaller market but fewer competitors.

Imagine that you wanted to bring a new dessert to the market. You might begin by abstracting the mental structure of that type of product. At the highest level in the structure would be the very general category of desserts. You could then divide that broad grouping into fattening and nonfattening types, and further subdivide fattening desserts into ice cream, pie, cake, and so on.[1] How you pitch your new offering will depend on whether you want to compete with all dessert makers for the vast market of all dessert eaters, ice cream makers for the smaller market of ice cream lovers, or somewhere in between.

No matter where you decide to enter the game, it is the act of constructing the abstract hierarchy that permits you to develop the best new strategy. You could even combine abstraction and conceptual combination by using abstraction to get you to the right level, and combination to help you decide what to merge. You may want to compete for the high-end, rich and fattening ice cream market by developing a new flavor that combines the most exquisite chocolates with the thickest of cream bases.

Using mental imagery to mentally merge separate components can also aid in crafting symbols to represent companies. In Chapter 3, we described an imagery technique for generating creative symbols and designs, using preinventive forms. This same technique could also be used to develop creative company logos. Some examples of how various companies might generate preinventive forms to represent their names or products are illustrated in Figure 6.1. Note that each of these logos was created by mentally blending the same three parts—a circle, a square, and the letter "D."

In general, you would want the logos to be as interesting, memorable, and meaningful as possible. This will depend on the extent to which the logo matches the type of product or the reputation of the company. Some recent experiments have demonstrated, in fact, that the way people interpret a particular logo

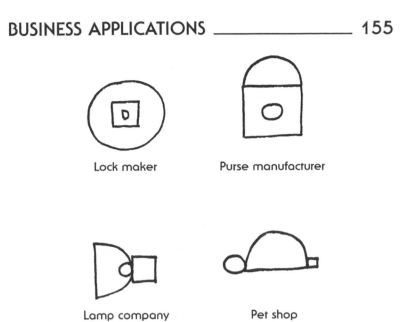

FIGURE 6.1. Potential company logos from preinventive forms.

depends on their knowledge about the company that the symbol represents.[2] For instance, consider the preinventive form shown in Figure 6.2. How appropriate would it be as a logo for a (1) car company, (2) chemical company, (3) clothing manufacturer, or (4) bicycle company? Clearly, the value of a particular logo would depend on the context in which it was used. Once designers decide to use preinventive forms to stimulate ideas, they can adapt the forms to meet their particular needs.

MENTAL MODELS OF THE PURCHASER AND THE USER

A young baby wails. A toddler screams in tearful protest. An otherwise brave adult winces, more in anticipation than from

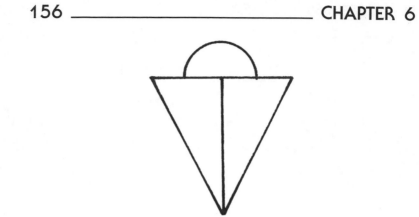

FIGURE 6.2. Preinventive form as source of ideas for company logos.

actual pain. What's wrong with these people? They're all being injected by a medical professional they had trusted just moments before.

Nobody likes being jabbed with a needle, in the arm or elsewhere. Even when we know injections will help us in the long run, we do not gleefully seek them out. The idea of having our skin punctured by a sharp object brings no thrill of anticipation. Some of us even fear becoming infected with the HIV virus or some other terrible agent, despite believing firmly that this particular needle has never been used before. For physicians and nurses, who surprisingly often stick themselves with used needles, the fear of infection is somewhat more justified.

But how else can we inoculate ourselves against the yearly onslaught of the flu, fend off dreaded childhood diseases, such as measles, mumps, and rubella, or quickly disperse large doses of antibiotics throughout the body? It seems obvious that to propel certain substances into the bloodstream, we have to drive a suitable tunnel through the skin, and the business end of a syringe serves that purpose. We have done things this way for centuries. The concept was introduced in the 16th century, and working models were available as early as the 17th century.

This is such a deeply ingrained concept, that it's hard to imagine anyone would question it. But now consider Biojector, a product developed by Bioject, Inc. that shoots doses of medicine through the skin with compressed carbon dioxide. No needles. No fear of accidental contamination. This type of device represents a startling creative leap, a rejection of a well-established bit of prior knowledge.

But the Bioject story doesn't end there, and its continuation is telling. It underscores the difference between innovation and success.

You would think such a marvel would be gladly welcomed by injectors and injectees alike. Despite providing improved safety and efficiency, however, the initial product did not sell well. Obviously, if a company cannot convince people to buy its products, all the innovation in the world will not help it remain competitive.

In retrospect the first Bioject model had problems. Its shape and the location of its trigger and safety device made it unwieldy, it could not deliver variable doses, and it made a startling hiss.[3] The common thread running through these problems is that, from the perspective of the people who give and receive injections, the gadget was not as "user-friendly" as it ought to have been.

Could Bioject have anticipated these problems? Perhaps they could have contemplated the mental models of the potential users more fully. Envision how patients would respond to the appearance of the product when they first see it. Work through how they would await a second injection after being startled by the hiss of their first one. Weigh, as a medical professional might, the relative advantages and disadvantages, the ease of use, the safety factors, and so on, of standard hypodermics and the Biojector.

Bioject now has a new model available. It's easier to use and more visually appealing, it can give variable doses, and it doesn't hiss. Whether the new version sells itself remains to be seen. One measure of its potential, however, is that *Business Week* named it a gold medal winner among medical and scientific products in its annual design awards for 1993.[3]

In the chapter on product development, we noted that inventors would do well to envision how people might actually use a new device. By taking a mental walk in a prospective user's shoes, an innovator can contrive a more appealing product. Advertisers, who must continually develop new ways to market products, can also benefit from seeing the world through the eyes of their audience.

Sometimes contemplating the perspective of potential buyers is as simple as thinking in their native language. You can imagine, for instance, the hilarity that would greet a foreign car manufacturer that tried to market a vehicle called the "Doesn't go" in the United States. We might judge it to be an unusual approach, but probably not a very creative one, because it would be unlikely to accomplish the clear goal of selling the product. But now consider the problem of Chevrolet attempting to advertise the "Nova" in Mexico. "No va" in Spanish translates as "doesn't go," and Spanish-speaking viewers could be excused if they rolled on the floor in spasms of laughter when they viewed the ads.

Maintaining an awareness of the audience is sometimes a more subtle process. There are cultural differences in the meanings of body motions, in the nature of greetings, and even in preferences for certain numbers, colors, shapes, sizes, and symbols.[4] A hawker of products who ignores these differences, who does not walk the proverbial mile in his or her audience's sandals, risks at best not attracting new buyers, and at worst offending an entire nation. Once again, knowledge is critical to the development of new ideas, in this case knowledge of how potential buyers view the world. Donald Norman's claim that developers of products should contemplate the mental models of potential users extends to marketing those products as well.

Sometimes the buyer and the user are different people, and this raises yet another challenge to those who would develop effective new marketing strategies. For instance, very few toddlers drive the family car to the local supermarket to buy their own food and diapers. Yet they represent a huge market for those products. Whose perspective should you take?

In the past, advertisers climbed into the minds of children to concoct ads aimed directly at their concerns. Consequently, they crafted ads that promoted foods as being sweet or otherwise fun to eat. The hope was that the tiny minions who saw these ads would carry the message forward to their parents, especially while seated in a shopping cart at eye level to cereal boxes. And it was a powerful strategy.

More recently, advertisers have embraced a compromise strategy. They now promote cereals, breads, snacks, and other foods as being tasty, thus satisfying to children, but healthy, thus consonant with the world view of the parents who actually spend the dollars. By considering the way both the buyer and the user think about things, a highly successful marketing approach has emerged. General Mills's advertisements for Kix are a particularly powerful example of this strategy with their simple, yet effective slogan: "Kid-Tested, Mother-Approved."

Sometimes, even the best efforts to accommodate the parent and child can go awry, however. Consider the omnipresent disposable diaper. Manufacturers have spent millions of dollars over the last several years to perfect this technological marvel. Their keen interest in baby bottoms is not surprising. In the United States alone, more than 4 million babies are born every year, and each requires anywhere from four to ten daily diaper changes. A company could absorb the costs of research and improve its bottom line by wrapping up just a small portion of the market.

From their crude beginnings, disposable diapers have seen a multitude of changes. Parents who cloaked their babies in disposables only 10 years ago are stunned when they hear about recent improvements contained in today's versions. These compact little miracles boast linings that draw liquid away from the child's bottom (and keep it away), filler material that can absorb several times its weight in water, leakage guards along the edges, resealable tapes, areas of absorbency strategically targeted for boys versus girls, and tailor-made shapes to ideally suit the changing body proportions of infants at different ages.

So fabulously absorbent are these modern throwaway diapers that any parent who has put a child wearing one into a pool has noticed that the child seems to weigh twice as much coming out.

Clearly, some of these improvements have the baby in mind. Others are directed at the parents. Mom and Dad, for instance, love diapers that can hold a whole night's output without either leaking or irritating the baby to the point of waking. Presumably, babies also appreciate the greater comfort of drier bottoms and fewer rashes.

But now let's consider the next step. Any parent will tell you that toilet training is no fun. Any toddler trying to gain control of the process will concur. Children want to grow up, but some fear sitting on the potty. Others have not yet learned to read the signals their bodies send them. In either case, once a child begins to venture out from the comforting confines of diapers, messy accidents happen. Parents become frustrated. Children can feel humiliated. What's a parent to do?

A clear need existed, and disposable diaper makers were quick to satisfy it. After perfecting ways to keep younger babies drier and more comfortable, diaper manufacturers went on to put all they had learned into disposables that children in the midst of toilet training could remove for themselves. They could use the potty when nature called, and then put the disposable back on. If an accident happened, it would be contained.

This was great in theory. It appealed to the child's sense of independence, and certainly enticed parents who would be faced with fewer messes to clean up. The only problem was that the technology was too good. The little would-be potty users often do not know they have wet themselves. They can have an accident and not even feel uncomfortable. Consequently, toilet training can be unnecessarily delayed.

So now for the ultimate irony. Manufacturers of these child-removable trainers have decided to introduce a new technological breakthrough: trainers that have a special lining to let the child feel wet! Before all of the improvements in modern diapers, this was easy to accomplish. Now it's an important innovation.

Could diaper makers have foreseen the potential problems with highly absorbent trainers? Possibly not. They may have needed to get further inside the child's head than any adult is capable of doing. It might have helped them to construct a mental model of a child using such a diaper, from the child's perspective, but only if the designers envisioned the child's reaction to having an "accident." This could have made them realize that the child might not even notice the accident. On the other hand, it may be asking too much of the designer, who, after all, is an adult many years beyond toilet training.

INNOVATIVE PRODUCTS AND INNOVATIVE PROCESSES

A new product fails. A business loses money. Heads roll. A sad tale indeed.

A different product exceeds expectations. A company reaps huge profits. Promotions follow. A happy ending.

The challenge for innovative thinkers is to compose stories of the second type and avoid those of the first type. Capitalizing on the techniques of creative cognition can help.

It's no secret that business today is ruthlessly competitive. Corporate executives find themselves navigating a harsh landscape in which a single misstep, a slight misreading of their guiding compass, can spell disaster. At the same time, a successful journey, a mapping out of a new market, can secure extravagant monetary rewards, and bring immense personal satisfaction.

In the previous chapter we concentrated on how people forge new ideas for inventions. But successful innovation in business—capturing market share or opening new territory—requires more than just a good, novel idea. It demands creativity in how people design, engineer, build, test-market, promote, and distribute a product. Moreover, it mandates that all of these disparate partners dance together to the same music in a smooth rhythm.

Changes in the marketplace have forced corporations to seek new ways for their divisions to work together. The life cycle of products, particularly in high-tech fields, is becoming ever shorter. This makes it more and more critical to bring products to the market quickly. It does no good to design and engineer a marvelously creative invention if a competitor beats you to the market. U.S. corporations learned this lesson all too well in the 1970s and 1980s, inventing one electronic wonder after another, but being left at the starting gate each time by more efficient Japanese firms that raced products out to consumers.

In other words, beyond cultivating original ideas for goods and services, corporations must find creative new ways to quickly manufacture products, and more generally, to run their entire organizations. They must reject their old knowledge of the way things "ought" to be done, the ways they have always been done in the past.

But as we've seen, breaking with the past is difficult. We typically build our visions of the future on the foundations of what has come before. In formulating new ideas, more often than not we merely impose modest variations on what we already know. Conjuring up images of anything wildly outside our experience is more demanding. This is no less true of executives and managers plotting a course to larger profits than of research subjects trying to visualize compelling extraterrestrials. Business people most often try to tweak existing corporate structures, rather than reject them entirely, in the same way that alien-builders simply adapt Earth animals, rather than summoning up something completely different.

The problem is that existing corporate structures put up walls, literal and figurative, between the people who need to work together. If we base new solutions on these structures, we will become ensnared in the same trap.

These structures are rooted deeply in the tradition of "division of labor." If there are different tasks to execute, different people, working in separate departments, perform them. Some people design. Others assemble. Still others market the products, order needed materials, keep track of inventory, hire new employees, pay bills, and so on. This strategy of dividing and conquering a large task made sense in an earlier era, but no longer applies in the current age of rapid change and increasingly sophisticated information technology.[5]

Communications software, shared data bases, advanced graphics displays, and expert systems can foster close ties among all people working on the same project—wherever they may be in the world. They can also aid a single case manager in overseeing an entire project from design to delivery, and they can equip a generalist to do the work usually reserved for several specialists in different departments. All of these benefits work in favor of bringing successful products to market quickly and with minimal cost. By promoting parallel or concurrent design, in which designers working on different components of a new product, manufacturing engineers, marketers, and those in charge of procurement all work together, businesses can bring an innovation to the marketplace with remarkable speed and efficiency.

What technology can't do is make people think differently. That has to come from within. In their recent best-selling book, *Reengineering the Corporation*, Michael Hammer and James Champy argue for a revolution in the way corporations are structured, and implicitly, in the way people think about corporations. They define reengineering in two words: starting over. Hammer and Champy propose that we reject Adam Smith's old notion of division of labor, and replace it with an emphasis on processes that would cut across traditional divisions. In effect, they argue for corporate imagination to escape the bonds of influence from prior examples.

The principles of reengineering fit well with our idea that abstraction provokes creative innovation. Hammer and Champy advocate "fundamental rethinking and radical redesign of business processes."[6] They exhort corporations to ask fundamental questions about themselves and how they operate. What do we do and why? How do we do it, and why do we do it that way?

You can answer these types of questions at many different levels. We make widgets. We supply a class of products. We take raw materials and convert them to useful goods for a profit. Abstraction helps to organize a hierarchy of answers, and makes transparent any implicit assumptions that may be holding back progress.

Fads come and go in the business world. Managers and executives constantly search for that new idea that will give them even the narrowest of competitive edges over their rivals. It is too early to tell whether "reengineering" is just another one of these fads, or a true revolution, but there is little doubt that it has taken the corporate world by storm. Because it urges people to think about the essence of what businesses ought to be doing, our bet is that it will continue to pay important returns well down the road.

SMALL STEPS AND GIANT PROFITS

When was the last time you went through a whole day without seeing a single aluminum beverage can? These compact containers are so ubiquitous, it's hard avoid them, and it's easy to take them for granted. Yet their popularity and seeming simplicity hide an intriguing world of design complexity.

Consider just the pressures a can must withstand. The tires on your car are designed to be inflated to a pressure of about 30 pounds per square inch, bicycle tires to about twice that much. But aluminum beverage cans, having skins only 0.003 inch at their thinnest point, and weighing in at less than half an ounce, must endure upwards of 90 pounds of pressure. Their ability to do so is a tribute to a long series of small but impressive technical innovations, including infusing the aluminum with other elements such as manganese and magnesium.[7]

An impressive innovation in aluminum cans is the integral rivet that holds the tab to the can. It isn't an extra bit of metal tacked on. It's actually part of the material of the lid itself that has been stretched upward. This and other innovations reduce the total amount of aluminum that must go into a single can.

In fact, a prime goal of redesigning cans is to reduce the amount of aluminum required by even by a miniscule amount. Is it possible do the same job, or better, with less material?

It's easy to see why this principle drives innovation. U.S. manufacturers punch out about 100 billion aluminum beverage cans each year. This mind-boggling figure translates to about one can per day for every man, woman, and child in the United States. Not surprisingly, then, tiny innovations in design and manufacture multiply into enormous increases in profits. For instance, because the aluminum in the can represents about half its cost, a new idea that would reduce the mass of the can by just one percent would save about $20 million a year.[7] It doesn't take a large step to bring about a giant leap in profitability.

But what this also means is that, unless someone dreams up a wildly different method for transporting soft drinks from producers to consumers, continued creative innovations are likely to take the form of small steps eked out by highly skilled experts. Despite their apparent simplicity, then, aluminum beverage cans are a prime example of how, in some industries, extensive expert knowledge is essential to making creative contributions. This highlights an importantly different face of creativity in the business world than we ordinarily think of. As with invention in general, creative innovation in business often happens in tiny increments rather than giant leaps.

WHEN TO CHANGE AND WHEN NOT TO

It was October of 1973. Spiro Agnew pleaded no contest to income tax evasion and resigned the Vice Presidency. Gerald Ford, Agnew's replacement, announced "I'm a Ford, not a Lincoln." And, the Organization of Petroleum Exporting Countries (OPEC) began to flex its muscles. In a bid to undermine U.S. support for Israel, OPEC imposed an oil embargo. The effect was immediate and devastating. A barrel of oil quadrupled in price in a matter of months. Gasoline prices went through the roof, and the makers of U.S. cars—Fords, Lincolns, and otherwise—would soon see their profits drop through the floor.

By early 1974 the Federal Energy Administration had printed gas rationing coupons, and fears of shortages compelled motorists to wait in lines for hours to fill their cars, even when they still had half a tankful remaining. But by far the most important impact was that consumers began to think about fuel efficiency, many for the first time in their driving lives. The coming demand for smaller, more economical cars should have been crystal clear to anyone who plugged into potential buyers' mental models of the driving experience.

The Big Three, Detroit-based auto makers either did not recognize the trend, or were unable to adapt to it in an innovative and timely fashion. They had difficulty breaking with their prior knowledge of consumer preferences and their past habits of making larger cars.

How did past history influence car makers' reactions to the oil crisis? Many readers are old enough to remember gasoline price wars. In the 1960s competing service stations ratcheted prices downward, sometimes dropping below 30 cents per gallon. They even tried to draw in customers by offering premiums, such as glassware, with each fill-up. Americans were in love with the open road. The low gas prices pushed their desires for ever larger and more powerful cars, and Detroit heeded the call with gas-guzzling behemoths.

With decades of tooling, and generations of engineering focused on power rather than performance, it's no wonder that the U.S. auto industry was shaken to its core by the upheavals of the 1970s. People were not accustomed to thinking smaller. The bulk of their existing models, technologies, and ideas worked against an easy transition to fuel-efficient vehicles.

The troubles of the auto industry sent shock waves well beyond Detroit. They had a profound effect on the economy in general and the American psyche as well, to say nothing of our relationship with Japan. Worse yet, early small-car offerings by U.S. firms bombed, and left a lasting impression that U.S.-made cars were somehow inferior to foreign ones. In other words, many consumers changed their mental models of American cars from being the "king of the road" to being the "bottom of the barrel." It has been a long hard climb back.[8]

Schwinn is another example of a company that failed to adapt to changes in the marketplace. Never has a society been more obsessed with its physical well-being than Americans have been over the last 20 years. Explosions in the health club and athletic shoe industries are just two bits of evidence for this trend. So, with an appropriate look at the market, one might have predicted an upsurge in the desire for mountain bikes as a natural offshoot of this trend. But Schwinn could not or would not notice and respond to the change. It patterned its future after its past, and stuck to producing traditional bicycles. As a result, its market share dropped precipitously during the 1980s.[9]

Clearly companies have a better chance of avoiding this type of turmoil if they are willing and able to break with the past, and to rapidly adjust to change. Keeping a finger on the pulse of consumer desires can help. Putting another finger to the winds of change in consumers' mental models can provide information about the direction in which to make a break.

But change has to be carefully reasoned. In April 1985, the Coca-Cola Company revealed its plan to replace its nearly 100-year-old formula with a new one. In a chapter aptly entitled "The Marketing Blunder of the Century," Mark Pendergrast has detailed the ensuing outcry.[10] Loyal Coke drinkers were outraged and observers were befuddled. In the following months, the company fielded thousands of angry phone calls and letters, protesters poured New Coke out in city streets, and crowds at sports arenas vehemently booed ads for the altered beverage. By

July of 1985 public pressure had forced Coca-Cola to reissue the original version under the name Coca-Cola Classic.

How could they have made such a tactical error? Millions of dollars of research had shown that people preferred the taste of New Coke to the original formula and, more importantly, to Pepsi-Cola. As Pendergrast puts it, however, the "taste tests had missed one crucial point. Roy Stout's researchers had never informed their respondents that the hypothetical new formula would _replace_ the old. Incredibly, no one had examined the psychological ramifications of withdrawing the old formula."[11] They had overlooked the fact that Coke drinkers loved Coke, and would respond to its withdrawal as to the loss of a close relation or good friend. No new acquaintance could take its place, no matter what taste tests said.

In creative cognition terms, when Coca-Cola changed the taste of Coke, they changed an essential property. New Coke simply was no longer Coke. And Coke was no longer it. The lesson is that, although innovation can open new markets, change that destroys the essence of a successful product can lead to disaster. Careful analysis of the way consumers conceptualize a product may shed light on what they consider to be unchangeable attributes, and may help companies avoid such debacles.[12]

Detroit could not, Schwinn would not, and Coca-Cola should not have innovated. How can corporations know when, how, and what to change? There are no magic solutions, but once again we argue for abstraction. What are the fundamental goals of the organization? What are the fundamental desires of consumers? How can we bring our actions in line with those desires?

A GROUP AND ITS INDIVIDUALS

Cognitive psychologists care about the workings of individual minds, such as your own. They are less interested in how your thoughts bend in the winds of influence from the people around you. We share this bias, and we have concentrated mostly on how you, as an individual, can use basic mental operations more effectively. Nevertheless, creative ideas do blossom forth from the combined efforts of many minds. They often sprout from seeds planted in our minds by other people. They are nourished in the fertile soil of old knowledge, and they flourish when we and others carefully tend and nurture them. Inventors pattern their new ideas after existing schemes. Prolific writers are prodigious readers. Scientists craft their new theories within existing frameworks, or as very specific rebellions against previous ideas. Artists build on styles and schools that have preceded them.

In the business world, the view of creativity as a collaborative effort predominates. Corporations often reward "team players," and they stress the value of group problem-solving techniques, such as brainstorming. In fact, from some writings you almost get the impression that the words *brainstorming* and *creativity* can be used interchangeably.

What is brainstorming in business? It's a procedure in which a small group of people work together on a particular problem. They toss out potential solutions, and a "recorder" is charged with noting all of them down. The group may have a nominal leader, but that person's job is more to facilitate and keep ideas flowing than to direct group members along some set path.

The most important principle in brainstorming is that criticism is forbidden. Quashing someone else's idea is the worst sin a would-be brainstormer can commit. This principle works sort of like a mental "keep off the grass" sign. Novel ideas are often fragile seedlings that are easily crushed under the heavy feet of criticism. Knowing that all ideas will initially be treated with respect helps participants feel freer about going outside the bounds of conventional thought. It helps the group overcome the unwanted influence of prior knowledge, because the most typical way of slaying a new idea would be with the weapons of existing knowledge and tradition. "It would never work (given my preconceptions about the way the world works)."

Delaying criticism does mean that many of the ideas generated will be nonsensical and have no hope of solving the problem, precisely because they don't touch base with what we already know. But this fits with two other principles of brainstorming: generate as many potential solutions as possible in the hope that quantity will lead to quality, and shoot for the wildest ideas possible.

Two analogies shed light on these quantity versus quality suggestions. First, many of us know people whom we admire as exceptional amateur photographers. Viewing their travel pictures is a joy, and we don't shudder when they ask if we want to see slides from their recent trip to Europe. What we may not realize is that they have taken the tedium out of viewing their pictures by only showing us a small fraction of the ones they have actually taken, the very best. When they go on a trip, they take as many photographs as they can. They don't just settle for one shot of a magnificent building. They capture it from different distances and angles, with different parts in and out of focus, with and without tourists, and so on. Like the faithful recorder in a brainstorming group they preserve as many views as they can, even if some may turn out to be supremely dull. Then, rather than boring us with all of the views they have recorded, they select only the very best, the ones that thrill and move us, the ones that capture a special nuance or reveal a truth.

A second analogy comes from nature. The problem all living things must solve is how to survive long enough to reproduce. Unless a species can meet this goal, it will quickly blink out of existence. One way to solve the problem is to produce a small number of high-quality organisms, but another is to produce so many that a few are bound to survive long enough in spite of themselves. Any native Texan will swear that June bugs, which actually begin to appear in April, are nature's ultimate example of solving the survival problem by way of quantity rather than quality. These peanut-sized insects spend their short little lives crashing into windows, bouncing to the ground, and spinning wildly on their backs, buzzing all the while in an annoying frenzy, like hysterical caricatures of break dancers. Their behavior is so random, it is a wonder how they continue. Yet they are so plentiful, it would be a greater wonder if, just by chance, they all died out.

So it is with brainstorming. If the group can beget a large enough set of ideas, even though most are silly and unworkable, some few will remain that might actually lead to a solution.

The rapid-fire production, the absence of criticism, and the emphasis on a bountiful supply of wild ideas all help people escape the bonds of conventional thinking. In this sense, the procedures are consistent with our view that one path to creativity is to circumvent the influence of existing knowledge.

One additional principle in brainstorming is that participants should "piggyback" on earlier ideas. They can either build on a single suggestion or merge two or more of them. This rule fits perfectly with the emphasis we have placed on conceptual combinations as a source of novel ideas.

Brainstorming has great potential as an aid to developing creative solutions, but it also has some drawbacks. The most serious is that it can actually inhibit productivity. Several well-controlled experiments show that individuals working alone dream up more ideas than the same number of people working together in a group.[13] This happens because, despite the best of intentions, when people build on earlier ideas, the thinking in the group will naturally tend to flow in a particular direction. Even though participants are encouraged to make a multitude of suggestions, they may inhibit themselves from stating ideas that do not continue moving the group in the same direction. Working by themselves, they would not experience the same inhibition. If the goal really is to propagate a bounty of suggestions, then it might actually be better to have people work alone.

Despite the possible disadvantage of promoting fewer ideas, brainstorming remains the most popular of all creativity training efforts.[14] One reason is that corporations believe it works. Unfortunately they are afflicted with the "compared-to-what" problem. If a brainstorming group discovers an effective way to reduce losses related to shoplifting or employee theft, to improve ridership on public transportation, to sell more boxes of a certain cereal, or to improve communication among divisions, it is tough to argue with their success. But the fact remains that we have no way of knowing whether an even better idea would have cropped up by assigning the same number of people to work on the task individually.

A second reason businesses stick with brainstorming is that they are interested in more than just breeding an abundance of ideas. For instance, because brainstorming groups can meet over an extended period of time, the technique can foster the goals of "team building" and nurturing a happy, cohesive work force. Furthermore, these long-standing groups might be more success- ful at avoiding the pitfalls of groupthink that stymie the groups studied in laboratory settings.

But, for whatever reason they do so, if corporations continue using brainstorming, they ought to exercise it to its fullest potential. Two procedures can help. First, to prevent any one person's ideas from being swept away in the rush down a different path, each group member should write down as many ideas as he or she can think of *prior* to meeting with the group. Before the group narrows its focus, all of these independently generated ideas must be aired.

The second procedure is that each would-be group member should hone his or her own thinking skills prior to participating in the group. The quality of solutions produced by brainstorm- ing teams can only be as good as the minds of the individuals who populate the group. If all participants are facile at merging concepts, using analogies and metaphors, envisioning images, pulling back by way of abstraction, and so on, they will be better able to move the group along toward constructive solutions. So even though we have concentrated mostly on how individuals can cultivate mental skills, it is clear that skilled thinkers can enhance group problem solving by exercising their talents in brainstorming sessions.

This chapter has explored the potential usefulness of creative cognition in the world of business; in particular, how to develop creative products, organizations, and marketing strategies. Conceptual combination, abstraction, and careful attention to the mental models of consumers can aid in all of these efforts. Any business concerned with its own capacity to innovate should be sure that its employees have mastered these skills and can bring them to bear on whatever tasks they have to perform. An important challenge is to harvest the talents of such individuals and make those part of the larger group effort of the corporation. Those who are aware of how to employ creative cognition are the business workers and administrators who will carry the corporation forward through the ever-changing future.

NOTES

1. We have borrowed the example of this hierarchy from Michael R. Solomon, *Consumer Behavior* (Boston: Allyn & Bacon, 1992).
2. David Green & Valerie Loveluck, "Understanding a Corporate Symbol," *Applied Cognitive Psychology* 8 (1994), pp. 37–47.
3. Dori Jones Yang, "A Shot in the Arm for Sales?" *Business Week*, June 7, 1993, p. 64.
4. William M. Pride & O. C. Ferrell, *Marketing* (Boston: Houghton Mifflin, 1993).
5. Michael Hammer & James Champy, *Reengineering the Corporation* (New York: HarperBusiness, 1993).
6. Hammer & Champy, *Reengineering the Corporation*, p. 32.
7. William F. Hosford & John L. Duncan, "The Aluminum Beverage Can," *Scientific American* 1994, pp. 48–53.
8. David Gelsanliter, *Jump Start* (New York: Farrar Straus Giroux, 1990); N. P. Kannan, Kathy K. Rebibo, & Donna L. Ellis, *Downsizing Detroit* (New York: Praeger, 1982).
9. Sandra D. Atchison, "Pump, Pump, Pump at Schwinn," *Business Week*, August 23, 1993, p. 79.

10. Mark Pendergrast, *For God, Country, and Coca-Cola* (New York: Charles Scribner's Sons, 1993).
11. Pendergrast, *For God, Country, and Coca-Cola*, p. 360.
12. The story does have a happy outcome for Coca-Cola. In the end, Coke Classic did regain the lead in the market over Pepsi-Cola. However, the turmoil and initial dip in market share might have been avoided with more careful planning.
13. Michael Diehl & Wolfgang Stroebe, "Productivity Loss in Brainstorming Groups: Toward the Solution of a Riddle," *Journal of Personal and Social Psychology*, 53 (1987), pp. 497–509.
14. Lloyd W. Fernald, Jr., & Pam Nickolenko, "The Creative Process: Its Use and Extent of Formalization by Corporations," *Journal of Creative Behavior* 27 (1993), pp. 214–220.

SCIENCE FICTION AND FANTASY WRITING

Stephen Donaldson, the noted science fiction and fantasy author, had a vexing problem, the sort of problem that most writers dread. He had an idea that he wanted to write about, but could not find a suitable way to convey it. He wanted to probe the abstract concept of "unbelief," an unwillingness to accept the possibility that fantasy worlds might exist. But, try as he might, he could not discern the story line, the vehicle that could transport this vague idea from mind to paper.

Unbelief nagged at him. It flirted with him. It poked its head out from behind a tree and then disappeared again, like some coy woodland nymph. But it would not be seized. How Donaldson ultimately captured the idea, and penned an exquisite set of books provides a classic example of the power of conceptual combination. In this chapter we will take a look at how authors employ that procedure and other techniques in practicing their craft.

175

Science fiction and fantasy writing are fertile areas for assessing the contributions that creative cognition can make. These genres call on authors to concoct not only engaging stories, but also fresh new alien life forms, cultures, and worlds. Thus, they provide a window on a vital aspect of creativity: how people conceive, amplify, and modify novel ideas.

We focus here primarily on how science fiction and fantasy authors hatch and nurture the ingenious ideas they convey in their stories. The chapter is not designed to make anyone a better writer, at least from the point of view of improving writing style. We claim no special expertise in handling matters of exposition, plot or character development, dialogue, or other technical aspects of crafting stories. Our goal is only to investigate how the basic processes described earlier manifest themselves in this highly creative arena. If readers also come away with tantalizing ideas for stories, or effective new strategies for giving birth to such ideas, then we have far exceeded that goal.

Some authors have claimed that they generate ideas for stories easily, and that the real difficulty in becoming a good storyteller is in mastering the skills needed to expound the ideas. Usually, however, the people who make such pronouncements are those who have already become prolific writers. Through years of practicing their trade, these authors have honed the cognitive skills necessary to come up with great ideas, making the task seem easier to them.

The procedures authors use to conceive initial ideas for stories are vital to crafting vivid science fiction, and are worth examining in their own right. The writing techniques authors exploit are also intimately linked to the imaginative process, which continues as they delve deeper into their germinal ideas in the very act of writing. Understanding where novel ideas come from, how they are structured, how they are extended and transformed, and how their form relates to existing knowledge can help us to understand the magic of science fiction writing.

CONCEPTUAL COMBINATION IN IDEA GENERATION

Science fiction and fantasy writers often report using conceptual combination in developing their stories. For example, Stephen Donaldson, in describing his general approach, writes that "for some reason, a fair number of my best stories arise, not from one idea, but from two."[1] He eloquently expresses the power of combinations by stating that "rather like a binary poison—or a magic potion—two inert elements combine to produce something of frightening potency."[2]

Donaldson also describes the specific combination of ideas that led to his stunningly imaginative series of fantasy books about Thomas Covenant, The Unbeliever, in which he was finally able to bring his concept of unbelief to fruition. After several years of fruitless effort, Donaldson realized one day that he could combine "unbelief" with the disease of leprosy. Immediately a compelling story line emerged. In Donaldson's own words, "As soon as those two ideas came together, my brain took fire."[2]

The resulting story is about Thomas Covenant, who has lost two fingers on his right hand to the disease of leprosy. Because leprosy attacks the peripheral nerves, its victims lose sensation in their extremities and can sustain serious injuries without knowing it. Consequently, infections and gangrene can set in unnoticed, and result in the need for amputation. This has already happened to Covenant's hand before we meet him in the first book of the tale.

After apparently being hit by a car and passing out, Covenant awakes to find himself in a strange and magical world, called the Land. In the Land, he is mistaken for a legendary hero, Berek Halfhand, but he refuses to accept the reality of the Land, and takes on the title of The Unbeliever.

The poignancy of the story derives from the contrast between Covenant's life as a leper and the magical properties of the Land. As the story opens, we find Covenant an outcast in his own world. Former friends and neighbors shun him. They pull their children out of his way when he passes. And most importantly, his physicians have warned him that to ensure his survival he must constantly monitor the condition of his own body. Because the nerves in his extremities will no longer tell him if he has sustained an injury, he must constantly perform visual surveillance of extremities (VSE) to know whether he has hurt himself.

By contrast, when Covenant is transported into the Land, he is welcomed as a hero. The Land also offers up from its bounty a magical substance called "hurtloam," which can heal injuries, and has apparently regenerated Covenant's nerves. Covenant can once again sense his extremities, and has never felt healthier in his life.

The Land provides a potential escape for Covenant, but at an extravagant risk. If he accepts the reality of the Land, he may exchange rejection for acceptance and illness for health, but he may also be tempted to give up the all-important VSE for a mere illusion of health in this fantasy world, thus putting his life in the real world at risk. This conflict between his desire for escape and the need for vigilance propels the story. Thus, the driving force behind the compelling, novel structure of the story emanated from the combination of two previously separate concepts, unbelief and leprosy. Donaldson rooted around in that structure to craft a disturbing yet penetrating tale.

We want to emphasize three points about this strikingly powerful instance of conceptual combination. First, the combination itself was merely a preinventive structure until Donaldson mined the rich vein of treasure that presented itself to him. He recognized immediately that the combination had enormous creative potential, but spent the next three months scrutinizing that potential, "taking notes, drawing maps, envisioning characters; studying the implications of unbelief and leprosy."[2] This underscores the fact that writing technique and imaginative processes are intimately intertwined: authors pounce on captivating initial ideas and then extend and transmute them to remarkable creative effect in the act of constructing a story.

Generally, although novel conceptual combinations may hint at intriguing possibilities, to unleash their potential requires this type of deliberate effort.

A second point is that Donaldson owned a rich storehouse of knowledge about leprosy, having grown up in India, where his father, a surgeon, treated many lepers. Without directly learning about the lives of leprosy sufferers, Donaldson would not have been able to understand the significance of combining that disease with unbelief. This reinforces a point we made earlier: To produce workable novel concepts, we must guide the development of new ideas with our broader knowledge frameworks. In trying to fulfill the promise of a conceptual combination, knowledge is a good thing. In the case of science fiction and fantasy, exploiting real-world knowledge is especially beneficial since one of the goals of those genres is to let readers see the real world in new ways through the prism of an imaginary world.

Our third point is that the potential of a combination depends greatly on its specific parts. The particular concepts that unite in a combination determine not just how alluring the resulting idea seems, but also the exact opportunities it presents for unveiling creative riches. It was critical to the Thomas Covenant series that the specific disease of leprosy was coupled with unbelief. When Donaldson married a leprosy sufferer's need for constant vigilance to his overwhelming desire for escape into a fantasy world they bore an offspring with a rich potential for anguish and emotional turmoil.

Donaldson captured this conflict compellingly in his description of the protagonist. "He understood part of what the doctors had been saying; he needed to crush out his imagination. He could not afford to have an imagination, a faculty which could envision Joan [his former wife], joy, health. If he tormented himself with unattainable desires, he would cripple his grasp on the law which enabled him to survive."[3] A reader can't help but feel the unremitting torment Donaldson was able to weave into the tale based on the fact that leprosy's unique demand for VSE conflicts so unequivocally with any form of mental escape.

To get a sense of how the potential of a combination changes when we alter one of its specific parts, try a brief exercise. Consider whether other diseases might combine as well with the concept of "unbelief." For example, would a character with diabetes, multiple sclerosis, hypertension, or cancer work as well? Would they provoke completely different story ideas and plots that might lead to riveting tales of a different sort? Might a protagonist with diabetes worry that the fantasy world was really just a delusion he was experiencing while lying in a diabetic coma? Might he do everything possible to escape from the fantasy and return to the real world to get medication before it's too late? One of the great fears of anyone who must take maintenance doses of medication is being trapped in a situation where the medication is unavailable. Could this give rise to the necessary tension in a fantasy story?

Must it even be a disease that is combined with unbelief, or might other human attributes, such as compulsiveness, empathy, fastidiousness, or procrastination, work as well? Might a compulsive person constantly check all of the "facts" of a fantasy world to determine whether they are mutually consistent? Might her escape from the fantasy world be triggered by detecting any slight inconsistency? Might she be hurled back into the fantasy world by noticing a tiny glitch in the logic of her "real world"?

Budding science fiction writers might test out various combinations of the concepts we have mentioned. Or they could generate their own lists of abstract concepts and human characteristics, and then randomly pair them to see if interesting story lines emerge. Some combinations would beg for further exploration, whereas others would seem drab and lifeless. Some might readily offer up their rich potential for story-building whereas others might require more coaxing. By courting and cajoling the most pliant among these combinations, an author might gain entry to a world of inspiration for new stories and plots. By tirelessly interrogating the other combinations that seem promising yet inscrutable, the writer might ultimately force them to relinquish their secrets as well. In either case the potential of a combination often will lie dormant until the efforts of a diligent explorer bring it fully to life.

Is it possible to specify the types of pairings that will lead to the most provocative outcomes? We noted earlier that to formulate workable novel ideas, we must enlist our knowledge as a guide, and Donaldson's exquisite wielding of his experience with leprosy supports this point. What this means is that writers should try to merge concepts that they know the most about. Classic advice to would-be writers is to "write about what you know." To that cliché we would add the heuristic, "write about a combination of two things you know."

Earlier we also noted that concepts that are further apart are most likely to lead to emergent properties, at least in laboratory research.[4] A statement by Orson Scott Card, author of several best-selling fantasy novels, seems consistent with this second point: "All but a handful of my stories have come from combining two *completely unrelated* ideas." (emphasis added).[5] So, in selecting ideas to combine, authors might do well to choose items that are seemingly unconnected.

Because knowledge is a vast network of interrelated concepts, however, it is natural that thinking about one idea will cause other highly related ideas to spring to mind. Thus, it may be difficult to think of two unrelated concepts to use in a combination. Part of the creative process, then, is to open your mind to the widest variety of combinations: dyslexia and cooking talent, stuttering and musical talent, and migraines and computer skills—an endless supply is available.

One way to procure unrelated ideas might be to impose the task of jotting down concepts on two separate friends. Choosing one concept from each friend's list should produce an unrelated pair. This procedure is reminiscent of "The Exquisite Corpse," a game played by surrealist artists in which each participant would write a word on a piece of paper, fold it over, and pass it to the next person who would do the same. The fun came in trying to make sense of the combinations, and the name of the game supposedly originated with one of the combinations. The surrealists used "The Exquisite Corpse" to elude conscious control over their artistic endeavors. Contemporary authors, too, can apply it to compose the incongruous combinations that often yield the most exciting possibilities.

Donaldson's afterword also highlights a type of combination that is likely to pay substantial creative dividends. He points out that he added the "familiar" concept of leprosy to the "exotic" concept of unbelief, and that other science fiction writers also tend to combine the familiar with the exotic. Such combinations may be especially evocative because the exotic concept interjects novelty while the familiar guides the progress of the new idea through an otherwise trackless wilderness of possibilities.

It is also noteworthy that unbelief is abstract and leprosy is concrete. It took the concrete concept to catalyze the writing process, and help bring the abstract concept to paper. Authors often need tangible ideas to wrestle their more abstract notions back to earth.

In the afterword to *The Real Story*, Donaldson also discusses the conceptual combination that led to the four novels that follow from that story. *The Real Story* uses a science fiction setting to tell the generic tale of a villain (Angus Thermopyle), his victim (Morn Hyland), and her rescuer (Nick Succurso). Donaldson expresses disappointment with the story, but excitement about combining it with another idea: to write a sequence of novels based on Richard Wagner's epic opera, *Der Ring des Nibelungen*. The exhilaration that can be engendered by conceptual combinations is captured in Donaldson's statement, "When I combined it with another idea which had already been in my head—alive, exciting, and totally static—for twenty years, I had a gusher."[6]

Donaldson's books reveal the power of conceptual combination to suggest the overall structure of a book, but concepts can also be merged for the more specific task of designing fanciful extraterrestrials. Some science fiction writers have produced intriguing aliens by combining very specific species of Earth animals. In *The Uplift War*, for example, David Brin skillfully blended birdlike physical features with humanlike sentience to produce the Gubru. These creatures preserved many aspects of birds, such as molting and competition for dominance, but those features played themselves out within cultural traditions, much like human cultural practices, rather than exclusively as part of the biological nature of the species as we tend to think of for birds.

Clarence Day provided another example of combining human intelligence with the traits of other species in *This Simian World*. Day speculated on what might have happened if species other than primates had evolved our mental skills and technologies. Consider the likely traits of a race of "super cats." They might have been solitary thinkers and explorers, with strong personal egotism. They might have constructed exceedingly clean and efficient cities. Their art might have been highly individualistic.

Consider the possible consequences if *bears* had evolved our intellectual abilities. What would their societies be like? How would their governments be structured? How would their science and art both resemble and differ from our own? As a further thought, how would they compare with us in the way they treated other species?

THE CASE OF THE NOT-SO-ALIEN ALIEN

When the movie "Star Wars" was first released, it was hailed by most audiences, and some critics, as a triumph, not just of special effects, but also of the imagination. The famous bar scene contains one of the most imaginative collections of aliens ever brought to the screen, including fanciful intelligent life forms from all over the galaxy. The creatures come in many shapes, sizes, and colors, and one cannot help but be impressed with the originality of each species, and the variety across species. Nor would anyone mistake most of the creatures for ones that might actually live on Earth. But closer inspection reveals that they also share some key properties with one another and with typical animals on Earth, including arms, legs, eyes, ears, and symmetry. The same is true for the bulk of creatures in the remainder of the "Star Wars" series, as well as in "Star Trek" and nearly all other science fiction movies and television programs.

Why do these creatures, despite the originality of their appearance, have so many of the same properties as Earth animals? There are, of course, some economic constraints that might limit the originality of the creatures. For instance, Gene Roddenberry formulated his "similar worlds concept" to convince programming executives that "Star Trek" could be produced cheaply.[7] The idea was that the *Enterprise* would visit only Class M planets, which are reasonably similar to Earth. By confining travel to Earth-like planets, expensive sets need not be built. Ordinary Earth scenery would do just fine.

In addition, because the creatures on Class M planets plausibly could be expected to resemble humans, they could be played by human actors wearing a minimal amount of makeup; the need to fashion expensive costumes or construct elaborate, mechanized aliens was minimized.

But, cost-containment cannot be the whole story. At least some of the standardized creatures in the "Star Wars" series were brought to life by way of expensive, elaborate mechanical and cinematic wizardry, which could have produced wildly different creatures. In addition, book authors need not worry about the costs of building a set or whether human actors could play their creatures. Yet, aliens from most science fiction books also share the central properties of Earth animals. For instance, *Barlowe's Guide to Extraterrestrials*, as noted in an earlier chapter, contains some excellent examples of otherwise unusual science fiction creatures that nevertheless sport several Earth-like features. And Barlowe specifically chose the aliens to be "challenging to the imagination," rather than picking from the endless supply of conventional dragons and such.

We want to emphasize that we are not being critical of these creatures or their creators. On the contrary, one must be impressed with how captivating and original many of them are. What we are noting is that even highly imaginative new ideas seem to inherit certain basic properties from existing knowledge.

Why does old knowledge play such a strong role in the generation and refinement of new ideas? The answer lies in the operation of some basic cognitive processes.

RULES THAT STRUCTURE COMMUNICATION

Writing about a creative idea is, after all, an act of communication, just like any other. So, naturally, the mental processes that determine the way we communicate will help to structure what we create in imagination.

Just as we tailor our words to suit our listeners in everyday conversations, writers must craft their ideas with an audience in mind. First, they must devise creatures and scenes that are engaging and believable enough that an editor will publish the story and a large audience will read it. An audience would find it difficult, for instance, to warm up to a gooey puddle of blue-green muck that simply lives alone under a rock, gradually dissolving it over a period of thousands of years, until one day when the rock is gone, the muck dries up and blows away. Such a creature would be decidedly unusual, but it would also have little hope of holding the audience's attention.[8]

To contrive and portray creatures that people care about, authors must either stick with familiar concepts or, at the very least, tie any novel properties to what the audience already knows. When we talk to other people, we often strive to couch any new information in terms of what is familiar, modifying or building on existing concepts. This tendency is called the *given-new strategy*. For example, if you were to inform a friend that "Ben and Jerry's now makes completely smooth flavors," you would be taking it as given that she knows that Ben and Jerry's makes ice cream, usually infused with large, outrageously delicious chunks of chocolate, nuts, or cookie dough. You would be building on her existing concept of their offerings by letting her know that they've introduced new, quite different varieties. You shared a common base of knowledge about the product and utilized it to communicate something new.

Likewise, when an author develops a creature with dozens of eyes located at the ends of long tentacles, he or she is communicating a novel physical feature based on our shared knowledge that vision is a useful sense that most creatures possess. When the author creates an alien species nearly identical to humans, such as a "Klingon" or a "Vulcan," he or she is relying even more on shared knowledge, and building in even less that is new.

The icky muck, sharing no obvious properties with Earth animals, provides no "given" information to help convey the "new." Thus, the need to communicate with an audience undoubtedly works against ideas such as this that are too novel. Furthermore, without tying a creature to some familiar hitching post, the author fails to accomplish a key goal of science fiction: helping people learn more about themselves and their world by trekking through a strange yet familiar alien landscape.

USING EARTH ANIMALS AS MODELS

Beyond the need to communicate is the simple fact that an easy way to produce a new idea is to take an old one and alter it slightly. If we wanted to create an intelligent alien, for instance, we could take humans as a model and change them slightly for the new situation. Because we know that humans are equipped with pairs of arms, legs, and eyes arranged symmetrically, we would likely wind up endowing our imagined extraterrestrials with those features. This is because we construct our new concept out of the information we recall about the old concept.

Many of our college students reported that they developed ideas for their alien creatures from typical Earth animals, such as humans, dogs, and elephants. Judging from the large number of similar creatures that occur in the science fiction literature, it is apparent that science fiction writers do much the same.

Some have criticized this approach of basing aliens directly on Earth species as indicating laziness, or a lack of imagination. George Ochoa and Jeffrey Osier, authors of *The Writer's Guide to Creating a Science Fiction Universe*, point out that evolution on other planets is unlikely to have led to creatures that closely resemble humans. "Slapping a few warts on a human will not help."[9]

Similarly, George R. R. Martin, a Hugo Award-winning author, notes that the bulk of science fiction aliens are not very interesting or innovative. He goes on to make the point that if an author is not going to make aliens considerably different from humans, it would be more sensible to just make them human.[10] Barlowe also complained that many authors take the easy way out by doing something simple, such as placing a cat's head on a human torso. Thus, much science fiction has earned a bad reputation for spawning creatures that are too familiar or conventional.

INCREASING UNUSUALNESS WITH ATYPICAL EARTH ANIMALS

As noted previously, it is easier to think of typical instances of a concept than atypical instances. This is true whether the concept is animals, vehicles, or tools. To test this, write down the first 10 tools that come to mind. Your list is likely to include hammers, screwdrivers, pliers, and the like. This same principle affects the imaginary creatures and artifacts we develop. We will be more likely to start with typical Earth animals than with atypical ones, because these are the ones that spring to mind first. Consequently, many imaginary aliens will resemble the most typical Earth animals.

One way to design a more innovative creature, then, is to resist the urge to make do with the first Earth animal that comes to mind. What are some extraordinary Earth animals that could be used as a model? One would be a starfish. Among its interesting properties are pentaradial symmetry, a mouth on the bottom and anus on top, rows of extending and contracting tubelike feet on each of five arms, a stomach that pushes out through its mouth to partially digest food before ingesting it, and receptors that respond to touch, smell, and light.

As Ochoa and Osier point out, the starfish would be an award-winning alien if it did not already exist on Earth. The differences between a starfish and typical Earth animals are far greater than those between typical earth creatures and most of the aliens imagined by science fiction writers. Knowing about the range of variations that exist on Earth can help in begetting novel aliens. An imagined creature that reflected this diversity would likely be regarded as novel, because the unusualness of the most atypical Earth creatures would contribute to the unusualness of the alien. A surprisingly wonderful variety of features and creatures are available to those who would exploit the most unusual and extreme examples from Earth.

In *Memoirs of a Spacewoman*, Naiomi Mitchison patterned her "Radiates" after starfish, and the result was a strange and compelling alien species. The Radiates are not identical to starfish; they boast a ring of bright blue eyes around their central brain case, and suckers that can grasp tools. In addition, rather than thinking in dualities as we do, they have a five-valued logic system. These interesting innovations reveal that even atypical Earth animals are just a starting point for creative ideas; they are preinventive forms. To expand the potential of a form, a writer must explore the dramatic possibilities to find all its creative implications.

In *Hen's Teeth and Horse's Toes*, Stephen Jay Gould eloquently describes another unusual Earth creature that has a parallel in science fiction. For certain types of anglerfish, the male is tiny. It attaches permanently to the underside of the female, and serves primarily as a sperm delivery system. Although Gould himself balks at the term, the male is often described as a mere parasite. This highly unusual fish violates the more typical tendency of males and females of the same species to be independent entities of roughly equal size.[11] In Donald Moffitt's "Cygnan" species, which he detailed in *The Jupiter Theft*, the parasitic male attaches to the belly of the female. It is not clear that Moffitt deliberately used the anglerfish as a model. The point is simply that there exists on Earth at least one species that could serve as a model for this more unusual type of alien.

INCREASING UNUSUALNESS THROUGH ABSTRACTION

As noted earlier, abstraction can often lead to greater innovation. Thus, instead of pressing into service specific Earth creatures as models for extraterrestrials, one might bring more abstract information to bear on the task. Three ways to put abstraction to work in writing science fiction are (1) to consider the general properties of living things on Earth, and how they might be altered, (2) to dream up a novel world and bestow on a creature the properties it needs to function there, and (3) to invent a particular story line, which would then call for creatures with particular traits to make the story work. All of these approaches require one to possess and apply broad knowledge.

The first approach encourages authors to take existing knowledge and turn it on its head. The technique grows out of one of the most consistent themes in advice to would-be science fiction writers: learn about and honor science fact. Without knowing the rules, it is difficult if not impossible to develop an idea that violates them in a convincing way.

Ochoa and Osier describe a method similar to this one in a section of their *Writer's Guide* entitled "The Alien-Builder's

Workshop." Ochoa and Osier list some central properties of Earth animals, including symmetry, sense organs, cephalization (senses located in the head), and movement. They also exhort would-be authors to explicitly consider those properties, and how they might be modified to fashion colorful imaginary species. Their suggestions highlight the special role abstraction can play in science fiction writing, and they support the more general point that an abstract approach can often lead to greater innovation by helping us to confront our implicit assumptions. When we force our assumptions about what living things are like out into the open, we can decide whether to accept, modify, or completely reject them in fashioning more innovative creatures.

By actively considering the fact that most Earth animals are bilaterally symmetric, we can ask whether animals on other planets must be. Could they be trilaterally symmetric, as are Damon Knight's "Tripeds," or entirely asymmetric? Must they take in the world through senses as we know them, or might they have no obvious sense organs, as is true of James H. Schmitz's "Old Galactics"? Must they move about on legs or wings, or might they roll on a wheel like Piers Anthony's "Polarians," float freely like Jack L. Chalker's "Uchjinians," or remain immobile like Philip Jose Farmer's "Mothers"? Must they even be bounded solids, or might they be vast interstellar intelligences like Fred Hoyle's "Black Cloud," or oceans like Stanislaw Lem's "Solaris"?

Bob Shaw, an award-winning science fiction author, argues for what he calls "inversion," which also relies on deliberate manipulation of knowledge.[12] An author using inversion would take some human attribute, such as a personality trait, and turn it around. If humans are highly social beings, the aliens might be social isolates. If humans are self-centered, the aliens might be selfless. One of Shaw's most compelling examples of inversion is an alien species that was unconcerned about dying, and perhaps even relished it. The very act of reversing this most basic of human preoccupations invites us to ask what such creatures would be like. Would they ardently hold religious beliefs about their role in the cosmos, or would they be scrupulously areligious? Would they perform any rituals surrounding the death of one of their own? Could they comprehend another species, or even a subgroup within their midst that feared death? The tension and conflict between such groups supplies a fertile soil in which a story might grow, and it arises from assessing and challenging a fundamental assumption about human nature.

Hal Clement, a noted science fiction author, favors the second abstraction approach: contriving a world and inventing creatures that could survive there. He states, "I get most of the fun out of working out the physical and chemical nature of a planet or solar system, and then dreaming up life forms that might reasonably evolve under such conditions."[13] The particular survival demands of the planet prod the author to contemplate novel solutions to those challenges, which may not always correspond to the ways Earth animals satisfy their survival needs. When properly guided by knowledge of physics, chemistry, biology, and ecology, the result is often a highly provocative and innovative creature. The new life form will also be appropriate for its surroundings. Since creative ideas must be appropriate rather than merely novel, applying knowledge to invent an adaptive organism will also help a writer satisfy this additional criterion of creativity.

Clement's own "Mesklinites" are a fascinating outcome of the world-building approach. Clement designed a world that rotates so rapidly it has been flattened to the shape of a disk. As a result, gravity varies enormously from the poles to the equator. The Mesklinites have 36 legs, are built low to the ground, are only 15 inches long, and have an extreme fear of falling. All of these unique attributes make Mesklinites especially well adapted to their circumstances. By building a world, and then hashing out how creatures would adapt to it, Clement was able to fashion intriguing, yet believable organisms.

Our research also demonstrates that this second abstraction approach is effective. In one study, we encouraged half of our subjects to develop their own imaginary animal by first thinking about what its planet would be like. We encouraged the other half to pattern their creatures after some known Earth animal. The first group devised much more innovative creatures. They were especially inclined to introduce unusual variations on the sense organs and appendages.[14] The practical advice given by authors, such as Clement, suggests that the approach has actual validity, and our laboratory experiments confirm these intuitions.

How else can an author utilize abstraction as a catalyst for creative ideas? A third approach is to fabricate a story line first. Once constrained to satisfy the logical requirements of a story, an author may be inspired to give life to an exquisitely appropriate creature. In this case, the properties of the alien are driven by the story the author wants to convey, rather than the properties of the planet. But, like the world-building approach, it spurs the author to construct the alien from broader knowledge rather than building it from scratch or simply patterning it after a single, typical Earth animal.

It may seem surprising that constraints can encourage creativity. We often think of them as blocking our paths, but ironically, this is why they work. They prevent us from taking the easy way out. If a typical Earth creature couldn't do what was required in a story, the author would have to dream up a novel creature that could.

Constraints also help in another way. The set of possible creatures is infinite. How are you ever able to narrow down that set and actually begin the task of writing? How do you ever find your way through the vast wilderness of possibilities? Constraints serve as field guides. A story line might require a creature capable of living for thousands of years, swimming a sea of molten rock to rescue a captured princess, or negotiating a settlement between a silicon-based species having only tactile and magnetic sensors and a humanlike species keen on mining their planet. What properties must a creature possess to meet these demands? By asking this type of question we can overcome the paralysis that results from having too many choices, and free ourselves to explore along certain fruitful paths.

KNOWLEDGE AND THE SYSTEMATIC EXPLORATION OF MENTAL MODELS

The three abstraction approaches all encourage authors to consult their world knowledge deliberately as they generate ideas for novel creatures. Authors can also exploit their knowledge to expand and sharpen their initial ideas. Nearly every author and critic who has given advice about how to write science fiction and fantasy has emphasized the need to fashion a consistent, coherent, integrated imaginary world. Without that structure, the story fails to hold itself together, and ultimately fails to hold the reader's interest.

In the formal terms of creative cognition, the most successful and ingenious authors carefully build and rigorously test "mental models" of their imaginary worlds by consulting their broad knowledge frameworks. These frameworks can include knowledge of physics, chemistry, biology, geology, ecology, psychology, economics, and sociology, as well as a lifetime of observations about "human nature." You may be what you eat, but as an author, you are what you know. Broad, general knowledge in all of these domains can help authors formulate tales that contain a tightly woven, mutually supportive, interrelated set of properties—tales in which the environment, its creatures, their interactions, and the plot mesh together nearly seamlessly like the strands of some glorious symphony.

One way to test a mental model of an imaginary world is to consider the consequences of changing one feature of an alien that might live there. For example, suppose we wanted to make our alien much larger than animals on Earth. This might be fine, but to make the alien believable, it might have to live on a planet with much lower gravity than Earth, which in turn would require the planet to be smaller, and so forth.[10]

The size of a creature might also have an impact on its other features. Enormous insects, for example, are not possible on a planet like Earth. They are confined to their small size by the fact that they breathe through invaginations in their surface, and by the more general fact that the volume of any object grows more rapidly (by the cube of the length) than its surface area (by the square of the length). Thus, an insectlike organism of very large size would not have enough surface area to take in the air needed to support its own body. An insect the size of a small mammal "would be 'all invagination' and have no room for internal parts."[15] In addition, a very large insect would collapse under its own weight, because its weight would increase with its volume whereas its supporting exoskeleton which would increase with its surface area would be unable to support the disproportionate weight. Again, one could change the planet, or the nature of the insect, but to be believable, the changes would have to form an integrated package.

Suppose we wanted to have an intelligent flying species. Because an intelligent creature would probably have a brain of some minimal size and complexity, these creatures would likely be reasonably large. For large creatures to fly well, flight on an imagined planet would have to be easier, either by having denser air, lower gravity, or some other variation. This in turn would mean that the evolutionary pressures on the planet would be more friendly to fliers. Consequently, there would be more fliers, and more varied types of flying creatures. All of this might influence how the various species would interact.

Exactly how a change in one factor would affect other factors may be debatable, but the issue can be addressed by constructing and testing mental models of the situation. If we discover that the various properties of our imaginary creatures and imaginary worlds are mutually consistent and supportive, then our mental model passes the test. If we find inconsistencies, we must introduce some additional changes.

Why bother taking these excursions through our mental models? Why should it matter if we get the "right answers" in a creative endeavor such as science fiction? One simple reason: readers will find believable creatures and worlds more appealing. They can suspend disbelief, but a story that shows a blatant disregard for known physical laws and makes no attempt to explain the apparent violations would not be captivating. "For many modern readers, a violation of the laws of thermodynamics by the author can spoil a story just as effectively as having Abraham Lincoln change a set of spark plugs in a historical novel."[16] Keeping accurate scientific knowledge in mind leads to more exciting, credible, and intellectually stimulating aliens and worlds. The best and most lasting science fiction is rigorously thought-out and tested, and the most ingenious authors know how to draw on existing knowledge to the highest dramatic effect.

Fantasy writers are less bound by science fact, and can invoke magic or mystical forces that violate known physical laws. Even in the fantasy genre, however, it is vital to stick with a consistent set of rules that can enhance a story. A world in which "anything goes" is less absorbing than one that sets clear limits. To capture a reader's imagination, even magic must adhere to some rules.

Orson Scott Card, a prolific fantasy author, paints a grim yet colorful picture of how fruitful it can be to place some restrictions on the use of magic.[19] He counsels authors to contemplate "the price of magic" as a way of setting up the rules of a system of magic. Requiring magic to have some price prevents its unlimited use and sidesteps the problem of a world in which anything goes. More coherent sets of rules open up more possibilities in a story.

To illustrate the price of magic, Card considers the possibility that magicians might lose parts of their bodies with each new spell. The type and size of the part might be unpredictable, or it might be related to the magnitude of the spell. In such a world, missing limbs would be a sign of great magical power, and reckless youth might pay to have parts amputated to create the illusion of power.

Just when you think Card has worked the idea for all it's worth, he continues to add other twists. Perhaps a whole trade springs up in which skilled artisans receive large sums of money to remove parts artfully. Perhaps a single individual avoids casting spells to preserve his own body, and is judged to be weak and cowardly. But later the society needs an enormously powerful spell for its own survival, one that will consume the entire sorcerer who casts it. The reluctant magician is now the only one who can perform the deed. A strict set of rules for magic has now laid the foundations for a tense drama of personal development and change.

In other variations on the theme, the price of magic might be a part of someone else's body. What story lines emerge if the other person is a random stranger, a relative, or a lover? What happens if the part must be given voluntarily versus taken by force? Again, having a clear set of rules gives rise to a wealth of intriguing ideas for stories.

J. R. R. Tolkien bestowed on the world of literature the great gift of the *Hobbit* and *The Lord of the Rings* trilogy, an exquisite set of books that give testament to the value of rules. The tale centers around the most powerful of all magical rings, a band that imparts an awesome authority to its bearer—the domination over all living things. "One Ring to rule them all, One Ring to find them, One Ring to bring them all and in the darkness bind them, in the Land of Mordor where the Shadows lie." The palpable, brooding menace of this omnipotent loop spurs a coalition of Elves, Dwarves, and Hobbits to mount a quest to destroy the ring. Frodo, the unfortunate hobbit who is designated as Ringbearer, and several companions undertake an arduous journey fraught with peril, not the least of which is the temptation to use the ring. For using the power of the ring corrupts the user.

The story derives much of its vitality from applying an old bit of wisdom to a fantasy setting. Power corrupts and absolute power corrupts absolutely. The mighty force of the band could help Frodo and his companions out of any difficulty on their quest. But in using it, Frodo risks absorbing and becoming the very evil he seeks to destroy. Without some cost to using the magic of the ring, there is no tension. There is no story. With the cost, a wealth of creative opportunities presented themselves to Tolkien, and he worked through them brilliantly.

USING ANALOGY TO GENERATE AND EXPLORE NOVEL ALIENS

An alternative way to assemble an innovative creature is by using analogies from some inanimate domain. Although most animals move by way of legs, wings, or fins, the most efficient inanimate equivalent is the wheel. What if we developed animals that had wheels? The result could be a highly creative alien, such as the Polarian or the wheeled creatures of Quopp from Keith Laumer's novel, *Retief's War*. What if the planet were very icy? Perhaps skates would provide a better analogy than wheels. The consequence might be innovative creatures, such as Alan Dean Foster's "Tran," which have skatelike curving claws that allow them to travel quickly across icy surfaces.

Are there other features from the world of artifacts that might be transferred to living creatures? What about creatures that have tools as appendages, such as hammerlike structures in place of hands?

There is a precedent for this approach of importing knowledge by analogy from other domains. For example, Gordon described the potential value of taking examples from nature to aid in developing artifacts. The approach we have described simply turns this procedure around; it takes examples of artifacts to aid in developing imaginary living things.

BREAKING AWAY FROM KNOWLEDGE THROUGH CREATIVE IMAGERY TECHNIQUES

So far, we have emphasized seizing on existing knowledge to create believable, imaginary creatures. As an alternative to this approach, one could try to avoid the influence of existing knowledge, at least in the earliest stages of generating ideas.

The technique of envisioning and interpreting preinventive forms, which gives rise to clever ideas for practical inventions, can also yield fresh insights for science fiction stories. Figure 7.1 presents some examples of preinventive forms derived from the same parts that we showed earlier. The figure also shows how these simple forms could be used as starting points for constructing novel, alien life forms. Various appendages and organs could be added to the forms, resulting in highly original creatures.

More original aliens might arise from preinventive forms that were generated simply to be aesthetically pleasing rather than from forms constructed specifically with alien creatures in mind. If you know that the forms are supposed to become alien creatures, you are more likely to structure them according to your knowledge about typical Earth creatures or familiar examples of what aliens should look like. By using preinventive forms generated by mentally melding simpler visual components, with no particular categories in mind, your starting point bears less resemblance to conventional types of aliens.

Preinventive forms can also be used to explore the kinds of tools and artifacts that aliens might use. Consider the form shown in Figure 7.2. Imagine that it represents some type of device that an alien creature commonly uses. What is the purpose of this device? How, exactly, would the aliens use it? Such explorations often stimulate insights into novel abilities and skills that your imagined aliens might possess.

CREATING IMAGERY FOR THE READER

Many writing teachers have emphasized the value of showing rather than telling, which helps the reader actually experience what the author is trying to convey.[17] Some have recommended specifically that fiction writers should try to visualize a scene before describing it, to make the details of the scene come alive.[18] We would add that visualizing a scene serves another benefit: It

FIGURE 7.1. Preinventive forms (left) and how they might be interpreted as alien life forms.

allows the writer to explore emergent properties of the scene that could lead to creative developments in the story.

For instance, try to imagine the following alien landscape: There is a green sun in the sky, and the planet is extremely dry.

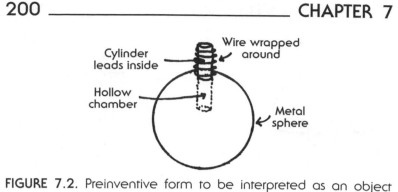

FIGURE 7.2. Preinventive form to be interpreted as an object used by extraterrestrials.

Tall, crusty, brown pillars rise up from the arid ground, and alien creatures soar from one pillar to another. Gravity is weak on the planet, and there is no detectable wind.

Using your image of this landscape, describe how these creatures might look and move. How would they search for food? How would they fight or protect themselves? What predators might prey on them? By scrutinizing your image, you can often discover things about the alien environment and its inhabitants that you would not have conceived of initially.

BEYOND ALIEN CREATURES

We have focused our attention on the subject of creating vibrant science fiction. Some of the same principles can also be applied to envisioning novel settings, social situations, and political institutions in other works of fiction. Combining two or more concepts can lead to unexpected insights, and judiciously applying and rejecting the basic assumptions of existing knowledge can foster compelling tales. Constructing and testing mental models can provide a check on the logical consistency of a story, and building knowledge-free preinventive images helps you to break out of the ordinary constraints of existing knowledge. Thus, these relatively simple yet powerful cognitive processes, available to anyone who would wish to exploit them, can provide a potent avenue for exploration and creativity to writers and visionaries from all genres of writing.

NOTES

1. Stephen R. Donaldson, *The Real Story* (New York: Bantam Books, 1992), p. 222.
2. Donaldson, *The Real Story*, p. 223.
3. Stephen R. Donaldson, *Lord Foul's Bane: The Chronicles of Thomas Covenant the Unbeliever, Book One* (New York: Ballantine Books, 1977), pp. 21–22.
4. Edward J. Wisniewski & Dedre Gentner, "On the Combinatorial Semantics of Noun Pairs: Minor and Major Adjustments to Meaning," in *Understanding Word and Sentence*, ed. Grog B. Simpson (Amsterdam: Elsevier Science, 1991), pp. 241–284.
5. Orson Scott Card, *How to Write Science Fiction and Fantasy* (Cincinnati, OH: Writer's Digest Books, 1990), p. 33.
6. Donaldson, *The Real Story*, p. 228.
7. William Shatner with Chris Kreski, *Star Trek Memories* (New York: HarperCollins, 1993).
8. If the puddle of muck grew larger, engulfed its surroundings, and became a threat to humans, as in the case of "The Blob," an absorbing tale might result. However, readers of science fiction have become more sophisticated over the years, and most would now want a convincing account of the creatures' means of survival, and so forth.
9. George Ochoa & Jeffrey Osier, *The Writer's Guide to Creating a Science Fiction Universe* (Cincinnati, OH: Writer's Digest Books, 1993), p. 161.
10. George R. R. Martin, "First, Sew On a Tentacle (Recipes for Believable Aliens," in *Writing & Selling Science Fiction*, ed. C. L. Grant (Cincinnati, OH: Writer's Digest Books, 1976).
11. Stephen Jay Gould, *Hen's Teeth and Horse's Toes* (New York: Norton, 1983).

12. Bob Shaw, *How to Write Science Fiction* (London: Allison & Busby, 1993).

13. Hal Clement, "The Creation of Imaginary Beings," in *Writing Science Fiction and Fantasy*, eds. Gardner Dozois, Tina Lee, Stanley Schmidt, Ian Randal Strock, & Sheila Williams (New York: St. Martin's Press, 1991), p. 132.

14. Thomas B. Ward, "The effect of processing approach on category exemplar generation." Paper presented at the meeting of the Psychonomic Society, Washington, DC (November, 1993).

15. Stephen Jay Gould, *Ever Since Darwin* (New York: Norton, 1977), p. 173.

16. Clement, in *Writing Science Fiction and Fantasy*, p. 130.

17. Peter Elbow, *Writing With Power: Techniques for Mastering the Writing Process* (London: Oxford University Press, 1981).

18. Stanley Schmidt, "Good Writing is Not Enough," in *Writing Science Fiction and Fantasy*, eds. Gardner Dozois, Tina Lee, Stanley Schmidt, Ian Randal Strock, & Sheila Williams (New York: St. Martin's Press, 1991).

19. Card, in *How to Write Science Fiction and Fantasy.*

SCIENCE AND ART

DISCOVERIES IN CHEMISTRY AND MUSIC

MULLIS AND THE POLYMERASE CHAIN REACTION[1]

Late one evening in April of 1983, Kary Mullis drove through winding hills to his ranch in northern California. Mullis was a biochemist employed by the Cetus Corporation to synthesize chemicals used in genetic cloning. The road wove to and fro through the hills, and the fragrance of wildflowers wafted in his window as Mullis toyed with notions in his mind. He had gotten an idea for a technique for working with chemical samples containing low amounts of DNA, and he was working out what might be wrong with his idea. In fact, his method would not have worked at all. Nonetheless, as he drove, the bumpiness of the road and the confinement of the car somehow seemed to encourage the chemical images as they continued to dance in his head, idly playing out possibilities. Then, in a sudden flash, an idea burst into his mind, an idea that would win him a Nobel prize and revolutionize the world of chemistry—the polymerase chain reaction (PCR).

BEETHOVEN'S DISCOVERY OF A MUSICAL CANON[2]

Returning from Vienna to Baden in a horse-drawn carriage one September evening in 1821, Ludwig van Beethoven suddenly remembered a dream. Riding in the same carriage on his way to Vienna the previous day, Beethoven had dozed in his seat, dreaming of the Holy Land, and then of the biblical name "Tobias," a man who had journeyed with the angel Raphael. The name reminded him of his Viennese publisher, Tobias Haslinger. In the dream the publisher's name had become incorporated into a musical canon that flashed into the composer's mind. Beethoven, on remembering the theme, wrote it down, and developed the canon into a finished work.

Mullis's discovery of the PCR and Beethoven's inspiration for his musical canon exemplify important principles of creative thinking discussed previously, including the playful or non-standard use of prior knowledge, the generation and exploration of preinventive forms, analogical thinking, conceptual combination, sudden insight, mental imagery, and noticing key relationships. We will return to these important discoveries and others to show how the principles of creative cognition can operate in both scientific and artistic arenas.

SCIENCE AND ART

Critics of our broad approach to creativity might object to our contention that similar patterns of creative thinking can be seen in all disciplines. Just look at how dissimilar disciplines can be, such as art and science. Art appeals to our emotions, whereas science deals with logic and mathematical relationships. A good scientist cannot be ruled by irrational emotions. Art is fundamentally subjective, whereas science relies on objectivity. Art is often wild and fanciful, while science needs to be rooted in reality. Nonetheless, as different as music and chemistry may seem, the circumstances that led Beethoven and Mullis to their astounding discoveries were strikingly similar. We maintain that the same cognitive approach to creative thinking can apply to such diverse spheres.

In addition to claiming that creative cognition is relevant to very different disciplines, we also assert that creative cognition speaks to experts as well as novices. The idea that learning about creative cognition could help serious artists and scientists make new discoveries, however, sounds preposterous to many experts in those fields. How could these principles possibly help someone discover new principles in chemistry or inspire a marvelous symphony?

The answer lies in the difference between having special knowledge about something and knowing how to wield that knowledge creatively. Most chemists, for example, are knowledgeable about chemistry, but few make creative discoveries in their field. Likewise, many artists who are highly skilled in technique fail to create innovative or influential styles. Expertise is necessary but not sufficient for making creative contributions to art or science. You have to know how to use knowledge creatively, and this is where creative cognition can help.

Consider, as an analogy, the way generalized physical training programs can help a pole vaulter jump higher, a linebacker tackle more assertively, or an ice skater flow more gracefully. Training techniques that improve stamina or strengthen specific muscle groups can help each of these athletes and many others use their special skills and talents in more effective ways. Similarly, learning how to generate preinventive structures, combine concepts, explore creative implications, and use contextual shifts can help both artists and scientists.

By highlighting a number of historically important discoveries and innovations, we will show how these two superficially distinct domains are actually quite similar, and how the principles of creative cognition are suffused throughout the important historical discoveries in both areas.

THE SCIENTIFIC PROCESS

The scientific method is a cyclic process. It consists of hypothesizing, or guessing what will happen in a scientific study, testing the hypothesis in a systematic way, observing the results of the test, and interpreting the results. To avoid subjective biases and misinterpretations, scientists strive to carry out the entire process in as objective a manner as possible. Stated this way, the scientific method appears to be a very orderly and predictable process.

In the real world, however, the scientific process is not as orderly as the above description suggests. Where do hypotheses come from? How do scientists know which way questions should be formulated? How do you build a theory? Purveyors of the scientific method usually do not even address these questions, much less answer them. There is no clear formula for cultivating scientific curiosity, no step-by-step method for thinking of ideas to test, no section at the end of the book that tells us where to search for answers. Explaining where scientific ideas come from and how to formulate questions is the domain of creative cognition.

ARTISTIC PROCESSES

The artistic process has not been so clearly articulated or agreed upon as the scientific method. Artists are often noteworthy for their eccentric or iconoclastic approaches to art. The "Exquisite Corpse" method described earlier is nothing like the methods used by ancient Byzantine masters, or those of modern hyperrealists. Van Gogh and Cézanne, both early Postimpressionist painters, contrasted greatly in their methods; whereas Van Gogh would complete as many as two or more paintings in a day, a feverish pace, Cézanne, his friend, might brood over his canvas and paint only a single calculated stroke in a day. No consensual method is apparent in the creation of art, as there seems to be in science.

Despite these superficial differences, however, there are some important similarities between art and science. These similarities include interactions between the two domains, parallels between the ways in which advances are made in the two, and similarities in the cognitive processes that give rise to these two important human endeavors.

ART IN SCIENCE AND SCIENCE IN ART

The claim that art and science have much in common is certainly not new. Many science writers, for example, have called attention to the way certain structures in science exhibit a kind of artistic beauty: The double helix of DNA is a fascinating, intriguing structure, even apart from its biological and genetic significance, and there is grace and elegance in the theory of relativity.

Art, in turn, has often been influenced by scientific principles and discoveries. The interaction of these two areas was embodied in the Renaissance artist and scientist Leonardo da Vinci, who excelled in both, using his studies of anatomy and mechanical physics to create some of the most beautiful artwork of all time. The Impressionist movement was inspired in part by scientific work on the way primary colors are combined in the human visual system. The "atomic" paintings by the Surrealist artist Salvador Dali, which depict objects disintegrating into their most minute components, were partly inspired by atomic physics theory. The mind-bending illusions created by M. C. Escher resulted from his masterful understanding of the principles of object perception. Many current artistic techniques are based on scientific principles of color mixing and contrast. The cinematic miracles that now grace our screens depend on countless scientific principles and discoveries, ranging from gyroscopic motion that can steady a rapidly carried camera, to the chemistry of pyrotechnics, and the principles of motion perception.

WHAT SCIENCE AND ART SHARE: SCHOOLS, MOVEMENTS, AND PARADIGMS

An important feature of both science and art is that progress occurs within and between schools of thought. A "school" of thought refers to a consensual way of thinking, exploring, and expressing ideas. Schools of thinking have been vital in the histories of both art and science. In the arts, schools have been referred to as "movements," such as the Impressionist and Surrealist movements, or as "periods," such as classical or baroque. In the sciences, a school is called a "scientific paradigm," a term given by the great philosopher of science Thomas Kuhn. Movements and paradigms have been powerful patterning forces in art and science.

One scientific paradigm differs from another in terms of the goals they try to achieve, the questions they ask, the methods they use, the phenomena they study to find answers, and even the language they use for description and explanation. In physics, for example, the Newtonian paradigm investigated the movements of objects having various masses, speeds, and directions. It ultimately gave way to quantum mechanics, which examines the physics of subatomic particles and forces. Geological science also underwent a startling paradigm shift in 1906 when Alfred Wegener proposed that the continents and mountain ranges of the planet were not nearly as solid as people had assumed, but rather that land masses consisted of vast tectonic plates. Geologists then began to study earthquakes and volcanoes in terms of geological activity along the edges of these floating plates, a fundamental change in scientific perspective.

Artistic movements undergo similar shifts, such as changing from religious to secular art, from baroque to classical styles, or from representational painting to abstract composition. Impressionism, Cubism, Surrealism, and Minimalism were at one time revolutionary new ideas that seized the imaginations of people everywhere. These movements arise and grow in popularity when a consensus of artists, critics, and aesthetes recognizes, celebrates, and explores the universality and meaningfulness of particular novel ideas. Even when the movements go out of vogue, their appeal and influence continue to enrich the world of art.

In addition to the many ideas and discoveries that have triggered paradigm shifts in science and new movements in art, it is equally important to point out that most scientific and artistic contributions occur within an existing paradigm or movement. The more people there are whose creative work is guided by general paradigms, the more historically important is the shift itself. Creative work within movements and paradigms and inspirations for new paradigms are both necessary components of creative endeavor. We will return to this distinction of within-paradigm and between-paradigm creativity to show their interdependence in science and art.

PATTERNS OF CREATIVE COGNITION IN SCIENCE AND ART

Beyond the similarities we have already noted, scientific and artistic endeavors share important cognitive processes. These include restructuring problems, achieving insights, exploring analogies, combining concepts, striking a balance between employing and rejecting old knowledge, and manipulating mental images.

INSIGHT AND RESTRUCTURING

Insight and Restructuring in Science

Scientists, as a group, have earned a reputation as conservative plodders, tinkering, testing, measuring, and repeating their observations. There have been times, however, when brilliant ideas have flashed suddenly into the minds of scientists, churning up the waters in this tranquil pool of stability. Although these unexpected scientific insights may represent only a fraction of what is known in the sciences, they nonetheless have provoked important discoveries. Understanding these earth-shaking insights can help us to fathom how the more commonplace, yet personally important inspirations come about.

There are striking similarities among the following insightful anecdotes. In each case the scientist, and others working in the field were initially stymied by some impasse that seemed impossible to resolve. The insightful ideas all occurred when the scientists were away from their typical workplaces, and not working directly on the critical problems. They were reported to flash suddenly into mind, rather than resulting from an incremental progression of planned steps. Finally, in each case, the insights were accompanied by an immediate feeling of certainty that the new ideas were sure to work.

Eureka![3] Archimedes was the greatest mathematical and scientific thinker of the third century B.C., and King Hiero of Syracuse, his relative, knew it. Archimedes had proved this to the King when he built a machine that, powered by one arm, could move a fully loaded ship out of a dock, whereas the entire Syracusan crew, without the machine, could barely budge the ship. King Hiero asked Archimedes to determine whether a gold crown he had commissioned had been surreptitiously alloyed with cheaper (and less dense) silver. Archimedes attempted first to determine the volume of the crown, so that he could compare it with the volume of an equal weight of pure gold. The crown was such a complex shape, however, that Archimedes was initially thwarted. When he neglected his personal habits in his absorption in the problem, his friends carried him by force to the public baths.

While in the bath, he noticed the water displaced by his body, and he realized that the crown would also displace an equal and measurable amount of water. Screaming "Eureka!," he is said to have run straight home in his excitement, without pausing to dress himself (and thus inventing the art of streaking, too).

Beer Bubbles. After earning his Ph.D. in 1949, Donald Glaser went to work in the Department of Physics at the University of Michigan. In his first three years there, Glaser worked with a team of scientists studying nuclear radiation at the subatomic level. The cloud chamber and the newer spark chamber were at that time the only known means of measuring subatomic radiation. Both methods relied on photographs of the trails of radiating particles through gas-filled chambers. Unfortunately, both devices gave very inexact readings because the vapors used were not dense enough. Glaser was frustrated with the problem and had reached an impasse when he experienced a sudden insight, one that may have been inspired by tiny streams of bubbles rising in a stein of beer. Glaser realized that a superheated liquid would form tiny bubbles along the tracks of subatomic particles as they emerged from a nuclear reaction, and that the liquid would be dense enough to give detailed measurements of the radiation. For his discovery of the bubble chamber, Glaser became one of the youngest scientists to win a Nobel prize in physics, at age 34.

Driving through the Hills. Kary Mullis, discoverer of the polymerase chain reaction, was 38 years old when he made his discovery. He insists that all of his best ideas come to him in a sudden flash. Mullis states that his breakthrough was like "seeing an idea out of the corner of your eye when the main channels are blocked." Amplifying a weak DNA signal (i.e., creating a lot of DNA from a minute sample) had been a problem for decades, and the sensible, tried-and-true methods for solving the problem had met with no success. Chemists could not see the solution by looking in their typical directions, because an implicit assumption in their approach was that chemical reactions happened only once, rather than repeatedly. Mullis could only see the solution by looking elsewhere. In fact, he was not even working on the DNA amplification problem at all when the discovery flashed into his mind; he was thinking about how to make a copy of a small segment of a DNA strand.

Mullis had first gotten an idea for how he might be able to copy a small DNA sequence, and he was considering some of the potential problems in his hypothetical solution. His solution used a molecule that, once the DNA strands were heated and split, would serve as a chemical anchor for the copying process. Mullis's twin realizations hit him in rapid-fire sequence: first, that entire DNA sequences could be copied, and, second, that the process could be reapplied iteratively to first double the amount of DNA, then quadruple it, and so on, amplifying the DNA at an ever accelerating pace.

Of his insight, Mullis wrote the following:

The Polymerase Chain Reaction (PCR) was discovered as
a possible consequence
of a proposed solution
to a hypothetical problem
which might have arisen in a planned experiment,
which itself contained an implicit assumption,
the truth of which would have denied the very existence
of the very important
and very real problem
which PCR so neatly solved.

In each of these cases, as with many insights, the traditional methods of pursuing scientific questions blocked solutions to the problems. As with inventors who repeat the flaws from earlier designs, and writers who pattern their creatures too closely on Earth animals, scientists too can be snared in the traps of existing, implicit assumptions. A paradigmatic pursuit of science can produce many important answers and ideas, but some problems require unusual and unexpected approaches.

It is also important to note that incubation spurred these sudden insights. Each idea occurred when the scientist was not working directly on the problem that was solved. Indeed, none were even at their workplaces when the ideas hit them. Archimedes was at the public baths, Glaser was having a beer, and Mullis was in his car. Other historical insights have also occurred away from the workplace. Kekule's sudden insight about the structure of the benzene ring came as he dozed before the fire. Henri Poincaré, the eminent mathematician, described one important insight as occurring as he stepped onto a bus, and another as he was strolling along seaside bluffs. Yung Kang Chow, a medical student, realized an idea for an AIDS treatment as he sat at the dinner table. These observations are consistent with the idea that blocks may be avoided or surpassed if you consider problems outside of their typical contexts.

Insight and Restructuring in Art

Insight experiences are also common in art. Beethoven's unexpected idea for a musical canon came to him as he rode in a carriage. The distorted faces of the prostitutes in Picasso's painting "Les Demoiselles d'Avignon" were inspired by his visit to a museum with displays of primitive sculptures and masks.[4] Early in his career, Alexander Calder had constructed many moving wire sculptures that depicted real objects, but his insight for the abstract mobiles that made him famous did not occur to him until he viewed an exhibit by the abstract painter Mondrian. As with their scientific counterparts, these restructurings happened not while the artists were at work, but when they were away from their workplaces.

It is also worth noting that these sudden insights were spawned by other events. We can sometimes trace insights to specific triggering events, such as an art exhibit.

CONCEPTUALIZATION

Analogy

Analogical thinking has been one of the most common and powerful tools for creative thinking in the history of science. Many of the greatest scientific discoveries have come from paradigmatic shifting from one scientific analogy to another.

For example, the structure of the atom was once thought to resemble a plum pudding; positively charged masses were thought to exist in randomly distributed lumps, like plums, while the pudding itself was analogous to a negatively charged medium. This analogy, disproven by Lord Ernest Rutherford's experiments, gave way to new analogies. Replacing the pudding model was the notion that an atom is structured like the ringed planet Saturn, or like the solar system, in which lighter objects orbit a central nuclear mass.

Physical laws that describe the relation between temperature and pressure in gases are based on the analogy of bouncing balls. In this analogy, molecules are seen as elastic balls that bounce more vigorously when the temperature increases. Having the balls bounce harder increases the force with which the balls strike the inside of their container, thereby increasing the pressure. In a similar analogy, Sir Isaac Newton thought of light as a stream of particles bouncing off reflective surfaces.

Throughout this century chemists have used a sort of Tinkertoy analogy for molecules. With Tinkertoys, grooved blocks are connected by thin pegs that fit into the grooves, allowing long branching configurations. Analogously, molecules are often thought of as branching structures of atoms connected by molecular bonds. This Tinkertoy analogy, now implemented in the form of elaborate computer graphics, permits chemists to form models of molecules that are helpful in predicting chemical reactions.

In cognitive psychology, the analogy of the mind as a computer has helped guide theories since the 1950s. Stimuli are thought of as input, our responses to stimuli as output, and our memory is envisioned as internal storage devices that retain, encode, retrieve, and decode information. Other analogies have compared the mind to a hologram or an interconnected network of nerves. These analogies help us to theoretically envision the mind, and they continue to stimulate research in cognitive science.

Artists and composers use analogy to portray particular ideas or emotions. Many composers, for instance, seek to tell definite stories, and they use either individual themes in a composition or specific instruments to signify particular events or characters. The interplay of the instruments then mirrors the way the characters in the story interact. In *Peter and the Wolf,* Prokofiev used instruments and words to tell how a boy's disobedience led him to a close encounter with a wolf. Just as the sun stands for the nucleus of an atom and a planet for its electron, strings symbolize the boy, French horns stand for the wolf, the bassoon represents the grandfather, and the kettledrums denote the hunters. And just as the relation "revolves around" connects the separate elements in the atom–solar system analogy, so too do the interactions among the instruments reflect the relations among the characters. Many other compositions of this type exist, including Beethoven's *Pastoral Symphony,* which tells a story about a day in the country.

Analogies also pervade the world of painting. These include simple physical analogies, such as mapping the relations among elements in a scene to correctly depict a three-dimensional space on a two-dimensional canvas. They also include the use of symbols organized in precise relation to one another to convey a specific message or abstract idea.

Filmmakers and playwrights also employ analogies, particularly when they adapt an older work to a new setting. It is often easy to trace how the characters and their relationships from an earlier creation map directly onto their counterparts in the new product. A classic example would be the tale of star-crossed lovers that descended from *Tristan and Isolde,* through *Romeo and Juliet,* to a play and movie version of *West Side Story.*

Conceptual Combination

Scientists and artists also combine existing concepts and procedures to make important discoveries, achieve stunning insights, and develop innovative forms of expression. One such discovery has already been described, the realization of the PCR. Writing many computer programs prior to his discovery of the PCR, Mullis had been impressed with the usefulness of recursive loops, a simple command that allows many repetitions of a computation. He was also toying with Tinkertoy images of the molecules in DNA replication. From a combination of these two ideas, recursive loops and DNA replication, the amazing possibilities of the PCR emerged. By recursively reintroducing the newly replicated DNA that he got from each chemical reaction, Mullis could increase at an exponential rate the amount of DNA he started with.

Another example described earlier was Donald Glaser's idea of using a bubble chamber to get fine-grained measurements of nuclear radiation. In this case, Glaser's discovery resulted from a combination of the concept of streams of bubbles in beer with that of radiation from subatomic collisions. Emerging from the combination was the possibility of tracking radiated particles by the bubbly tracks they left as they shot through a superheated liquid.

Albert Einstein was also known to play with conceptual combinations as a way of stimulating theoretical ideas. In one exercise, Einstein considered that an object dropped by someone in free-fall would be in motion relative to the Earth, but it would be at rest in relation to the person who dropped it. Einstein's theory of relativity, in fact, appears to have been inspired in part by his simultaneous consideration of these seemingly contradictory concepts: the idea of an object being in motion while also being at rest.

Scientists have not been alone in the creative use of conceptual combination. The "Exquisite Corpse" method used by Surrealist artists, described in an earlier chapter, is a remarkable example of the use of conceptual combination in art. Artists in a group would take turns, each contributing any word that occurred to them to a "sentence" without seeing what the others had written. The resulting "sentence" was a combination of concepts, one of which happened to be "exquisite corpse." The combination was then interpreted by the artists, who hoped to get a glimpse of their own unconscious minds. The artists believed that unconscious thoughts can provide subtle and profound inspirations for artistic works. A similar method used by "Action painters" was to combine drawn lines and shapes, and examine the combinations for interesting shapes and themes.

Indeed, conceptual combinations are so plentiful in art and music that a multitude of examples could be listed. We note just a few here. Consider Calder's insight, mentioned earlier, to couple his early moving wire sculptures with abstract forms. From this combination emerged the mobile, a now familiar hanging wire sculpture with counterbalanced abstract forms. Paul Klee combined the influences of cubism, children's drawings, and primitive art to fashion his unique style. Salvador Dali also used combinations, and his *Nature Morte Vivante* provides a striking parallel to Einstein's combination of motion and rest. The painting depicts several different objects simultaneously in motion and at rest.[5] An example from the musical sphere is Mozart's exquisite merging of chromatic and diatonic progressions.

As an exercise, you might try exploring conceptual combinations in art for yourself. For example, what new art forms might result from combinations such as "landscape jewelry," "sonic paint," or "rhythmic portraits"? We have already heard of rock operas, country and western bands, and electronic Bach; what would a country and eastern band sound like, or a Gregorian rap, or heavy metal sitars? The possibilities seem endless.

SHOULDERS AND RUTS: THE ROLE OF KNOWLEDGE

"Imagination is more important than knowledge." So stated Albert Einstein. Although he undoubtedly recognized the importance of knowledge in scientific discovery, Einstein's words underscore the point that knowledge alone is not always sufficient.

Creativity presents us with a paradox; knowledge is essential for creativity, yet an automatic adherence to knowledge can blind you to creative ideas. When we take advantage of knowledge that has accumulated over time, we are "standing on the shoulders of giants." Exploiting knowledge from others and that which we acquire for ourselves is essential if we want to be creative.

On the other hand, our patterns of thinking can fall prey to mindless, habitual routines if we rely solely on existing knowledge. Getting "stuck in a rut" can cripple your thinking when you are trying to solve new and different problems.

Which of these two seemingly contradictory wisdoms should you use to guide your creative thinking? Hopefully, it should be obvious by now that the answer is both. Sometimes creative advances are made in small but sure incremental steps, by the sweat of your brow, or in Edison's words, the "99% perspiration" that goes into creative work. At other times creative ideas come in an unexpected flash, as if inspired by some incorporeal muse, or more likely by a portion of the mind that works beyond our conscious awareness. Perhaps more often than not, creative discoveries stem from an interplay between periods of building on existing knowledge, and getting unexpected insights in the course of playing with that knowledge. As described by Roger Schank, a noted explorer of artificial intelligence (AI), creative thinking involves a "playful misuse of knowledge."

Computer Programs That Manipulate Knowledge to Make Discoveries

Albert Einstein was not only a scientist but also a philosopher. He once said, "The whole of science is nothing more than a refinement of everyday thinking." Some find reassurance in these words, which indicate that great scientific works do not require extraordinary genius or special abilities. Obviously, everyday thinking in and of itself does not yield important scientific discoveries. Nonetheless, cognitive psychologists have identified some of the mental operations that scientists use in making discoveries. As we will see below, using these operations turns out to be relatively easy for most college students, who are no more likely than the rest of us to be geniuses.

Computational approaches to science attempt to capture the mental operations of scientists in systematic formulas that can manipulate existing knowledge to make scientific discoveries. Most noteworthy have been the computer programs devised by Allen Newell, Herbert Simon, and their colleagues.[6] These AI programs are fed systematic observations of phenomena, and they apply various heuristics and algorithms to uncover scientific laws. Examples of their computer programs include BACON, HUYGENS, and DALTON, acronyms that link programs with the scientists whose thinking processes they have modeled.

Although the computer programs designed to simulate scientific thinking are varied and intricate in detail, they share certain features. Taking systematic observations, such as might be produced by experiments, the programs select, manipulate, transform, and summarize the data using heuristics, or general rules. The heuristics vary in terms of their specificity; the rules intended specifically for one type of scientific problem or another are called "strong" rules of inference, whereas more general rules that apply to many types of problems are referred to as "weak" methods. These heuristics notice or identify certain regular patterns of data, such as those that recur, or those that fit into simple mathematical relationships.

For example, Kepler's third law of planetary motion states that $D^3/P^2 = c$, where D is the distance between the sun and a planet, P is the period (the time it takes for a planet to complete an orbit), and c is a constant. How could a computer discover this law? By knowing the distances and periods of the planets and applying the following heuristics to test out possible rules: (1) if the values of a term in an equation are constant, then assume that the term always has that value; (2) if the values of two terms increase together, then try dividing one term by the other; and (3) if the values of one term increase as those of another decrease, then try multiplying the two terms. If you observed the distances between planets (one term in the equation), and the time it takes for each planet to complete an orbit (the second term), then applying these simple heuristics could lead you to the same law that Kepler discovered.

These AI programs have had remarkable success in "discovering" scientific laws that are already known. That is, given the same observations that a scientist might have available, the computational systems can produce the same laws that great scientists have identified. Examples of the many successes, besides Kepler's laws of planetary motion, include discoveries of Galileo's laws of momentum, Boyle's law that relates pressure to volume, Ohm's law of electrical resistance, Black's laws of temperature equilibrium, Coulomb's law of electric attraction, Joule's law of energy conservation, Kreb's cycle, and even Archimedes's celebrated law of displacement.

Are these scientific discoveries only possible for computer programs and a few geniuses? Apparently not. Studies by Simon and his colleagues reveal that college students with no special training are often able to discover the same laws if they scrutinize the same experimental observations. The students often describe using thought processes that resemble the heuristics applied by the AI programs.

The scientific achievements of AI programs are, for the most part, within-paradigm discoveries, what we might call normal science. Using terms that we introduced earlier, such inquiry addresses well-structured problems operating within a stable problem space. That is, the programs take scientific laws that are already known, and use them in appropriate ways to answer other questions. Whether AI programs can suggest new scientific paradigms or unknown scientific laws remains to be seen.

Computational methods have not been used as extensively to simulate artistic processes as they have been for scientific reasoning, but computer programs are beginning to have some success in creating aesthetically pleasing pictures and musical compositions.[7] For example, graphics programs now exist that can determine sensible layouts of objects in landscapes, such as placing near and far forms into proper perspective, depicting human figures in natural and realistic postures, and placing lighter objects on top of heavier ones. These heuristics, and others, have helped computer programs produce sensible and pleasing visual effects. Music composition programs are now able to determine features that define styles of various composers, and write new compositions that sound as if they had been penned by the human composer. Other programs can create variations on themes or compose in particular styles, such as jazz or reggae, by using specific heuristics. As in the AI simulations of scientific reasoning, the operations used in these programs show us that some of the methods used by the best human experts can be understood and learned by others.

Noticing: The Prepared Mind

The "prepared mind" was a term used by Louis Pasteur to describe the idea that as a scientist, you need to know a good deal about your subject matter, and you must be prepared to recognize the significance of chance observations. That is, you need to have knowledge and an actively searching attention to the world.

There are many examples of chance events that triggered important scientific discoveries, all involving prepared minds.[8] Pasteur's method of vaccination was one such discovery. Angered at first when his laboratory assistants had gone on a holiday and let a cholera culture go sterile, he then pondered the result. Experimenting with injecting the dead cholera bacteria into animals, he discovered its effectiveness in preventing disease. Alexander Fleming conceived of using penicillin as an antibiotic when he noticed that the mold growing on an undiscarded petri dish had dissolved the staphylococci in the dish. Luigi Galvani, who had been experimenting independently with a machine that generated electricity, and with dissected frogs, noticed that the disembodied frog legs twitched when he used the nearby machine. Galvani realized the importance of the finding, which led to what we now call electrical current. Joseph Priestley's discovery of oxygen happened when by chance he stuck a lit candle from his worktable into a gas he had trapped during a chemistry experiment. Surprised that the flame burned brilliantly rather than going out as he had expected, Priestley recognized that he had discovered a new element. Kary Mullis's discovery of the PCR also required a mind that was knowledgeable and prepared enough to realize the implications of his chance idea for amplifying tiny amounts of DNA.

Noticing important relationships and events has also been an important ingredient for artistic creativity. For example, as a child, Max Ernst was fascinated by the patterns he saw in the grain of the wood on the floor of his bedroom. He would place paper on the wood and rub it with graphite to make a tracing that he would sometimes embellish with painting. This idea led Ernst and other Surrealist painters to try similar methods of working with natural patterns and "found objects," that is, ordinary objects that seem to possess a beauty of their own.

Leonardo da Vinci, a Renaissance artist, broke with the tradition of drawing divinely beautiful faces when he noticed the richness of character in the faces of anonymous commoners. He spent hours in the public squares sketching the faces of chance passersby, using the sketches later in his paintings.

Noticing the potential usefulness of other artists' techniques has led to many achievements and innovations in art, as in the cases of artistic insight noted earlier. The faces of the women in Picasso's "Les Demoiselles d'Avignon" were inspired by his visit to an African art exhibit. Calder's idea for mobiles was triggered by seeing Mondrian's abstract paintings. Jackson Pollock's development of pouring paint was inspired at a workshop he attended where he saw artists trying out unusual methods of applying paint, such as dripping or airbrushing.

The prepared mind has been vitally important in creative artistic and scientific discovery. Without an open sensitivity to our world, we will never notice the fascinating events and objects all around us, and without any knowledge, we will never realize the significant implications of our observations.

THE ROLE OF IMAGERY IN SCIENTIFIC DISCOVERY

Mental imagery has also played an important role in scientific creativity. Roger Shepard, a noted authority on imagery, has described many cases in which scientists discovered important principles by way of relatively simple, imagined structures and forms. Einstein, for instance, reportedly came to his basic insight about relativity by using mental imagery, such as picturing a person dropping an object while in free-fall, or imagining how the world would look to someone riding along a beam of light. Faraday developed the concept of "force fields" after imagining what lines of force might look like once they emanated from charged objects. Tesla claimed that he could tell how well a particular machine would work by letting the machine run in his imagination.

Imagery may foster important discoveries by allowing scientists to explore properties that emerge in their images. As noted above, Einstein could readily picture the consequences of moving near the speed of light by using his imagination to "see" what would happen. Faraday was able to determine the direction and concentration of lines of force that would describe the nature of electrical fields. Tesla, simply by picturing a new machine at work, was able to predict when it was likely to work or fail. Although discoveries that result from mental excursions are not always valid, they often provide fundamental insights that later result in more precisely formulated theories.

Imagery also encourages imaginative divergence, an important component of creative realism. One is more motivated and engaged in looking for new scientific possibilities when one can vividly imagine the consequences of a new idea. Mental images are often dynamic and compelling, engaging your creative involvement; they can be combined in creative ways, which invites combinational play, and they can bring many elements together at once, encouraging you to see complex interactions and relationships. For instance, the theory of relativity has many far-reaching implications that excite the imagination in a way that most theories in science fail to do. You can visualize the consequences of living in a world in which time is expanded or compressed. Or, you can contemplate the very real possibility of leaving Earth at high speed and then returning hundreds of years in the future. The creative possibilities are intriguing and therefore more likely to lead to further discoveries.

Another important aspect of creative realism is structural connectedness, the patterns and systems that make up the components of creative ideas. For example, Einstein's theory of relativity has structural connectedness because it is based on mathematics and physics, systems that have been shown very reliably to explain events in our world. Astrology, on the other hand, lacks structural connectedness because there is no clear way in which stars or planets could have the systematic influences on people claimed by astrologers. In many scientific discoveries, structural connectedness emerges following the creative insight, rather than being imposed initially on the creative process. That is, you often begin to see the important connections to previous ideas only after the insight has already occurred. It is in this later "postinsight" stage of creative thinking when expert knowledge can most effectively come into play, allowing you to recognize the meaningful connections and implications that already exist in nature.

DISCOVERIES USING PREINVENTIVE FORMS

Simulated Scientific "Discoveries"

Previously we described how playing with preinventive forms can spawn ideas for inventions and fictional creatures. This technique also holds promise for hatching original scientific concepts.

For example, in a laboratory experiment, students who were not science majors generated preinventive forms, such as the one shown in Figure 8.1. They were then given a scientific category, such as physics, biology, or medicine, and told to try to interpret their preinventive form as representing a new concept or theory

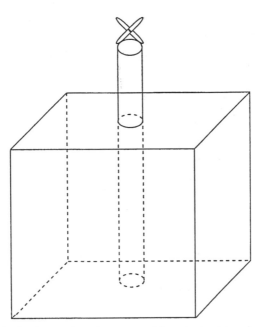

FIGURE 8.1. Preinventive form used by student to develop concept of "viral cancellation" (from Finke, 1990).

in that particular field. When given the category "medicine," one subject interpreted the form shown in Figure 8.1 as representing the concept of "viral cancellation." The idea inspired by this form is that two viruses attempting to invade the same cell might inhibit one another, thereby curing or preventing a disease.

Even though the subjects were not experts in these scientific fields, they were still able to probe their preinventive forms to discover interesting possibilities within those fields. The validity of these ideas is not at issue. They could be verified or refuted by marshalling existing facts or collecting new data. The inspirations of experimental subjects, in terms of the cognitive operations that led to them, were not different in essence from those reported by eminent scientists who had sudden flashes of insight while daydreaming or playing with mental images. The advantage that professional scientists have is that they possess the expert knowledge for recognizing the true significance of these emergent, imaginative possibilities, and for distinguishing the creatively useful from the merely fanciful.

Emergent Structures in Art

In art as well as science, there are many examples in which preinventive structures are first generated and then scrutinized to uncover their creative potential. Beethoven, as we have already noted, often became intrigued by melodies that suddenly came to him, and then varied them extensively to survey their creative possibilities. He later incorporated these melodies and variations into his major compositions, although this was not his explicit intention when he first conceived of the melodies.

For example, one day Beethoven was traveling home after a devastating love affair had just ended (a not uncommon occurrence for Beethoven). Wallowing in despair, he suddenly conceived of a wonderful melody that seemed to capture the very essence of his bleak mood, and frantically wrote it down. Later that evening, he developed the melody into the opening movement for the Apassionata piano sonata, which became one of his most famous compositions. Instead of starting out with a conscious decision to write this sonata and then developing an appropriate melody, Beethoven began with a "preinventive" melody, one that seemed to him intensely meaningful and full of potential, and then found a suitable way to cultivate it.

There are many other examples of musical compositions that arose as emergent structures, rather than as deliberate, planned creations. However, there are also many examples of great musical works that resulted from commissions to compose specific types of pieces. Creativity can work both ways; you can start with melodies and find creative outlets for them, or you can begin with an overall structure and then find the melodies that will fit.

There are also many examples of emergent structure in the visual arts. Impressionist painters, such as Seurat and Pissarro, were able to create powerful, emergent effects as a result of the way they combined and contrasted thousands of tiny points of color to create shapes of people or landscapes in Pointillist paintings. Visitors to art museums can readily discover the objects that emerge from the points of paint when they back away while viewing one of these masterpieces. Other artists who have used creative emergence include M. C. Escher, who systematically used perspective cues in novel ways to create unreal and fascinating impossibilities, and Dali, whose dreamlike paintings sometimes depicted figures (such as a bust of Voltaire) that emerged from combinations of other objects in the picture. Emergent structures can also be awakened by seemingly arbitrary processes, as in the sense of swirling movement in some of Pollock's famous "drip" paintings, or the subtle suggestions of objects in Ernst's wood grain tracings. In each case the total effect is greater than the sum of its component parts.

CREATIVE REALISM AND STRUCTURING IN SCIENCE AND ART

In addition to generating preinventive structures and exploring them in the search for emergent properties, professionals engaged in the arts and sciences share something else, namely, a concern for creative realism. Previously, we discussed the concept of creative realism and how it bears on the problem of guiding creativity in practical and realistic directions. Structural connectedness and imaginative divergence, two aspects of creative realism, apply to both science and art.

In science a successful theory must be connected to those ideas that have worked in the past. Even radically new theories are structured in meaningful ways by earlier, successful ideas. The theory of special relativity, though wildly original and imaginative, did not arise out of a vacuum. It was inspired in part by Maxwell's theory of electrodynamics. Similarly, most successful movements in art and music stem from or arise in reaction to forms and techniques used in previous styles. Most new forms of music retain at least some of the qualities of previous musical styles. Composers such as Beethoven and Tchaikovsky have incorporated folk themes into some of their major works. When science or art begins to dissociate itself from past accomplishments, it risks becoming arbitrary and inconsequential.

Besides structural connectedness, imaginative divergence is also needed for science and art to achieve creative realism. To be considered a creative success, a scientific theory must do more than simply provide some alternative account of a set of findings; it must also provide a meaningful, enlightening interpretation of those findings that inspires the imagination. The theory of relativity, the theory of evolution, and the quantum theory are all imaginatively divergent. The theory of evolution, for example, has had implications far beyond the original patterns explained by Darwin; it has given us an understanding of how bacteriological strains become resistant to antibiotics, it has made psychologists consider the evolution of behavior, and it has given sociologists ideas about how cultures thrive and disappear. In the arts imaginative divergence is also essential; the works that are best remembered are those that not only are interesting compositions, but also inspire the imagination. Picasso's "Les Demoiselles d'Avignon" was not just a fascinating painting; it also inspired others (such as Braque and Léger) to use Cubism and other methods to abstract and decompose shapes in paintings. The Celtic romance *Tristan und Isolde* was more than a marvellous play; it inspired countless other dramas of forbidden and tragic young love, such as Shakespeare's *Romeo and Juliet* and the modern musical *West Side Story*. To be successful, creative endeavors in science and art must strive for creative realism.

SUMMARY

In spite of the enormous differences between science and art, we have shown how the principles and methods of creative cognition can describe and explain diverse discoveries in both domains. In chemistry and physics, as in painting and musical composition, sudden insights can arise that shatter old paradigms and lay foundations for new perspectives. These insights have often occurred as a result of incubation, at times when people were away from their typical working contexts, and not directly trying to answer the problems eventually solved by their ideas. New insights have also been produced by analogical thinking and tinkering with combinations of concepts and preinventive forms.

Applying existing knowledge in novel and playful ways can foster the development of new ideas within an artistic movement or scientific paradigm. The fact that AI computer programs can imitate discoveries of scientific laws shows that fairly straightforward heuristics can be used to generate creative ideas. We have also shown that generating creative ideas or stumbling across important events is useful only to those with enough expertise and vision to realize the full implications of their discoveries. Although knowledge of your field is important, you do not have to be a superhuman genius to make contributions to art and science; you need only apply the principles of creative cognition.

NOTES

1. Kary Mullis, personal communication, September 27, 1994.
2. Brewster Ghiselin, *The Creative Process* (Berkeley: University of California Press, 1952).
3. Robert M. Hutchins, *Great Books of the Western World (II): Euclid, Archimedes, Apollonius of Perga, and Nicomachus* (Chicago: Encyclopaedia Britannica, 1952).
4. Robert W. Weisberg, "Case Studies in Creative Thinking: Reproduction versus Restructuring in the Real World," in *The Creative Cognition Approach*, eds. Steven M. Smith, Thomas B. Ward, & Ronald A. Finke (Cambridge, MA: MIT Press), pp. 53–72.
5. Albert Rothenberg, *The Emerging Goddess: The Creative Process in Art, Science, and Other Fields* (Chicago: University of Chicago Press, 1979).

6. Pat Langley, Herbert A. Simon, Gary L. Bradshaw, & Jan M. Zytkow, *Scientific Discovery: Computational Explorations of the Creative Processes* (Cambridge, MA: MIT Press, 1992).
7. Margaret M. Boden, *The Creative Mind: Myths and Mechanisms* (New York: Basic Books, 1991).
8. Mary Batten, *Discovery by Chance: Science and the Unexpected* (New York: Funk & Wagnalls, 1968).

JUST HAVING FUN

The principles of creative cognition clearly come into play when inventors, writers, artists, and scientists perform their creative magic. We can also put the same principles to work in everyday life, even if we hold other kinds of jobs, or labor at home to keep a household running smoothly. Many day-to-day situations clamor for imaginative solutions, and we can call basic cognitive processes to the rescue. Furthermore, we can engage the same procedures even when we simply want to derive more enjoyment or satisfaction out of life. Not all creative endeavors have to originate in a pressing problem, or culminate in a clever solution. One of our most splendid traits is our capacity to plunge into creative play, for its own sake. Creativity can be its own reward.

Here we explore some ways creative cognition can add the spice of variety to everyday activities of a more personal or recreational nature. These include playing sports and games, having fun with language, and conceiving ideas for useful personal objects. These activities need not be practical, productive, or economically profitable. But they nevertheless can help us to lead richer and fuller lives and to enrich the lives of those around us.

GAMES, SPORTS, AND AMUSEMENTS

In a scene from the popular comic strip *Calvin and Hobbes*, we find Calvin running away from Hobbes yelling "OLLY-WOLLY POLLIWOGGY UMP-BUMP FIZZ! Ha Ha! I stole your flag!" Bill Watterson is treating readers to yet another episode of "Calvinball," a wild and wacky game played out in his delightful comic strip world of *Calvin and Hobbes*. Hobbes, in hot pursuit, claims that he hit Calvin with the Calvinball, and that Calvin must return the flag and sing the "I'm Very Sorry" song. Calvin protests that he was in the "no song zone" at the time, but Hobbes counters that he had transformed it to a "song zone" by touching the "opposite pole" and declaring the change oppositely by not declaring it. After some additional tortuous twists, the strip ends with Calvin proclaiming that "the only permanent rule in Calvinball is that you can't play the same way twice," and Hobbes helpfully noting that "the score is still Q to 12."

This hilarious episode, and others in the same series draw attention to an interesting fact: for the most part, we do not play games like Calvinball. Virtually all of our games and sports, from Chutes and Ladders, to sandlot baseball, to professional soccer are structured by clear rules that change very little over time, and always stay the same within a single performance of the game.

Let's try to formulate ideas for a new sport using several creative cognition techniques. We can first abstract out some of the central properties most sports have in common: competitors, a contested object, and a fixed goal area. Some examples of typical sports and their properties are shown in Table 9.1.

TABLE 9.1. Common Sports and Their Properties

Sport	Competitors	Object	Goal
Football	Two teams of 11	One ball	End zone
Baseball	Two teams of 9	One ball	Home plate
Tennis	Two individuals	One ball	Court
Hockey	Two teams of 6	One puck	Net
Soccer	Two teams of 11	One ball	Net
Basketball	Two teams of 5	One ball	Hoop
Golf	Many individuals	Balls	Holes
Track	Several teams	?	Finish line
Bobsled	Several teams	?	Finish line
Skiing	Teams/individuals	?	Finish line
Gymnastics	Teams/individuals	?	Ratings
Swimming	Teams/individuals	?	Finish line

This abstract representation unmasks some of the implicit ideas lurking in the shadows of our "sports" concept. Note that sports such as football and tennis pit only two rivals against one another on the same playing surface at the same time, whereas golf and skiing might bring together several individuals or teams. Now notice that whenever more than two contenders vie with one another in the same match or event, they do not directly contest the possession of a single object. Nor do they openly interfere with a competitor's progress toward a goal. That type of combat is reserved for a pair of adversaries going head to head. Skiers, for instance, compete against many foes, but do not jostle one another or bump one another off the course; golfers do not try to catch an opponent's ball before it drops into the cup; and gymnasts do not shake the high bar to dislodge another athlete. In contrast, football players pummel each other senseless, but need only concern themselves with a single opposing team.

Now that we have made this implicit idea explicit, we can decide to reject it. What would happen if three or more teams clashed more directly? Envision a game resembling soccer, but with three contending teams battling over the same ball. How would the dynamics of the game change? Would opposing squads attempt to form alliances? Would they concoct strategies to set the other two teams against one another, leaving themselves a relatively unobstructed path to a goal? Perhaps an analogy from the alliances that countries form in fighting wars would provide some insights.

Note also that when opponents directly struggle for possession of something, it is always a single object, such as a ball, and generally one that has a highly predictable pattern of movement. What would happen if our triadic soccer game included two balls? What if one of the two balls moved erratically like the faddish children's balls that have battery-operated motors and are weighted so that they scurry wildly along the ground? Would scoring a goal with the unpredictable ball yield more points?

In traditional sports, the athletes can also rely on the end zones, nets, hoops, and finish lines to stay put. A recent commercial for a sports drink highlights this point humorously by depicting an aged superstar who tells his grandchildren that basketball was easy until they put in the moving baskets. How would our triadic, dual-ball soccer change if the nets roved around the field rather than remaining stationary?

But wait, there's more. Note that there are always the same number of competitors on each side in a typical sport. This seems fair enough, but we could nevertheless change it. Teams of size 11, 9, and 7 seems like a good place to start, but there is an infinite number of possibilities.

We have invented triadic, dual-ball, roving goal, variable squad soccer. And we have yet to consider the shape and size of the field, where the goals would be placed, how many there would be, whether all would move or only some, and so on. Like Calvinball, our fanciful sport is unlikely to catch on. It probably varies too many central properties at once, making it difficult for athletes to attempt it or fans to watch it. Nevertheless, this playful excursion is an example of how one can use abstraction to identify and modify the implicit assumptions in virtually any concept for the sheer joy of doing so.

We also may learn some things in the bargain, such as an appreciation of how sports are structured and the underlying reasons for that structure. Why do direct confrontations pit only two opponents against each other? Why do rival teams have the same number of members?

And once again, we reinforce the point that even wildly unusual ideas are grounded in some central aspects of existing knowledge. Our hybrid game does, after all, incorporate the concepts of teams, balls, goals, and a field. Perhaps you can envision a game that challenges even these key features.

Finally, consider yet another central assumption that we could challenge: that the rules never change within a single episode of a game. What if we had a game in which key rules were reversed sometime during the event, either at random or in response to some triggering condition? In most sports, for instance, the team with the highest score wins. What if it were possible, though not certain, that the rule could change to "low score wins"? What if it switched back and forth several times so that it was never clear which rule would be in effect at the end of the game? How might this affect a team's strategy? Would they seek a moderate score rather than a high or low one?

We can also use analogy and conceptual combination to devise new sports and games. Indeed Monopoly, one of the most popular board games of this century, originated as an analogy to the financial turbulence of the Great Depression. Charles Darrow, himself unemployed, incorporated the real and ever-present threat of sudden bankruptcy and ruin, along with the fantasy of easy cash, into a game that was to bring him an enormous real-world fortune. The more recent Acquire reflects the frenzy of corporate mergers and takeovers so evident today, and Risk embodies the concepts of world conquest and domination that were prevalent during the Cold War. A series of computer simulations, such as SimCity and SimLife, stem even more directly from real-world concerns. SimLife, for instance, allows people to use their imaginations to build entire ecosystems from scratch, specifying the conditions that exist on a planet and the plants and animals that inhabit it. People can learn about the interdependence of life forms and environments, and gain an appreciation of the fragile and delicate balance of life on Earth as we know it.

Can you envision other games that could be generated from analogies to contemporary situations? Perhaps something like "SimDeficit" would help people realize the complexities involved in developing a sensible federal budget. The simulation would have to be detailed enough to let people trace out the exact implications of cutting funds from various programs. It would force people to confront dead-on the issue of what services they want and what they are willing to pay for them. What sacrifices are people willing to make, for themselves or others, in exchange for lower taxes? All in all the game might help players to recognize some of the political rhetoric being thrown around these days as the grossly oversimplified smoke screen it really is. And who knows, maybe a dedicated player will devise some creative new way to bring about a balanced budget without causing anybody any pain. Wouldn't that be great?

Games also tend to borrow from previous ones, and their progress mirrors the slow incremental change that typifies other sorts of inventions. For instance, though it may be heresy to true believers, Abner Doubleday almost certainly did not invent baseball out of the clear blue. Baseball evolved from an earlier English game called "rounders," in the same sense that the cotton gin developed from the earlier charka. Baseball is an enormously popular sport, as demonstrated by the widespread gloom over the cancellation of the 1994 World Series and the continuing stalemate. So, we see again that even exceptional new ideas grow naturally from the fertile soil of earlier concepts.

How does conceptual combination contribute to new games and sports? One example of an emergent game is Frisbee Golf which clearly blends two existing activities. Consider some additional mergers of the sports listed in Table 9.1. What elements of each component sport would carry over into the combination? What new rules and strategies might emerge?

Contextual shifting, envisioning existing ideas in new situations, can also give rise to new games. For instance, what happens if we take a game played indoors and move it outside, or vice versa? Street hockey played on in-line skates, and indoor soccer are two recent examples of these types of shifts. Both of these offspring sports resemble their parents, but they also bear significant traits all their own. For instance, the more confined indoor environment works against the slow buildup to a perfect shot so characteristic of scoring in outdoor soccer. Instead, indoor soccer is played at a frenetic pace, and strategies revolve around quick strikes.

How might we change the context of other sports to produce fundamental changes in the nature of the game? What if soccer were to be played in a space station? One intriguing consequence would be that players could move in all three dimensions rather than being pinned by gravity to a two-dimensional playing surface. Perhaps the game could be played in the full area of a cube, 100 yards on a side. Maybe all of the walls would be glass so that spectators could view the contest from all six sides. The cube might easily rotate in zero gravity, giving fans an ever-changing perspective on the proceedings. Perhaps the goals would be anchored midway between the floor and the ceiling, or drift about freely. Mentally moving the familiar game of soccer to the exotic location of a space station begets a dizzying array of possible variations that can be considered just for the fun of it, or even with an eye to the future.

So far, we have emphasized how knowledge can be abstracted, modified, borrowed by analogy, combined, and dragged into a new setting to invent new games. But we can also try to sidestep existing knowledge entirely by using preinventive forms. For instance, using the methods described in previous chapters, you could generate a preinventive form, with no specific plan in mind, and then try to interpret it as a new type of toy or game.

Figure 9.1 depicts a game called "UFO Ring Toss" that one of the authors dreamed up using a preinventive form. The ring and the post both glow in the dark. The object of the game is to toss the ring so that it lands on the post, which creates the illusion of an alien spacecraft approaching a space station. One intriguing aspect of this game is that, in the dark, we cannot detect the cues that normally tell us how far away objects are. Thus, players would have to formulate new strategies for throwing accurately. The idea could be further developed by having multiple landing posts of various sizes, locations, and colors, as Figure 9.1 suggests.

FIGURE 9.1. "UFO Ring Toss," a game developed by Ronald Finke.

Preinventive forms could also be used to hatch games for more specific purposes, such as those that you could use with children, pets, or alone. You could also try to imagine toys and games that a blind or disabled person could use, again by exploring and interpreting your preinventive forms. Perhaps the posts in the UFO Ring Toss game could emit sounds so that blind players might participate.

Mental models can enhance many of the tactics we've described. For instance, part of the fun in imagining triadic soccer, or zero-gravity soccer comes from trying to envision exactly how the game would be played by constructing and running mental models. We can also use mental models as a way of discovering new forms of amusement. For example, one of the authors envisioned the following as a mental model for a new type of roller coaster, which allows for a virtually unlimited number of unique rides. The idea, as illustrated in Figure 9.2, is to have several branching points along the track, with the specific sequence of turns being randomly selected for each ride.

The intriguing feature of such a roller coaster is that every ride would be a true adventure—you would never know exactly how long the ride would last, or what the particular course of the ride would be. As a result, people would want to go on the ride repeatedly, since no two rides would be exactly the same. The only constraint would be a maximum time limit on the ride.

As another example of using mental models to explore creative amusements, suppose you had the power to create your own amusement park. Imagine how it might look. In particular, try to imagine the kinds of rides you would have, how the park would be laid out, and how it would be landscaped. Imagine how people might respond to any new themes that your park expresses. You could do this by taking a familiar park and changing it, or by imagining an entirely unique combination of rides and features. You might even envision games or rides without real-world constraints, and then contemplate how to actually implement some of them.

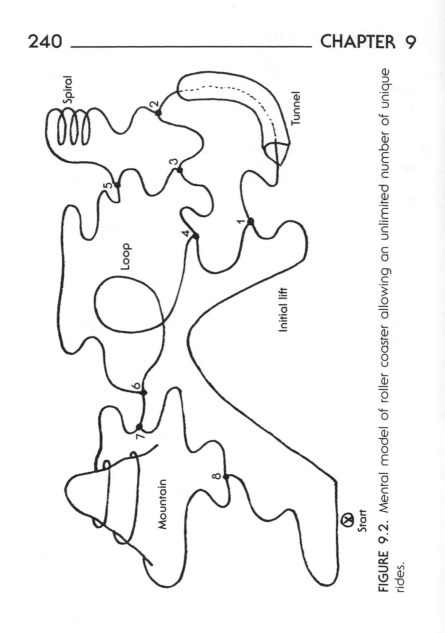

FIGURE 9.2. Mental model of roller coaster allowing an unlimited number of unique rides.

If you were a sports fan, you could imagine that you had suddenly become the manager of a major-league baseball team. How would you run the team? How would you assign players to the various positions, hold workouts, and establish club rules? You could even try to imagine how an actual game might unfold, to explore the consequences of your managerial decisions, and how you might have to change your policies. This is yet another example of how fantasies can often be explored by creating and testing out mental models.

HAVING MORE FUN WITH LANGUAGE

PORTMANTEAU AND THE SENSE IN NONSENSE

Charles Dodgson, writing under the pseudonym Lewis Carroll, delighted readers with nonsense poems, none more famous than Jabberwocky. Its sounds tickle our ears, and beckon us, like Sirens, to approach and unveil their meaning. Consider the resolute warning in the second verse.

> Beware the Jabberwock, my son!
> The jaws that bite, the claws that catch!
> Beware the Jubjub bird, and shun
> The frumious Bandersnatch!'

Here, as elsewhere in the poem, Carroll has engaged in serious word play to contrive new terms. In the preface to *The Hunting of the Snark*, he lays out the derivation of one of them:

> Take the two words 'fuming' and 'furious.' Make up your mind that you will say both words, but leave it undecided which you will say first. Now open your mouth and speak. If your thoughts incline ever so little towards 'fuming,' you will say 'fuming-furious;' if they turn, by even a hair's breadth, toward 'furious,' you will say 'furious-fuming;' but if you have that rarest of gifts, a perfectly balanced mind, you will say 'frumious'.[1]

With this derivation in mind, ponder the meaning of *frumious*. It might evoke an image of an angry beast, blasting hot breath from its mouth and nostrils. Or it might convey an emotionally intense vision of a different sort.

Carroll's preface confirms the charming "portmanteau" theory of word meanings put forth by Humpty Dumpty in *Through the Looking-Glass*: terms such as *frumious* pack two meanings into one word, much as we pack many items into the same suitcase or "portmanteau." Thus, Carroll playfully exploited a form of conceptual combination to compose fanciful nonsense.

Readers might also take a verbal romp through the meanings of combined words to concoct novel concepts of their own. Would *cheerful* and *curious* form *churfulious*? What would it mean? What are some other terms to merge? Would Janusian thinking, a melding of opposite concepts, foster more intriguing possibilities? Perhaps interested readers could even use these types of words to craft their own nonsense poems.

In a class exercise, one of the authors asked each student to write down an adjective. Two students, chosen at random, had written *melancholy* and *radiant*. They then used Carroll's "perfectly balanced mind" technique to compose *meladiantoly, meladianly, radiancholy, relodencholy, meladiant,* and *meradiancholy* as possible blends. They also crafted several definitions including (1) a condition of sadness so profound that the person projects (radiates) the sadness and infects those around him with the same condition, (2) a state of awareness and enjoyment of one's sadness, a kind of wallowing in or relishing of depression, and (3) a type of manic-depression in which the person's mood swings back and forth between deep sadness and immense joy.

The first definition amalgamates the terms completely into a new mixture that means something like "radiantly melancholy." The last one joins them together, yet preserves their separate integrity. But, either method of combining opens the door to a world of colorful new concepts. The concepts might be useful and provide penetrating insights into a problem, or they might simply amuse and entertain us.

Are there heuristics for hatching clever combined concepts? One is the *offspring* heuristic. Imagine that you are in the delivery room to witness the birth of the offspring conceived from the marriage of the two parent words. The outcome is likely to be a smooth blending of their traits. It may, by another analogy, resemble a "morphing" of two pictures, as when a computer programmer gradually transforms the pixels in each of two images to form a homogeneous composite. Alternatively, one could make use of the *add-on* heuristic, in which separate parts of each concept are appended to one another.

BUZZWORDS AND EXPRESSIONS: CALLING A SPADE A SHOVIT

The verbal playground is open to all who would enter it. Beyond the literary gems crafted by Lewis Carroll and other writers, we often hear clever expressions and buzzwords, developed by people from all walks of life. A marvelous example is *tourons,* which park rangers recently coined to describe tourists who act like morons. *Touron* may never appear in a poem, but the term undoubtedly gives some pleasure to park rangers, and relieves some of the stress of having to cope with the antics of inconsiderate vacationers. And we can dream up such buzzwords just for the fun of it.

One method for coming up with these types of novel expressions is to test out various conceptual combinations. Consider *touron,* an obvious blend of *tourist* and *moron.* Some synonyms for tourist are *traveler, vacationer, visitor,* and *sightseer.* Alternative disparaging terms for a thoughtless person are *cretin, dimwit, ignoramus, imbecile,* and *idiot.* We could convey similar sentiments with additional mergers such as *vacwit, visiot,* or *travoramus.* Readers can play with other possible combinations.

Perhaps your profession brings you face to face with other types of difficult people such as shoppers, accountants, or managers. In verbal self-defense, you might originate *shopecile, accountoramus,* or *managetin.* What about words for poor drivers, newscasters who can't pronounce foreign names, people with last year's sense of style, or people who call at dinnertime to sell you something?

Of course, the new terms need not be derogatory, though there is a perverse joy in crafting them. You might, for instance, combine _genius, master, virtuoso,_ or _prodigy_ with different groups of people who make your life easier. Would a superior sandwich maker be a _lunchuoso,_ or a clever mechanic an _engenuis_?

The main message here is that we need not always use the first term that springs to mind to express our thoughts. Through verbal play, we can suppress the commonplace, and embrace the unusual. Suppose, for instance, you simply wanted a colorful way of referring to everyday goods such as shampoo or beer. You might try another form of conceptual combination by envisioning how people in different professions might playfully refer to such products. An auto mechanic might refer to shampoo as "head grease," perhaps in saying, "I took a shower this morning and ran out of head grease." A neurologist might refer to drinking alcohol as "killing brain cells," and invite friends out for a drink by saying "Let's go kill some brain cells." By taking the perspective of those in other professions, and exploring the emergent features that might result, you can discover novel ways of expressing common objects or things. Of course it helps to have at least some sense of the interests and inclinations of people in those professions. On the other hand, this procedure might also allow you to confront your own stereotypes about members of a profession.

You can also use this method to develop unusual expressions for everyday events, such as going to the dentist or getting married. For instance, a farmer might refer to having a tooth pulled as "having your gums plowed." A zookeeper might refer to marriage as "sharing a cage."

THE PAINFUL JOY OF EXTENDED PUNS

When is a car not a car? When it turns into a driveway. This familiar pun exploits the fact that language is inherently ambiguous. If "turn into" had only one meaning there would be no pun.

It doesn't work as well to answer "when it pulls into the garage," as one delightful four-year-old did recently. Nor is it as effective to ask "When is water not water?" and answer "When it turns into ice."

The ambiguity of language sets the stage for it to sometimes frustrate and sometimes amuse us. When we accidentally miscommunicate about something important, we legitimately become upset. When someone deliberately plays with the alternate meanings of an expression, they can make us laugh, or at least groan. Creatively toying with the ambiguity of language can provide endless hours of amusement.

Robert Rhodes, a former newspaper editor, dedicated punster, and all-around great guy, has perfected an extended version of punning. He takes a common expression and crafts a long, tortuous tale to bring us face to face with a deliciously twisted variant on the well-known phrase. Bob has graciously agreed to let us include one of his efforts, and we quote it here verbatim, for to paraphrase it would be comparable to painting a mustache on the Mona Lisa of puns:

> A little known fact about the great jazz trumpeter of the '20s and '30s, Bix Beiderbecke, is that he was not only proficient in jazz but was extremely interested in, and competent in, the classical field. In fact, a record company producer of the time had Bix make a recording of one of Bach's Brandenberg concertos and was astounded with the quick and eager reception it was accorded in the marketplace. The record sold like beer at a bowlers' picnic.
>
> Naturally, the producer was interested in an encore. This time he had Bix give his special treatment to a Handel opus. Same response. Fantastic.
>
> They tried again. This time with a Beethoven sonata. Strangely, however, this never caught on with the public. So they gave Beiderbecke a Brahms rhapsody, and this, too, fell flatter than the disc it was on.
>
> The promoter couldn't understand it. He tried the Beiderbecke treatment again on a Bach fugue, and the

record soon hit number one on the charts. Sold over a million copies. Encouraged, the promoter had Bix go back to Beethoven and coupled it this time with a Chopin waltz. Nothing. The people just didn't buy it.

Another Handel record—big sale. Another Bach—big sale. But anytime Beiderbecke put his horn to any of the romantic composers, he bombed. This led the promoter to the inevitable conclusion. And he came up with the truism that is good, even today: If it ain't baroque, don't Bix it. Ugh.

You can imagine other variants on this same theme. Consider the persnickety musician who would only play pieces by Bach and Handel. One day he arrived late for a concert only to discover that he had left his music behind. In desperation, he called his agent who happened to have a fax machine available and asked him to quickly send some scores. The agent had the works of many composers to choose from, but knowing this particular musician's proclivities, the agent was able to follow a simple rule. "If it ain't baroque, don't fax it."

You can try these extended puns with any common expressions or book titles. Part of the fun comes in distorting the phrase, and part in walking listeners down the path to that inevitable conclusion. Generally, the longer and more elaborate the tale, the more fun it is to concoct, and the louder the audience will groan.

MAKING CONVERSATIONS METAPHORICAL

Metaphors can also be employed creatively to make conversations more interesting, meaningful, and open to new explorations. Instead of taking a direct, literal approach to conversations, it may be more entertaining and fruitful to express ideas in terms of metaphors or indirect associations.

For example, instead of saying, "I hate my job. I answer to other people, and can't make my own decisions, but I also can't leave it right now," you might simply say "My job is a jail." More elaborately, instead of saying "I'm depressed. My arms are flabby, my hair is falling out, and people are avoiding me," you might say, "I feel like that old tree over there. Its branches are sagging, its leaves are falling off, and even the birds are starting to avoid it." These types of metaphoric statements invite others to explore their symbolism with you. You might even discover how you really feel about things by searching for a metaphoric way to express your thoughts.

You could also take what others say and try to interpret their statements as metaphors, as a way of exploring alternative meanings and implications. For instance, suppose someone said, "I really like going to the mountains." Instead of simply agreeing with the person or talking about what you like to do, you could explore whether the person enjoys taking on the challenges that nature offers, is involved in environmental issues, dislikes urban life, is fascinated by wild animals, or simply enjoys spending some time alone—all of which might be connected to the person's interest in going to the mountains.

UTILIZING THE NATURAL FLOW OF CONVERSATIONS

In taking this approach, you would try to treat your conversations as if they were preinventive forms. The idea is to pick up on the interesting features of the conversation and then explore their implications, instead of trying to impose a particular plan for how you would want the conversation to go. Often, people will try to plan in advance exactly what they want to say to someone, and then commit themselves to executing that plan, regardless of the context or how the person is reacting. This is another example of how prior knowledge and expectations often impair creative exploration and discovery.

In many types of conversations, it might therefore be better not to stick to specific plans for saying what you intended to say, but to utilize those emergent aspects of the conversation that seem interesting and potentially meaningful. This would allow the conversation to develop in a more natural and spontaneous way, which would allow you to make new discoveries within the conversation. In addition, it would help you to seem more interesting to the other person, as someone who is willing to explore other perspectives and share new insights.

A POTPOURRI OF PERSONAL PRODUCTS

Consider some of the minor irritants that afflict your daily life. Or, more positively, try to reflect on what might make your life easier.

Sometimes people have difficulty dredging these ideas up; often they pop up only when we find ourselves in the problem situation, cleaning newspaper ink off our hands yet again, or holding the sole remaining member of what used to be a pair of socks. We find ourselves chanting a familiar mantra, "They can put a man on the moon, why can't they make . . .."

But, when this situation crops up again, stop and ponder the following: If you have the problem, many other people are plagued by it too. Let's call this the *"im"personal problem heuristic*, because paying attention to a personal problem can lead to ideas for products that many people might want to buy.

King C. Gillette and Levi Hutchins, for instance, each had an obsession: Gillette's was to invent something that was disposable, and Hutchins's was to wake up at four o'clock each morning. While shaving one day in 1895, Gillette noted that his razor was dull and would need professional sharpening, and this event triggered his vision for the disposable razor. Hutchins occasionally overslept, especially in the long New Hampshire winters that provided no sunny stimulant. Being a clockmaker, Hutchins was always surrounded by clocks. But one day he noticed them in a different way, and realized that it would be easy to rig the mechanism of a timepiece to set a bell in motion at a prescribed hour. Gillette patented his safety razor and became rich; Hutchins never patented his alarm clock, but always arose on time until his death at age 94. Apparently, being early to bed and early to rise, made Hutchins not wealthy, just healthy and wise.

Many readers will wake tomorrow to an alarm clock, and shave with a disposable razor. Indeed, these tools are so embedded in our daily routines, we generally do not even take the time to contemplate their existence.

Other examples also illustrate the potential in recognizing common need. One company, for instance, makes a profit selling small plastic disks designed to unite a pair of socks and prevent them from divorcing one another in the dryer. In addition, a woman recently made a tidy fortune by marketing the "topsy tail," a device for making ponytails that turn in on themselves. She searched for an easy way to form the right kind of tail, borrowed from her knowledge about knitting needles to concoct a deceptively simple hoop on a stick, and sold it to hordes of eager followers.

We now humbly offer two concepts instigated by the impersonal problem heuristic, and augmented through the techniques of creative cognition. We apologize if someone else has already patented these products outside of our awareness. We also hope that if they are truly novel, and someone strikes it rich by selling them, we will receive a small reward for our generosity.

Two of the authors sport beards, and one of the two occasionally trims his. The natural locale for performing this odious task is the bathroom sink. So how does one prune an unruly beard with an electric clipper without coating the sink with tiny hairs and instigating marital discord?

The author has adopted several make-do solutions, such as draping a towel over the sink, or tearing a paper or plastic shopping bag to cover the area. None are especially satisfactory. The towel needs to be shaken out, the paper bag refuses to tear evenly, and the plastic one carries so much static electricity that the hairs refuse to descend to the bottom of the bag.

Assuming he could not be the only person with the problem, the author hatched an idea for "the hairbag." This is a simple paper product shaped to fit conventional bathroom sinks and extend slightly over the edge. The most basic model would simply be used for dry shaving and would be discarded before any water would be run.

Envisioning a mental model of how a person would actually use the hairbag, raises the possibility that someone might want to combine a dry cut using clippers with a more detailed trim using water, shaving cream, and a razor. Thus, a more sophisticated version would borrow an analogy from coffee filters and be porous enough to let water run through, but sturdy enough not to disintegrate. Yet another version would borrow from the sticky substances football receivers spray on their hands to facilitate catching passes. A shaver would spray the substance on the hairbag to firmly trap the hairs against it.

Consider the origins of our second contraption, a contact lens remover. Jalapeno peppers can really ignite your taste buds, so just imagine what they would feel like on your eyes. One of the authors found out exactly how it feels when he removed his contact lenses after eating jalapeno slices with his fingers (don't try this!). From the throes of ocular agony, however, arose an idea; a contact lens remover and applicator that keeps your fingers from directly touching your eyes! Not only could individuals have them at home, but restaurants could offer little sterile packets of disposable applicators after spicy meals, and oculists could use them on all of their customers. Here is an idea that was evoked by an urgent necessity that resulted from an unusual combination of events, eating peppers and removing contacts. Interestingly, as noted in a previous chapter, just such a device was also suggested by a student who was playing with interpretations of a preinventive form in an experiment. Innovative ideas can arise from many different origins; there is no one set path that we must trek to reach a creative goal.

In keeping with the theme of this chapter, the concepts for these personal items might be silly or salable. Most importantly, however, they show how heuristics, mental models, and analogy can beget fresh ideas.

SUMMARY

Previous chapters focused on the practical side of creative cognition. Here we have considered its lighter side. Our view is that creative play, for its own sake, is valuable. It is clear that we can abstract central properties, borrow analogies, merge concepts, change contexts, and exploit preinventive forms to cultivate new ideas for sports, games, expressions, and personal products. Moreover, even if we never actually develop these ideas into realities, merely thinking about the creative possibilities can often be entertaining, rewarding, and enlightening.

Playing with creative cognition may seem frivolous to some, but consider some analogies. When kittens play with yarn, or roughhouse with each other, they are really honing hunting skills they may need as adults. When children dress up, and play other games of imagination, they are practicing to take their place in society. Likewise, even if creative play is not valuable in itself, it surely has value in helping us to cultivate the skills needed to be creative in more practical endeavors.

NOTE

1. Lewis Carroll, *The Hunting of the Snark* (New York: Mayflower Books, 1980), pp. x–xi.

LOOKING BACK AND LOOKING FORWARD

LOOKING BACK

Those first creative ancestors who picked up sharp rocks and contemplated their usefulness also might have pondered that soft round light that appeared periodically in the night sky. They certainly would not have realized that the source of the light was the sun's rays reflecting off the celestial satellite that we call the moon. Nor could they ever have anticipated that children of today would handle rocks that a much later band of human pioneers brought back from that fair orb.

But from our vantage point, we can look back and see in their efforts the first glimmerings of human creativity. The first steps along that path that diverged so radically from the ones taken by any other species on our planet. No, they did not anticipate where their stone tools might lead. Perhaps they didn't even think as far ahead as the next stone. But they did

253

pass on a natural curiosity and inventiveness that has been expanded and refined over countless generations.

That inventiveness is reflected in all we do, not the least of which is the way we use our language. Nobody knows for certain just when human language, as we know it, began. What we do know, however, is that our language is one of the hallmarks of our creativity. From the bedrock of a modest collection of words and a handful of grammatical rules, we can form and comprehend a nearly infinite variety of sentences that express our thoughts. If we don't like the taste of chicken, for instance, we can say "I don't like chicken," "The taste of chicken doesn't appeal to me," or in Deana Ward's case, "Chicken is stupid!"

Even as young children, we construct novel statements unlike any we have heard before. To be sure, we sometimes get hung up and keep repeating the same small set of words and phrases. As our kind editor pointed out, the first draft of this book would have been considerably shorter if we eliminated all instances of just two words: *new* and *exciting*. But our potential to produce and understand an enormously flexible and infinitely variable set of verbal constructions is truly staggering. Language is a creative phenomenon; we almost always produce something new with it. And it is also at the core of being human, a reflection of how our minds work; all humans learn language. Human cognition, then, at its core, in essence—in its very nature—is creative.

Our creative minds have moved us, in tiny steps and giant strides, to a world of startling diversity, replete with exquisite works of literature, art, and music, astonishing scientific discoveries, amazing labor-saving inventions, and marvelous medical advances. At the same time, it is quite clear that we do not always make the best possible use of that exquisite tool atop our shoulders. Many of our most challenging problems still lie ahead, and even our creative ideas can sometimes be improved. A second part of our message, then, is that we can do even better than we have so far by grasping the mental operations that lead to creativity, and utilizing them to their fullest potential.

We did not write this book to be a self-help manual. Yet creative cognition has much to offer anyone who wants to tap into and mine their creative powers. By identifying the aspects of thought that inhibit and enhance innovative thinking, we can highlight the mental skills a person ought to cultivate to become an expert in creativity.

THE COGNITIVE SKILLS OF THE CREATIVE EXPERT

George Santayana observed that those who cannot remember the past are condemned to repeat it. When we apply this gem of wisdom to creativity, we see that learning from past mistakes can help us to steer clear of similar foibles in the future. What can we learn from running boards on early train cars, hordes of uninspiring science fiction creatures, 80-column computer displays, and the business troubles of Schwinn? As we have shown, they are all woven on the loom of excessive reliance on prior knowledge.

There is no doubt, however, that past knowledge is essential to future advances. Clearly the awe-inspiring progress we have made from stone knives to food processors, from contemplating the heavens to launching probes to investigate them is a tribute to our remarkable capacity to remember and apply our past experiences.

As we journey down the path to creative expertise, a key element is learning to use abstraction to differentiate between the parts of the past we want to retain and the parts we ought to shun. We can use abstraction to help lay bare the essence of a problem, and to identify the necessary features of a solution. Abstraction prods science fiction writers to dream up more intriguing extraterrestrials, engineers to design more innovative complex systems, inventors to analyze and extend existing tools, executives to reengineer their corporations more productively, and people from every walk of life to solve everyday problems more effectively and to have more fun.

To develop creative expertise we must also employ a set of techniques for sparking new ideas. Where do novel thoughts come from? Sometimes they spring forth when we combine earlier concepts. As with the magical transformation that takes place when a sperm cell penetrates a mature egg, merged concepts give birth to new thoughts. And like their physical analogues, these mental offspring necessarily resemble their cognitive parents in some respects, but they also take on a life of their own.

We have shown how conceptual combination has brought us claw hammers and Combos, breathtaking fantasy tales and cars that dreams are made of, the art of Calder, the music of Mozart, and the scientific advances of Einstein. It is, without doubt, a powerful source of creative energy that can be applied to an unlimited range of problems.

Analogies also give rise to new possibilities. They have brought us working models of the atom as a solar system and the mind as a computer. They also prompted the Reebok Pump, Velcro, a working electric distribution system, and wheeled science fiction creatures.

It is also important to remember that when you are stumped, getting up and moving away from the situation, or even just immersing yourself in something else can help. By booting out from your conscious mind the old information that's been holding you back, you can make room for new ideas, and open yourself to notice potentially helpful clues. As we have seen, incubation has inspired many stunning insights such as the concept of specific gravity by the bathing Archimedes, the structure of benzene by the dozing Kekulé, the polymerase chain reaction by a driving Kary Mullis, exquisite symphonies by a grieving Beethoven, and the printing press screw by the wine-festing Gutenberg.

Incubation should be part of the bag of tricks any creative expert carries around. But there is an important proviso. Great insights usually occur only after people spend considerable time diligently working on their problems. In fact, in addition to any creative mental operations they might have in common, brilliant innovators share an overwhelming knowledge of their subject areas. Kekulé, for instance, would not have realized the significance of his self-consuming snake if he had not already worked extensively on the nature of benzene. Archimedes would not have noted the importance of his spilling bath water had he not prepared his mind with prior conscious thought. Similarly, it is unlikely that you will have any great insights if you simply nap or bathe regularly. Like a plowed field, a prepared mind is ready to let seeds take root and grow to fruition.

Building mental models and testing them by envisioning how they might work over time are also tools of the trade for the creative expert. The Wright brothers' flying machine, Einstein's theory of relativity, and the contemporary scientific view of the place of the Earth in the universe all sprang from these mental operations. These are sophisticated strategies that may be essential to innovation in complex systems. In addition, they are crucial for contemplating not just how a new device might work, but also how an audience of consumers might respond.

One final technique to keep in mind is the generation and exploration of preinventive mental images. What makes this procedure unique is that you essentially start with an answer and then see what question it can help you with. Instead of beginnning with a problem, you can playfully manipulate mental images with no particular goal in mind. Solutions to problems you might not even have considered may then present themselves to you as you probe the significance of those images. Future creative experts may begin to realize the value of this technique in a variety of practical situations.

We all need to be creative sometimes, and we all have the potential to do so. Whether you are an artist, a scientist, an inventor, or a homemaker, these techniques will help you assess and extend your own creative resources.

LOOKING AHEAD DOWN THE INFORMATION SUPERHIGHWAY

Consider the way we express our ideas. More than 100,000 years ago, humans engraved on bone, and more than 25,000 years ago we engraved and painted on stone. The earliest true writing systems—cuneiform, hieroglyphics, and ideograms—all date from about 3000 B.C., and over the succeeding 2000 to 3000 years, a series of alphabets were developed. We have recorded our thoughts on stone, papyrus, parchment, and then paper. Books were printed as long ago as 868 in China, and the Gutenberg printing press was developed in the mid-15th century. Today, of course, we have desktop publishing, and we may one day no longer have books in paper form at all, but only in some magnetic medium. Indeed, it's difficult to envision having taken this book through its various metamorphoses without the aid of sophisticated computer hardware and software. It is even more startling to consider that if we were to write this book five years from now in electronic form, it might be a completely different work, full of animation, full-speed video, and sound.

Few recent developments have been the subject of more hype than the so-called information superhighway. Exactly what this expressway to the future is, where it's going, and how quickly remain to be seen. The road sign might read, "Construction Ahead, Next 10 Years. Be Prepared to Stop—and Scratch Head." There is no doubt, however, that the times are changing. We are well into the information age, in which knowledge is power.

To get just a small hint of uses of the internet, consider the following. While writing this book, we also organized a major conference on creative thinking. Eighteen of the world's most prominent cognitive psychologists were preparing to descend on quiet little College Station, Texas. They would come from several cities in the United States, as well as Canada, England, Germany, and Italy. The logistics of coordinating such an event could have been a nightmare. We had our share of headaches along the way, but they were like a breeze to a hurricane compared to what they would have been without the modern Infobahn.

When it came time to ask our prospective visitors about their talk titles, travel preferences, and other assorted details, we simply wrote a message, stored it as a computer file, then sent it with a few keystrokes to everyone concerned via a distribution list that contained all of their e-mail addresses. Within seconds, our messages arrived to each participant, and we often had their replies back the same day. No printing of individual letters. No waiting for a week, or several in the case of our European colleagues, for letters and replies to travel by surface mail. No need for 18 separate phone calls just to get a single piece of information from each presenter.

What is more startling is that what we did is not particularly new or sophisticated. Anyone with a computer, modem, and phone line can travel virtually anywhere in the world in seconds without leaving the comforts of home. Through services such as America Online and Compuserve, you can instantaneously send a note to a friend in London, check out the weather in Paris, see how the dollar is doing against the yen, study recent earthquake activity in California, consult stock quotations from New York, Frankfurt, or Tokyo, or keep up with a dizzying array of newsgroups on every imaginable topic. And if you decide that you really want to visit some of those other places, you can look at schedules and fares, and book your own reservations.

As we cruise on down the information superhighway it may be useful to ask ourselves if we're going the right way. Are we traveling in the best possible vehicle, specially designed for the new world, or are we stuck in a Model T, or worse yet, a modified stagecoach complete with running board? As we begin to exploit this new information technology, is there anything we can learn from mistakes we've made in other major transitions? Can we avoid carrying over ideas from the past that will have little relevance in the new situation, or worse yet, interfere with progress? Must we repeat sequences like carrying 80-column limits over from punch cards through magnetic tape to personal computers?

Creative cognition can provide a candle to guide our search. By formulating an abstract analysis of the problem we can determine where we want to go and what we have to do to get there. What exactly do we want to do with our new technologies? With our ability to transform virtually any sight or sound into digital form and send it anywhere a wire, fiber-optic cable, or microwave signal can travel? With our electronic marvels smaller than a breadbox that can execute so many steps so quickly that they can calculate a complex business projection in the blink of an eye or flash up a photographic-quality image in a heartbeat? With modern-day micro-Towers of Babel that will translate among languages? With scanners that can pass over a page of text and read it aloud to a blind person or store it in an ever-growing electronic library? With multimedia programs that can integrate all of these marvels?

In the broadest sense, we want to make it easier to generate and transmit information, but the goals may be slightly different for different applications. Scientists may be more concerned with developing new knowledge, and educators with imparting it to young minds. Corporations may be more concerned that the right people receive the right information at the right time, whether or not they remember it when a given project is finished.

Many readers have probably used an electronic encyclopedia, but just consider a scenario from the not-too-distant future: You want to find out a little something about John F. Kennedy. You turn on your home computer and, through a modem, activate a connection to your favorite online communication service. Next, you travel in an ethereal world to a library of multimedia encyclopedias. You type in the name "Kennedy," and after a series of choices, a whole world of sight and sound opens up to you. You can read text, hear narration, and view photographs. You can even click on a video clip selection and see JFK giving his famous inaugural speech. "And so my fellow Americans, ask not what your country can do for you. Ask what you can do for your country." Another clip shows you the tragic scenes of Kennedy's funeral procession. There's Jackie, in the icy November air, standing as the ultimate symbol of dignity and grace under unbearable adversity. Surely a child would gain a better appreciation of history from this type of learning tool than from a standard printed encyclopedia. School systems are just now beginning to put these types of technological advances to work to help children from kindergarten through high school learn about history, math, and science.

If we can dramatically change the way children learn, then surely we can change the way scientists communicate with one another. Over the last 100 years and more, the dominant mode of scientific commerce has been the bound paper journal. The single base unit of currency has been the scientific article. Articles generally report background literature, findings, and a discussion of their significance for the field. Often these works are accompanied by figures depicting especially important aspects of the data.

Currently, many fields are flirting with or rushing headlong into electronic journal publishing. But it's interesting to examine what many people mean by this form of publishing. Much of the debate about the future of electronic journals centers around doing the same things we do in paper journals, only perhaps a little faster or cheaper. With some rare exceptions, most people who have talked about it have implicitly assumed that the goal of electronic publishing is to find a way to bring the standard scientific article, complete with all its unnecessary paper baggage, to readers in this brave new medium. Most seem less inclined to consider what new possibilities these advanced technologies can provide.

For instance, some people argue that a drawback to electronic publishing is that different mainframes and personal computer systems have different conventions for displaying graphical information. While standardization certainly is a problem we need to confront, a bigger problem is that worrying about the best ways to display a static graph on a computer narrows our thinking. It makes us focus on how we can do the same old things a new way, and it diverts us from thinking about what new things we can do with our new technology to improve the way we share scientific information. It's a bit like worrying about where we're going to store the plowhorse's oat bag on a motorized tractor. Why should we concern ourselves with displaying the same old graphs in a new medium? Why not consider the dazzling possibilities available to us and utilized in multimedia encyclopedias to completely transform scientific publishing?

Imagine you have just conducted an experiment on techniques for improving memory performance, and you want to tell your colleagues about it. Certainly you will write a paper, and you might even include some graphs of the data. But, why not have some special features in your electronic report? For instance, if you ran the experiment on a computer, you could include the program you used to present the materials and collect your subjects' responses. That way anyone "reading" your paper can automatically access the same program, load it onto her computer, and run the exact same experiment in her laboratory. Since one of the goals of science is consensus through replication, this simple new addition advances an important goal in a new way.

But let's not stop there. You can include all of the data in an electronic appendix. Other researchers could then load your data into their own statistical packages, test any ideas you didn't consider, and convert their analyses to graphs they are interested in seeing. Maybe you could videotape subjects as they participate, and with their permission of course include clips that interested readers could pull up and examine. Perhaps there ought to be a special icon a reader could click that would automatically generate your e-mail address so he could forward you a question, suggestion, or related paper. We have a completely new technology available. It's up to us to see what we can do new with it rather than simply transferring the same old things from one medium to another.

Again, we guide our search for new applications by way of abstraction. What are our most fundamental goals? Communicating findings? Testing theories? Advancing the field?

Multimedia technology also has the potential to transform college education. Several universities are experimenting with electronic courses. A professor records his lectures on videotape and they can be electronically stored as video clips complete with any relevant photographs, animated sequences, and sounds. Students can access these on their own computers whenever they find it convenient, even if it's 3:30 in the morning. If they have questions, they can e-mail the professor, who in turn can send an electronic reply which may or may not include another video clip. Best of all, the clips, questions, and replies are all stored so that future students can see if others have had the same questions, and how they've been answered.

Is this the future of education? Perhaps. On the other hand, we want to make sure that the e-mail course does not become the New Coke of the nineties. We want to make sure that we don't give up anything critical to college education by charging down this path blindfolded. For instance, most courses now occur in classrooms. With many students sharing the same space at the same time, social interactions are possible. Are these gatherings in any way important to the educational experience? If we eliminate these face-to-face social interactions, might we change the essence of education? We are, after all, social beings.

Will other types of interactions arise to take the place of the classroom experience? Electronic courses certainly can set the stage for a broad range of interchanges. In electronic writing courses, for example, students might comment on each other's work via e-mail, and offer suggestions and criticism that the professor might not even see or think of.

So with fast enough hardware and sophisticated software, an electronic community might form, but it is not yet clear whether something crucial might be dropped from the mix. As an object lesson, however, many businesses have been way ahead of academia in their use of teleconferencing. The initial idea was that a company might save on its travel budget if employees met via teleconferencing rather than traveling thousands of miles to work together. And clearly, teleconferencing has some benefits. But corporations still spend as much on travel.[1] Why? Because they've discovered that the kinds of subtle and extended interactions that occur when people are physically in the same place are crucial to effective communication. The chat over a sandwich. The banter over a beer. An idea that springs to mind while strolling the street or riding an elevator with a colleague. Perhaps some future version of a virtual world in which collaborators across the continent can spend the whole day in the same environment will replace good old-fashioned human contact. But until that time, moving people from one location to another still has its benefits.

Corporations are discovering anew that technological advances are not just for doing the same things faster, more efficiently, or more cheaply. They are for doing new things. So now, corporations use teleconferencing as a complement to other ways of working long distance. People from different locations who work on the same project still travel to visit one another just as much. But they supplement those visits with periodic teleconferences. At least two benefits emerge. First, colleagues can hash out any issues that were left unresolved in a face-to-face meeting without having to make a new trip, and they can quickly deal with any new problems that have arisen. Second, more people at more levels in the process can be directly involved in the collaboration. For instance, higher-level executives can sit in on the teleconference and remain close to the project without taking valuable time away from their home base.

But now let's take one more step. Teleconferencing and related technologies are designed to move "us" from one place to another electronically. But why limit ourselves to sending our boring old selves? We can do that with cars, airplanes, and other old technologies. If we're going to send out electronic emissaries, why not transmit digitally enhanced ambassadors that represent not just who we are, but who we might want to be? Why not send a virtual Tom Cruise to do your bidding? He could say your words in your voice but sway people more effectively with his good looks and other assets.

If you want to leave a message of apology to your loved one you might send a video clip. But rather than just a plain shot of your face, perhaps you could run yourself through a graphics program first. Adding an electronically produced clown suit might allow you to say, "I'm sorry I was such a clown" in such an engaging way that you can break through the anger barrier and move on to real communication.

Perhaps you could morph images of yourself with celebrities or your personal heroes. Maybe you could use this for self-analysis, self-promotion, or even (hopefully harmless) self-delusion. By finding the middle ground between you and your idol you might be able to see new things about yourself, and see aspects of that person in you. Wouldn't it be nice to discover the Julia Roberts in you? Or the John Wayne? Or the John Kennedy?

POLITICS

In the perpetual quest to win the hearts, minds, and votes of their constituents, politicians often seek to redefine or reinvent themselves. In the 1980s, after vicious attacks by the far right on the patriotism of liberals, and equally ignoble charges by the left of racism and heartlessness on the right, some politicians scurried for the cover of the middle ground. They tried to walk a fine line between "a government of bleeding hearts, on the one hand, and of no heart, on the other." Thus, political animals of many stripes rushed to transmogrify themselves into curious creatures called social-liberal-but-fiscal-conservatives. This is an interesting political version of merging, at least in image, two opposing tendencies. What should the resulting critter be called? A libervative? A conserveral?

What features of the libervative might clash with one another? Professing a concern for the less fortunate members of society, but being unwilling to spend large sums of money to help them? Striving to preserve ecologically sensitive areas, protect endangered species, ensure clean air and water, and expunge toxic waste, as long as these actions do not inhibit business development?

Whether true libervatives ever really existed, and if so, whether any survived the purge of the 1994 elections is not critical. What's important is that the combined concept itself sets up conflicting tendencies. On a more serious note, from opposing forces, constructive ideas for change might emerge. How can we provide a safety net that ensures adequate food, clothing, shelter, and medical care to all who need it but that doesn't ensnare the people it's designed to help, and that doesn't bust the budget? How can we protect the land, water, and air and discourage the exploitation of workers by businesses without crushing economic growth? How can we curb violence and still protect the rights of hunters, the accused, the victim, and so on? How do we acknowledge the atrocities committed by one set of grandparents on another without driving the grandchildren to perpetuate the cycle.

We don't pretend to have the answers to these pressing concerns. We do claim, however, that by applying the same types of mental operations that inspire creativity in invention, business, literature, science, and the arts, we will move closer to creative solutions.

It is easy to see how, with laboratory-based problems, or even with the real-world problems we've examined, the right representation can lead to an effective solution. For example, consider a simple experimental problem in which there are two trains 50 miles apart. They begin to approach one another each traveling at 25 miles per hour. At the same moment a bird springs into the air at the front of one train and flies at 100 miles per hour to the second train, then back to the first and so on. How far will the bird have flown when the trains meet?

If you have gotten out your calculator to try to determine how far the bird went on the first trip and how much distance is left for the second trip, and so on, you have not structured the problem correctly. But if you restructure it by thinking that it will take the trains one hour to meet, the answer that the bird will fly 100 miles is obvious.

In the same vein, we can see that transforming kinetic energy is the best abstract representation for designing new brake systems. It involves fundamental physical laws, and we can all agree on the goal. But what about complex social problems? What is the best abstract representation of poverty, ethnic cleansing, drug abuse, and assorted forms of mayhem? Clearly the answers we will achieve will depend on the abstractions we form. Hopefully, those abstractions will force us to confront our most basic implicit assumptions so that we can challenge them and move on.

SUMMARY

Creative thinking is essential for scientific, technological, and artistic accomplishment, and it enables us to handle the personal, professional, and societal challenges that confront us daily. The fruits of creative thinking provide practical solutions to difficult problems, and they enrich our lives in countless ways.

Cognitive science can forge the keys to unlock the secrets of creativity in all spheres of human activity. The task has only just begun, and the advances we have highlighted here are a mere scratching at the surface of this great mystery. The cognitive exploration of creativity must go on. It will remain an exciting and imperative area of research, and the insights it provides will be as relevant for engineers as for artists, for fiction writers as for scientists, for homemakers as for corporate executives.

We must begin to assess whether abstraction always leads to the most innovative results, or whether it can sometimes let us down. Might there be some problems so intricately detailed that we simply must rely on exact prior solutions to make sure we include all that is relevant? Consider designing the human body from scratch. Even if you could list all of the abstract principles that would need to be included, could you envision putting all the pieces together in a single system that would function even remotely as efficiently as the one that has evolved over the eons? On a more mundane level, might we find architects designing strikingly innovative houses but forgetting to include the bathrooms?

We must also determine exactly which types of combinations lead to the greatest amount of originality in a variety of circumstances. Even though incongruous combinations seem effective, it is by no means certain that this will be true in all creative endeavors. Why might some combinations of art techniques or musical forms captivate and others revolt us?

Other research will have to flesh out the details of when it is best to draw away from a problem, and what are the most effective means of doing so. Can stumped scientists, blocked writers, and blank-canvas artists learn how to leap over the barriers to their goals?

Still other studies must assess the utility of the preinventive form procedure in practical settings, and determine when it is best to let function follow form, and vice versa. As we perform a painstaking analysis of basic cognitive structures and processes we will discover more about the nature of our minds and we will increase ever more our creative potential.

As we expand our efforts to understand creative thinking, we necessarily must focus both on the boundless possibilities of using our potential to its fullest and on identifying some of the traps we can fall into. Focusing on the summits we can reach should inspire us, but pointing out our mistakes should too. They should not discourage us. Rather they should challenge us to do better in the future, and struggle to overcome all limitations.

Can we ever anticipate all the possible problems in a new technology, a new discovery, a new domain of inquiry? Of course not. Failures are an inevitable outcome of striving for a better world.[2] As we grope our way in the darkness toward the future, we are bound to bump into a wall now and then. But we must keep striving, even knowing we will stumble. If we let a fear of making mistakes stop us from trying, we might as well decide that human progress stops with us.

As a species, we have journeyed a long way from our first tentative efforts at using tools. And as authors and readers, we have traveled a long way in this book, from our basic look at cognitive skills to showing how they apply in domains from engineering to art, from science to science fiction. Much of the journey still lies ahead. How will future generations remember us? Will they look back in wonder at our accomplishments? Will they wonder how we could have made such colossal mistakes? How well we study creative cognition, and how well we learn its lessons will determine not only our own futures but also what great gifts we will be able to bestow on future generations.

NOTES

1. Michael Hammer & James Champy, *Reengineering the Corporation* (New York: Harper Business, 1993).
2. Henry Petroski, *To Engineer Is Human* (New York: Vintage Books, 1992).

INDEX